T0296388

Now the Chips Are Down

Now the Chips Are Down

The BBC Micro

Alison Gazzard

The MIT Press   Cambridge, Massachusetts   London, England

Set in Filosofia and Helvetica Neue by Toppan Best-set Premedia Limited.

Library of Congress Cataloging-in-Publication Data

Names: Gazzard, Alison, 1982- author.
Title: Now the chips are down : the BBC Micro / Alison Gazzard.
Description: Cambridge, MA : MIT Press, [2016] | Series: Platform studies |
    Includes bibliographical references and index.
Identifiers: LCCN 2015038328 | ISBN 9780262034036 (hardcover : alk. paper)
ISBN 9780262552028 (paperback)
Subjects: LCSH: BBC Microcomputer—History. | Computer literacy—Great
    Britain—History.
Classification: LCC QA76.8.B35 G39 2016 | DDC 004.0941—dc23 LC record available at
    http://lccn.loc.gov/2015038328
ISBN: 978-0-262-03403-6

Contents

Series Foreword

How can someone create a breakthrough game for a mobile phone or a compelling work of art for an immersive 3D environment without understanding that the mobile phone and the 3D environment are different sorts of computing platforms? The best artists, writers, programmers, and designers are well aware of how certain platforms facilitate certain types of computational expression and innovation. Likewise, computer science and engineering have long considered how underlying computing systems can be analyzed and improved. As important as scientific and engineering approaches are, and as significant as work by creative artists has been, there is also much to be learned from the sustained, intensive, humanistic study of digital media. We believe it is time for humanists to seriously consider the lowest level of computing systems and their relationship to culture and creativity.

The Platform Studies series has been established to promote the investigation of underlying computing systems and of how they enable, constrain, shape, and support the creative work that is done on them. The series investigates the foundations of digital media—the computing systems, both hardware and software, that developers and users depend upon for artistic, literary, and gaming development. Books in the series will certainly vary in their approaches, but they will all share certain features:

- a focus on a single platform or a closely related family of platforms
- technical rigor and in-depth investigation of how computing technologies work
- an awareness of and a discussion of how computing platforms exist in a context of culture and society, being developed on the basis of cultural concepts and then contributing to culture in a variety of ways—for instance, by affecting how people perceive computing.

Acknowledgments

The BBC Micro was my first computer. It is a machine I will always remember taking pride of place in our living room as I sat with my dad playing the games he would program. He would later show me how to program my own simple games and animations, as I typed in line after line of code from listings found in books, or we would spend afternoons working our way through countless plays of *Granny's Garden* and *Repton*. That original machine now takes pride of place in my own living room, and the archive of those games, books, and manuals remain in my loft. So first and foremost I would like to thank my parents for buying the family Micro, and for many of the memories that found their way into this book.

Those memories were sparked once again in 2012 during my first visit to The National Museum of Computing (TNMOC) in Bletchley. It was there that I met Owen Grover, who replaced the burned-out capacitor in my Micro, and Chris Monk, who runs the educational program at the museum and encourages visiting school groups to spend an hour programming the Micros using BASIC. Chris provided many valuable insights into the BBC Micro, and went out of his way to find some of the many manuals that I worked my way through while researching this book. I am thankful to the museum for providing access to its archive as I read through racks of magazines, and to the visitors who provided their own recollections of the machine on the Sundays that I would help out in the BBC Micro classroom. I will never forget the Sunday, not long before Christmas, when Chris, Dave Sussman, Steve Clark, and I sat programming a Christmas-tree graphic in BASIC to show to visitors in the classroom, and how it took four programmers a good half hour to find where a comma had been omitted in the code.

TNMOC also led me to David Allen, who not only gave an insightful talk into his time working on The Computer Literacy Project but also allowed me to follow up with further questions, which I am truly thankful for. The insights provided by those who helped to develop the platform and those who created content for it were extremely helpful to me while I was writing this book, and for these insights I would like to thank Sophie Wilson, David Braben, and Tim Tyler. Sophie's detailed comments on the draft of my manuscript provided further commentary into the development process, for which I am very grateful. I would also like to thank Jon Silvera at FUZE for not only providing his own history of the Beeb but also supplying me with my own Special Edition FUZE casing to go alongside my Micro in the living room.

At the UCL Institute of Education I would like to thank those who attended my lunchtime seminar at the London Knowledge Lab during the early stages of writing this book. Your questions and own memories of using the machine in the classroom all helped to shape some of the research in this book. I would like to thank my colleagues Andrew Burn, John Potter, and Diane Carr for their support while I was writing the book, and John and Andrew for their comments on some of the chapters. I would also like to thank Neil Selwyn, Jussi Parikka, and Tom Apperley for recommendations, advice, and feedback during the writing process.

Some of the material in part II of this book was presented at the 2013 History of Games conference and at the 2014 Game History Annual Symposium, both held in Montreal. I would like to thank not only the organizers of these events but also the attendees and panel members for their insightful comments about computing in various parts of the world in the 1980s. Some of the research presented in chapter 4 about the game *Elite* was published as "The Player and the Platform: Exploring the (Hi)stories of *Elite*" in *Game Studies* 13, no. 2 (a special issue devoted to the History of Games conference), and some of the research presented in chapter 5 about the game *Repton* was published as "Remembering Repton: An alternative history of co-creativity in 1980s Britain" in the June 2015 issue of *Kinephanos* (a special issue devoted to the cultural history of video games).

This book would not have been possible without the early comments provided by Ian Bogost and Nick Montfort, the editors of the Platform Studies series, and by Doug Sery at the MIT Press. I would like to thank them for their help in the early stages of preparing the book. I would also like to thank the anonymous reviewers and everyone at the MIT Press.

Last and by no means least, I would like to thank Steve for giving me the space and time to write the manuscript, for listening to me talk through ideas, for his own history of microcomputing in the 1980s, for reading multiple drafts of the book, for providing me with many cups of tea, for his continued support, and for proposing a week after I had finished the first draft. This book is for him, as although it was the ZX Spectrum that started his journey into programming, it was, in many ways, the Beeb that brought us together.

Introduction

[This is] not some distant future, which we and our descendants can blissfully ignore, but one which is imminent and whose progress can be plotted with some degree of precision. It is a future which will involve a transformation of a world society at all kinds of levels, and while taking place slowly at first, will gather pace with sudden force. It's a future which is largely moulded by a single, startling development in technology whose impact is just beginning to be felt. The piece of technology I'm talking about is, of course, the computer.

Christopher Evans, *The Mighty Micro* (Gollancz, 1979), 1

The political, social, and economic climates of Britain in the 1970s were bleak. It is a decade remembered for power cuts, a lack of waste disposal, miners strikes, union opposition, and changing governments. As the end of the decade neared, broadcasters and journalists began to create a wave of panic about Britain's place in the global economy. While other countries were already positioning themselves within the electronics and microelectronics market, Britain was seen to be falling behind. Disheartened by a lack of government response to the issue, the British Broadcasting Corporation (BBC) and other media outlets began to expose some of the issues and fears related to this perceived lack of technological advancement, including the 1978 episode of the BBC's television series *Horizon* titled "Now the Chips Are Down" and Independent Television's 1979 series *The Mighty Micro*.

Both the *Horizon* episode and the ITV series were seen by some as casting the growth of microcomputing in a pessimistic light for future workers, yet at the same time Britain needed to be seen to position itself as a country at the heart of innovation within a global context. And a generation of users needed to be educated as to how to understand and use this new wave of technology. In 1980 the Microelectronics Education Programme (MEP) was announced and financed by the Departments of Education for England, Northern Ireland, and Wales with the aim to "help schools to prepare children for life in a society in which devices and systems based on microelectronics are commonplace and pervasive."[1] Subsequently it was also discussed that a more general education about microcomputers was needed, and who better to do this than the British Broadcasting Corporation, the company that had sought to "entertain, educate and inform" us about the world we live in.[2]

From this the concept of the BBC Microcomputer was born. In January 1982 the BBC launched its Computer Literacy Project with the aim "to introduce interested adults to the world of computers and computing, and to provide the opportunity for viewers to learn through direct experience how to program and use a microcomputer."[3] It was this philosophy that ran through the development of the scheme. In addition to developing a series of television programs, the BBC would support a range of courses, books, and software for both teachers and learners along with the licensing of its own microcomputer to use throughout the campaign. After an outline of the proposed machine was given to various microcomputing manufacturers in the UK, Acorn Computers was chosen by the BBC to develop the machine that would be connected to the Computer Literacy Project—a machine that would subsequently be named the BBC Microcomputer. Therefore, not only was a nationwide computer literacy program developed and rolled out, but so too was an accompanying piece of hardware developed by Acorn Computers and subsequently recognized as being at the forefront of the campaign.

In contrast with other microcomputers designed in Britain during the 1980s, much of the BBC Micro's final design was influenced by the Computer Literacy Project. This gave the machine a particular ethos for those envisioning its use in both the home and educational markets, thus leading to questions about what computer and digital literacies might or should be. At the same time, the design of the platform was based not only on what the BBC thought the public and the schools might need but also on a wider media campaign. The machine had to be capable of being displayed on both pre-recorded and live television programs, and therefore its functionality had to allow for recording the output signal to show viewers on-screen examples clearly so that they could potentially follow along at home. Furthermore, beyond the home use of the platform, the Computer Literacy Project places the BBC Microcomputer into a wider discussion about not only technological determinism but also how the political and media climates of the late 1970s became directly related to the machine's production, to its supply, and in many ways to its legacy. Therefore, this book places the birth of the BBC Microcomputer in the context of 1980s Britain—that is, of a country undergoing political and educational change as it was trying to erase dystopian views of the perceived future. As Paul du Gay et al. state in their book *Doing Cultural Studies*, "Throughout the 1980s Margaret Thatcher's radical programme of reform was represented in large part as a cultural crusade, concerned with the attitudes, values and forms of self-understanding embedded in both individual and institutional activities. The Conservative Party's political project of reconstruction was simultaneously defined as one of cultural reconstruction, as an attempt to transform Britain into an 'enterprise culture.'"[4]

In parallel to this the BBC Micro is remembered as a machine designed as part of a centralized project envisioned by a media corporation and Acorn Computers, the company that created and manufactured the machine. Instead of focusing on single entrepreneurs, the creativity of the platform and potential enterprise created from it are examined in light of the uses of the hardware and software developed for the machine. It is for this reason that the origins of the BBC Micro have to be explored via an examination of the early capabilities of multi-platform content generation and consumption in the 1980s. These factors were central to the BBC Micro's influence on the public, but this is not the only focal point for the multiple literacies that this approach enabled. Literacies related to computer programming and software creation were encouraged, but so too was an understanding as to how to access information across a wide range of related media services, hardware literacies, and "do-it-yourself" computing. This led to the dissemination of ideas related to how to use the machine among local communities as a way of continuing to develop the possibilities of this new learning not originally anticipated by the Computer Literacy Project, or even by the hardware embedded within the BBC Micro itself.

This is not a book about firsts in the timeline of microcomputing, nor is it a history of the BBC Micro or Acorn Computers. It is a book about particular platform-specific case studies identified through hardware and software innovations facilitated by the machine. As Paul Atkinson notes in his discussion of "firsts" related to the evolution of computers, "it has to be accepted ... that for such complex technological products there is no relevant, single 'first'—rather, there is a series of related innovations, taking place in different locations, often at very similar times, each having a claim to having pushed the development of computing forward in one of a number of ways."[5] Although it is possible to understand what was unique about the BBC Micro via its platform-specific characteristics, and how these characteristics were used and sometimes manipulated by others in an attempt to push the boundaries of what the machine could offer, these characteristics of the machine can also be situated in light of other events within microcomputing cultures. Therefore, instead of attempting to write a comprehensive history of the BBC Micro, I have attempted to provide snapshots of particular components unique to its design and placement within a microcomputing market while being aware of other influences for both producers and consumers during the microcomputer explosion in 1980s Britain.

Microcomputers in 1980s Britain

One of the most important points to consider is just how the BBC Microcomputer was created by both the BBC and Acorn Computers. Understanding some of the initial developments surrounding the BBC Micro requires first discussing the BBC's Computer Literacy Project.

Founded by John Reith in 1922, the BBC created the "template for public service broadcasting in Britain."[6] The service is primarily funded by a license-fee structure. Anyone who purchases a television set in Great Britain or Northern Ireland must pay a fixed fee in order to watch television content. The license fee enables the BBC to produce content in the public interest and keeps it from having to accept advertising, as commercial television channels must. In response to this funding structure, the BBC as a corporation is, in many ways, defined by its responsibility to produce radio and television content for the masses that adheres to a set of conditions. Reith fought hard to fend off politicians' attempts to influence the BBC and to make it the BBC's mission "to enrich people's lives with programs and services that inform, educate and entertain."[7]

In the 1960s, a series titled *Horizon* was born. According to its mission statement, "The aim of Horizon is to provide a platform from which some of the world's greatest scientists and philosophers can communicate their curiosity, observations and reflections, and infuse into our common knowledge their changing views of the universe. ... We shall do this by presenting science not as a series of isolated discoveries but as a continuing growth of thought, a philosophy which is an essential part of twentieth century culture."[8] It was this philosophy that led to the airing of the 1978 *Horizon* program titled "Now the Chips Are Down."

"Now the Chips Are Down" is often cited as having been the starting point of a wider discussion about the integration of the microcomputer into British society and of a drive toward increased computer literacy among the public.[9] It painted a picture of a new wave of technology, starting with a computer reading a book to a blind man, following a trajectory of the development of computing from valve technologies through to silicon chips and the microcomputer. But rather than offer a positive outlook on the benefits of the microprocessor and the rise in computing power, the program offered little consolation to its viewers. Instead, the wording became increasingly negative. It spoke of a "new war" arising from the development of arcade games generating an income of a quarter of a billion pounds, and how the rise of the microcomputer would result in "100 petrol pump attendants [being] unnecessary." In an article titled "Computing for the Masses? Constructing a British Culture of Computing in the Home," Tilly Blyth writes that the program "tapped into a bigger culture of concern about the nation's response to its changing economic position and developing technology."[10] As the program unfolds, so does the scaremongering. Word-processing software is said to be taking jobs from typists, and it is observed that even the skills needed to paint a chair can be "absorbed into the machine." In a dissertation titled "The Making of the Micro," Thomas Lean observes that the program "on one hand [promotes] more leisure time, easier lifestyles and greater productivity [but] on the other, massive unemployment and other unpleasant social implications, and a Britain further in decline in the face of computerised foreign competition."[11]

In October 1979, one of the other major television channels in Britain, ITV, aired *The Mighty Micro*, a series of six programs about the development and some of the possible effects of the silicon chip.[12] *The Mighty Micro* was written by Christopher Evans, who published a book with the same title; the front of its jacket included the sentence "This could be the most important book you ever read—it might even be the last."[13] Again, in a time of scaremongering, both the book and the television series not only detailed the past and the present but also attempted to predict the future in the short, medium, and longer terms. (The "long-term future" referred to in the last chapter of Evans' book is the period 1991–2000.) Not only did Evans focus on the possible evolution of the microcomputer; he also tried to predict political, social, scientific, psychological, and even "bizarre" issues (meaning moral and ethical problems that the misuse of computing power might provoke). According to various media outlets, computers (often unnamed ones) were about to infiltrate daily life.

Coincidentally, the United Kingdom entered another phase in its political history around the same time. Margaret Thatcher, who had become the leader of the Conservative Party in 1975, became the UK's first female prime minister on May 4, 1979. Moving into the political limelight at a time of unrest among the media about the role of computing in industry, culture, and society, the newly formed Conservative government had members who were eager to understand this phenomenon and who thought "something should be done."[14] France, Sweden, Denmark, the United States, Canada, and Japan were all more advanced in their thinking about supporting their national microcomputing industries. Histories charting the rise of the microprocessor in the US often dominate accounts of what was happening at this time. Martin Campbell-Kelly and other historians noted that in the mid 1970s, in parallel to the development of Intel's 8080 microprocessor, "other semiconductor manufacturers were starting to produce their own microprocessors—such as the Motorola 6800, the Zilog Z80, and the MOS Technology 6502."[15] The development of such processors has subsequently been linked to the development, in 1977, of the Apple II, characterized by Campbell-Kelly et al. as a "real personal computer" after an era of hobbyist computing. However, from the British perspective the UK was already falling behind, even though British companies were manufacturing a variety of microcomputers. The Conservative government wanted to promote computing and information technology in order to be seen as forward thinking, but also as a way of showcasing Thatcher's new economic policies related to entrepreneurial thinking.[16] A new position was created: Minister of State for Industry and Information Technology. The first to hold it was Kenneth Baker. In his biography, Baker writes that "the microchip … was to affect not just the technological and electronic industries but every industry in the country, through revolutionising the processing of information, the design of its products and the control of the manufacturing process."[17] The government decided to support research and development in the field of information technology by increasing the amount of funding available from 1979 to 1984 by £250 million.

Although these events did not directly influence the development of the BBC Micro, or even influence the BBC in its original decision making, the political climate at the time did help to promote the possibilities offered by new microcomputers. Neil Selwyn cites 1979 as a "turning point" in the UK's relationship with the computer for numerous reasons, including "the election of Margaret Thatcher's Conservative government," "the early development of UK-produced computers," and "a rising media interest in new technologies."[18] For Selwyn these factors allow for the "discursive formation of educational computing," yet the BBC Micro was only one of the microcomputers driving this shift.

Before the BBC campaign promoting an understanding of computing even began, a microcomputing race was getting underway. The evolution had already begun for those in the know about these new processors, with the ability to assemble do-it-yourself home computing kits and eventually ship them to others in the know. Although not new, and formed within a long line of mainframes and other larger computing systems, the microcomputer was seen in Britain as accessible. Whereas in the United States hobbyist computer kits such as the TRS-80 had seen a wave of computing culture emerge, to be replaced by consoles such as the Atari VCS or more powerful machines such as the Commodore 64 and the Apple II, in Britain in the 1980s interest in computing was, for many, centered on home-grown computing cultures. According to Campbell-Kelly et al., in the US "during 1977 three distinct paradigms for the personal computer emerged, represented by three leading manufacturers: Apple, Commodore Business Machines, and Tandy, each of which defined the personal computer in terms of its own existing culture and corporate outlooks."[19] However, in the UK there were other companies manufacturing microcomputers for home use, among them Sinclair, Newbury, Tangerine, Research Machines, Transam, Nascom, and Acorn. Though some companies were more successful than others, each had a role to play in the British microcomputing scene.

Part of that scene began in the communities of Cambridge, where groups of people were already excited by the possibilities that smaller computing systems could offer. Cambridge as a site for engineering and technological innovation was nothing new. According to Kirk and Cotton's introduction to *The Cambridge Phenomenon*, "around 4,000 companies exploiting technology and innovation in some form or another have been set up around Cambridge since Tim Eiloart founded Cambridge Consultants in 1960."[20] However, according to Kirk and Cotton there had already been a "handful of engineering companies" before 1960, including "The Scientific Instrument Company (founded 1881), the Pye Group (1896) and Marshall of Cambridge (1909)."[21] The Cambridge scholars Charles Babbage and Alan Turing are both widely recognized in the history of computing in Cambridge.[22] However, it was after Labour Party leader Harold Wilson's "white heat of technology" speech, delivered at a conference of the party in 1963, that technology companies really began to grow in the Cambridge area.[23] Yet for those inside the Cambridge computing scene during the late 1970s and the early 1980s the future was now, the possibilities were endless, and the need for more than one company offering computers to consumers started to become a desirable concept for those with the expertise to do so.

In the 1980s, microcomputers were seen as a "potent symbol of 'new technology.'"[24] In fact 1982 was declared the British Information Technology (IT) Year, coinciding with Kenneth Baker's appointment as the Minister for Information Technology in the Department of Trade and Industry. As Maureen McNeil notes, the terms associated with microelectronics and microcomputers were replaced with the term "information technology" as a way of broadening the spectrum of the new information revolution and focusing not only on hardware but also on the "conceptual nature" of what was being produced alongside its innovative qualities.[25] In line with Margaret Thatcher's proposals, 1980s British computing is in many ways recognized for entrepreneurs and their machines—for example, Clive Sinclair's ZX80 and ZX Spectrum computers and his C5 electric car. As a way of trying to convince the general public that Britain could survive the recession of 1979–1983, which resulted in the loss of manufacturing jobs and in some ways drove the dystopian views of the rise in microcomputing, "the positive associations with IT were further amplified through other vocabulary extensions—the 'sunrise' industries, Britain's 'sunbelt' (the area of the country in which the high-skill end of IT industries were concentrated)."[26]

The promotion and media coverage of IT entrepreneurs in Britain at the time not only helped to demystify the microcomputer but also helped to educate consumers about microcomputers. The BBC campaigned for general computer literacy but this was not the only way of educating the public. The publicity that Sinclair received in the media directed the public's attention toward the new revolution. "At the end of 1981," according to Maureen McNeil, "200,000 households in the UK had computers. By the end of 1983, there were 2 million such households and Britain had the highest number of home computers per capita of any nation in the world. By early 1984, somewhere between 11 and 14 per cent of UK households were equipped with these machines."[27] Although the BBC Microcomputer was by no means the only machine to be used by the British public, its inception is a prime example of how such a project came to life when other machines were already on the market.

Aware of the current media climate and of debates about computer use and subsequent literacy of microcomputing in the UK in early 1980, Sheila Innes, then Head of Continuing Education, sent two people from her team, David Allen and Robert Albury, to investigate what could be done in order to drive microcomputing education in the UK. In a recent retrospective, David Allen recalls Innes saying "There's this thing called microelectronics, I want you to see if there's anything in it."[28] The BBC had already delivered an Adult Literacy Campaign from 1972 to 1976, and had broadcast an associated television series titled *On the Move*. Indeed, the history of the BBC's links with educational programming goes back to 1971 and a partnership with The Open University. Offering distance-learning courses, including degrees, The Open University used the BBC as a means of transmitting programs for its students to watch. However, it was *On the Move* in particular that influenced the BBC's attitude toward computer literacy. As David Allen notes, the television program was used as a stimulus for more hands-on education. The BBC had a strong belief in the hands-on philosophy. As Allen states, you had to "use it to control it."[29] This philosophy formed the backbone of the Computer Literacy Project and the BBC Microcomputer: controlling the platform was very much at the heart of where users began their journey into what the machine could do.

Excavating the Platform

For many reasons the BBC Micro was more than just the hardware platform. The widespread adoption of sharing the responsibility of the Computer Literacy Project across several BBC and government departments is discussed in *The Legacy of the BBC Micro*, a report, published by the charity Nesta in May 2012, that lists the BBC Education Officers, BBC Enterprises, Engineers, the Department of Industry, and the Departments of Education and Science as all playing roles in the project.[30] Alongside this, the Computer Literacy Project was also enhanced by a range of television and radio programs broadcast by the BBC, educational programs run in schools, a correspondence course, and a range of books and magazines published by the BBC and by various publishing companies.

These multiple outputs potentially encouraged linked forms of learning by users drawing on similar examples in a variety of ways. This multiple-platform approach can be seen as an early example of what Henry Jenkins and others define as "convergence culture," with the BBC Micro platform at the heart of the campaign (see figure I.1).[31] As the flagship machine for the range of television shows that were aired by the BBC, the BBC Micro was seen as a vehicle to educate the general public about using microcomputers. Although the BBC is not allowed to actively advertise products in its programs, its links to the BBC Micro were apparent from the symbol of the owl found both on the machine and in the opening titles

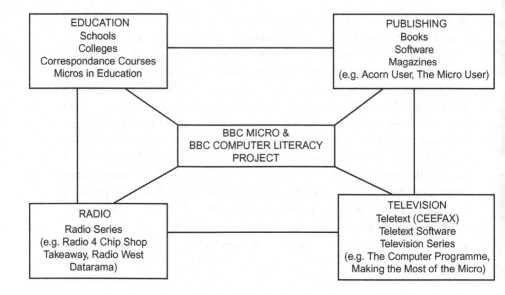

Figure I.1
The BBC Micro and the Computer Literacy Project in the context of other services and media outlets.

of *The Computer Programme* and of the follow-up series, *Making the Most of the Micro*. Although the BBC Micro was not directly advertised as part of the television shows, the links to the platform were there in small parts of the design of related media content. Subsequently, the project relied on the convergence of multiple outlets that could be used to promote the machine indirectly as well to aid in general learning about a range of microcomputers in Britain. The widespread use of different media outlets—television, radio, and home education courses—encouraged further conversations among the public and wider engagement and participation in the generating of knowledge about the machine.

Today, as we are so often reminded, we live in an age of "participatory culture."[32] The development of the Internet and, in turn, the World Wide Web has seen many participants fuel their creativity in a variety of ways, among them blogging, writing Wikipedia entries, uploading YouTube videos, and "modding" (modifying) video games. However, this creativity is not a new phenomenon. Although hack spaces, game creation, co-creation, and sharing software are all current topics of media discussion and debate, these practices occurred before these terms became part of our popular culture and of what is often defined as a "new media" vocabulary. As many have written, new media often draw on older forms of media.[33] The computing technologies of today would not have been possible without previous developments in microcomputers, processing powers, memory, and disk space. Beyond technological progression, our cultural understandings of these machines have grown with the familiarity of processes and with the acknowledgment of the change through our societal uses, embedding computers at the heart of most of what we do in the digital world. The integration of these systems into our workplaces, homes, and social spaces relies on the audience's understanding, recognition, and use. The ability to understand how to use some of the many computers of the time was made possible by access to computer clubs, information transferred among friends on school playgrounds, and dedicated magazines related to each platform. All these scenarios enabled a form of offline "collective intelligence" for users to seek help beyond the more media-driven outputs and thus now enable a further way of being able to examine the role of a particular platform at the time.[34] In order to understand the link between the platform and its uses, this book takes a media-archaeological approach to Platform Studies as a way of excavating the archives of the components that were connected to the BBC Micro, not only in terms of hardware, software, and pieces of code, but also by documented user accounts and the multitude of platform-specific magazines that were published during the time the Micro was in use.

In their discussions of what defines the study of platforms, Nick Montfort and Ian Bogost emphasize the importance of the relationships among creativity, design, expression, and culture, all potentially leading to the underlying features of platforms in terms of both the hardware and the layers of operating systems, software, and peripherals.[35] "In addition to allowing certain developments and precluding others," Montfort and Bogost write, "platforms also function in more subtle ways to encourage and discourage different sorts of computer expression."[36] Therefore, to understand the platform it is essential not only to understand the basic underlying technological processes of the machine but also to understand how it could be manipulated and developed further by the user. Though we can't time travel back to the 1980s to get a full understanding of the user in relation to the machine, we can place the BBC Micro within a larger historical context surrounding computing at the time, including what has been documented through television programs, magazines, user manuals, games, software and the progression of the hardware during the lifespan of the platform. Examining archives in this way allows for a greater understanding of the processes, functions, uses, and experiences of the platform that media archeology allows over more general media-historical narratives.[37] Similarly, this approach highlights how elements of the platform, examined in this way, continue to link to some present-day practices across present-day platforms. "Media archaeology," Erkki Huhtamo and Jussi Parikka write, "rummages textual, visual, and auditory archives as well as collections of artifacts, emphasizing both the discursive and the material manifestations of culture."[38]

It is through the study of the platform that these discussions can begin. In the case of the BBC Micro, much of the research has to take place through archives, noted histories, and in some cases fan nostalgia through online web communities. The source material for these investigations will include magazines held in the archives of the National Museum of Computing and by dedicated users who have scanned and archived documents for others to download and/or read online. Thomas Lean notes the importance of magazines during the 1980s microcomputing era: "The communication they facilitated between different groups made magazines an integral component of the microcomputing system."[39] Platform-specific magazines such as *The Micro User* and *Acorn User* contained game code, DIY examples, reviews, and general news, all of which help to paint a larger picture of the role of the BBC Micro in both culture and society. In line with Erkki Huhtamo's methods of exposing "alternative histories" of media practices, this book not only examines the BBC Micro platform in its capabilities as a computing machine but also examines the surrounding cultural, industrial, and educational histories as part of its creation and its limited success within the boundaries of the United Kingdom. Although the histories of the BBC Micro platform have been preserved through countless retellings of the Computer Literacy Project and related nostalgia to regenerate a new age of computer programming literacy, there is often little or no discussion beyond these factors. Even at the time of its inception the BBC Micro was not always given as much page space as cheaper machines such as the Sinclair ZX Spectrum, especially outside Britain. The BBC Microcomputer is allocated less than half a page near the end of *The Personal Computer Handbook: A Complete Practical Guide to Choosing and Using Your Micro*, in a section titled "A guide to other machines,"[40] whereas entire pages were devoted to Apple, IBM, Sinclair, Commodore, and Atari machines . Tracing what Huhtamo calls the "topoi" or common "cultural vessels" of recurrent themes that run through the histories of 1980s British computing and those of other global microcomputing cultures both past and present gives each chapter a focal point for discussion in light of the unique qualities offered by the BBC Micro that led to platform-specific innovation and creation.[41] These case studies also piece together another facet of microcomputing through an examination of the BBC Micro platform in order to place British computing cultures within a wider global context so often focused on more popular and therefore more dominant machines.

However, in constructing "alternate histories" there has to be some degree of caution as to what one is finding, how it could be interpreted, and the resultant projected reading that is then implied. For Huhtamo, the meaning of media archeology is a "critical practice that excavates media-cultural evidence for clues about neglected, misrepresented, and/or suppressed aspects of both media's past(s) and their present and tries to bring these into a conversation with each other."[42] It is by uncovering some of these lesser-known global histories through the connected hardware and software practices facilitated by the BBC Micro that we can start to see the role it played in early hypermedia, game creation, digital mapping, networking, and creativity as its users found ways of adapting and creating content for the machine. For although all platforms enable creativity, it was through modifications, software creation, and the overcoming of technological hurdles by both users and companies that the BBC Micro became a machine of many possibilities rather than one directed solely at education.

The Plan of the Book

The book is divided into three parts, which draw upon one another and upon the central theme of the BBC Micro as a platform for users to potentially access multiple literacies. Part I, titled Hardware and Software Literacies, consists of chapters 1 and 2, which examine the BBC Micro's introduction into the mainstream market, how the Computer Literacy Project played a pivotal role in this development, and how communities of users embraced the machine through hardware and software practices. Chapter 1 develops a more extensive look at the histories of the Computer Literacy Project, examining the links between the British Broadcasting Corporation and its role in raising national awareness of the cultural and technological implications of microcomputers. Chapter 1 also highlights the role of Acorn Computers as the chosen developer and manufacturer of the machine, and how that role helped to shape the design of the hardware. Chapter 2 opens with a discussion of the integration of BBC BASIC as one of the software literacies that the machine enabled before focusing on the hardware development associated with the BBC. These developments include the use of ROM expansions as workarounds for limited memory within the system. Discussions surrounding earlier cultures of hardware hacking, software copying, and DIY communities are further developed by understanding the outreach and capabilities of the machine through its use within schools and colleges, as well as through a growing number of households. Present-day discussions of maker spaces and hack spaces are challenged through an examination of 1980s DIY principles seen in terms of the inbuilt input and output capabilities that were unique to the BBC Micro.

Part II, titled Making and Playing Games, develops the idea of communities and literacies further by examining three case studies. Chapters 3–5 all explore Bobby Schweizer's discussion about how "specifications for platforms influence rather than determine."[43] Chapter 3 takes a look at *Granny's Garden*, an educational game that was used in primary schools. Although the primary focus of chapter 3 is on the game itself, the role of the platform and limited supply of machines in schools are also discussed. Economic and political constraints are traced through government incentives surrounding the purchase and use of microcomputers more generally. *Granny's Garden* is situated in among a wave of educational games that arose in the 1980s, in the UK and elsewhere, as a way of developing computer literacies and problem-solving skills. However, the development of learning seen in *Granny's Garden* was not necessarily always about the software itself; in some cases it was about other extensions of using the software, such as using the game as a different form of "litersture." Chapter 3 examines *Granny's Garden* in the context of more current dialogues about the role of media and games in education as a wider area of debate that continues in educational discourse. With this in mind, chapter 4 takes the idea of learning and games in a slightly different direction, examining the world of independent programmers and software innovation through a case study of *Elite* and of that game's links to the software publisher Acornsoft. *Elite* is a seminal game that was developed on the BBC Micro platform. Many people could not afford the BBC Micro for their homes, so it was not always seen as a machine purely for game-playing activities; for that reason, *Elite*'s links to the BBC Micro are often lost in later writing about the game. *Elite* not only paved the way for *Eve Online* and other space-trading games; it is also often recognized as an important game to come out of the 1980s British game development scene. The ingenuity of *Elite*'s developers, David Braben and Ian Bell, is evident from how the BBC Micro's hardware limitations were overcome so that the capabilities of the game's final design could be realized. These themes are continued in chapter 5, where the game series *Repton* is examined in more detail.

The theme of obsolescence and ingenuity continues in part III, titled Extending the Platform. The shift in focus toward peripherals used in connection with the BBC Micro is discussed in chapters 6 and 7. The Teletext adapter, which allowed for computer programs to be downloaded via television aerial systems and the BBC's CEEFAX service for free, is discussed in chapter 6. The Teletext adapter could be used as a basic software distribution system before the Internet and the World Wide Web came into wider use, and shortly after its introduction the term "smart television" was used. Chapter 6 examines the use of the Teletext system in light of how content is downloaded and distributed today via the Internet through a variety of platforms. The Teletext adapter is placed within a wider context of the networked capabilities of the BBC Micro and other microcomputers including systems and services such as local-area networks, Prestel, bulletin-board systems, and email. The history of Teletext and the development of Mode 7 on the BBC Micro are discussed in order to provide further links between the design of the BBC Micro's hardware and other technologies that were available before the BBC Micro was designed. Chapter 7 goes on to examine the next incarnation of the BBC Micro, the BBC Master, and the integration of the Philips Laserdisc player in the 1986 Domesday Project. The BBC's Domesday Project, initiated to mark the 900th anniversary of the Domesday Book, was a large-scale collaborative project in which students in schools all over the UK were invited to submit short descriptions of their day-to-day lives in the towns and cities they lived in, and photographs to go with them. The information collected from the schools was combined with Ordnance Survey maps of the UK, as well as video footage in order to create an early hypermedia-like experience. Laserdiscs were used as storage media in order to link the still photographs and the video, showcasing not only the limitations of the computer hardware but also the solutions used to work around them. The Domesday Project also highlights earlier forms of participatory culture in the context of our current abilities to digitally map content using services such as Google Maps.

Chapter 8 examines the legacy of the BBC Micro platform and the recent developments of the Raspberry Pi in order to recreate some of the original purpose of the BBC's Computer Literacy Project and the BBC's move toward increasing awareness of programming literacy through its new Micro Bit computer. The chapter charts Acorn's developments from the Archimedes to the ARM chip now often used in "hidden packages" (such as smartphones). By using a combination of hardware- and software-specific examples, and by examining some of the advertised and known uses of the BBC Micro, chapter 8 considers the Micro's place in history as a vehicle for various literacies but also as the machine for and of the user that pushed the boundaries of what could be achieved in order to produce something completely new.

The book offers not only a discussion of the BBC Micro platform as a piece of hardware, but also discussions of its creators, its users, its critics, and its advocates. As Katherine Hayles wrote, "Technologies do not develop on their own. People develop them and people are sensitive to cultural beliefs about what technologies can and should mean."[44] It is by tracing these cultural contexts that we can start to see some of the ethos of the BBC Micro platform continuing in conversations and debates today.

A website to accompany the book, available at www.bbcmicrobook. com, contains examples and images mentioned in the text as a nod to the multiple-media approach that the Computer Literacy Project facilitated.

A Note on Terminology

The BBC Microcomputer was often referred to as the BBC Microcomputer, the BBC Micro, or even just the Micro. These terms, along with the more colloquial name "the Beeb," are used interchangeably throughout this book. Where microcomputers other than the BBC Microcomputer are discussed, "microcomputer" and "micro" are not capitalized. Variants of the platform's name will be used throughout this book in order to avoid repetition and to highlight how the machine was discussed in other forms of documentation.

Hardware and Software Literacies

[I]

The Beeb Is Born

On December 1, 1981, the BBC Microcomputer was launched. It was unlike other computers released before and since. Now often fondly referred to as "the Beeb," the BBC Micro is a symbol of computer literacy and computer education in schools in 1980s Britain. Although its inception was due in large part to the BBC's Computer Literacy Project, the production, manufacture, and design of parts of the machine were possible only because of Acorn Computers, the company responsible for the BBC Micro's creation. The media storm of the late 1970s that evoked panic about the growth of microcomputing and the related economic and social impacts allowed the BBC to begin positioning itself as one of the companies that could think about resolutions to this problem.

Beyond the known links with the Computer Literacy Project, the BBC Micro was a highly advanced machine upon its release and an even more advanced one after some development. Much of this was attributable to its underlying hardware and to the expertise of the Acorn team. Therefore, in this chapter the BBC Micro is discussed not only in relation to the initial set-up prompted by the BBC, but also in relation to Acorn Computers and that company's earlier microcomputers. Similarly, beyond the role of educating the public about microcomputing, the BBC Micro came with a Welcome Pack that enabled various types of exploration into the possibilities of this particular machine. It is through an investigation into the hardware and initial set-up of the Micro that this chapter will act as a starting point for further discussions later on in this book, including the multiple literacies that the machine enabled.

During the inception of the proposed Computer Literacy Project, Sheila Innes was the Head of Continuing Education and one of the people coordinating these developments at the BBC. After David Allen and Robert Albury, two BBC employees working for Innes, were sent out to investigate microelectronics, a series of three mid-evening programs titled *The Silicon Factor* and presented by Brian Fawke was aired on BBC2 in 1980. Much like television programs from the 1970s about the rise in microcomputing technologies, *The Silicon Factor* aimed to inform the public about the current uses of microcomputers and how they were being integrated into society, mainly through work-based activities. Then in 1981 the BBC produced five programs for small businesses, presented by Brian Redhead, titled *Managing the Micro*. Focused on "opportunities for businesses," such as tracking supermarket sales data and stock lists, *Managing the Micro* also helped to educate the business community about the developments in microcomputing around the country and the potential impact of these developments. However, developing and producing television programs was not enough for the team at the BBC, and a report titled Microelectronics was written and distributed in August 1980. The report was circulated to policy makers and to members of Parliament. The initial work at the BBC was backed by the Department of Trade and Industry (DTI), by the Department of Education and Science (DES), and by the Manpower Services Commission (a quasi-autonomous nongovernmental organization, set up to identity the needs of national training in the UK, that in 1979 had commissioned a report titled Something Must Be Done in response to the heightened awareness of the microcomputing industry).[1] It was the response to the Microelectronics report that started some of the initial developments of having a nationwide Computer Literacy Project.

At first the BBC attempted to construct a project around a common programming language that could be used across microcomputers already on offer. Tilly Blyth writes:

Rather than create their own machine, the Department of Industry (DoI) and the BBC Education team originally tried to persuade the British computing industry to all implement a common language— ABC (Adopted Basic for Computers). All the manufacturers were brought into a room in Cavendish Square, London and were told that if they did this their machines could be used as part of the project. The manufacturers refused to do this unless there was some financial support for the development of the chips. The government was not forthcoming, so the BBC began to look at alternative arrangements.[2]

The BBC, after recognizing that it wouldn't be able to develop its own entirely new machine to act as the flagship microcomputer for the project or to convince manufacturers to use the ABC programming language, approached various companies that were already manufacturing micro-computers. Between Christmas 1980 and New Year's Day 1981 the members of the team wrote initial specifications of what they wanted from a microcomputer for the project. David Allen and John Coll distrib-uted the specifications to seven manufacturers: Sinclair, Newbury, Tangerine, Research Machines, Transam, Nascom, and Acorn. The speci-fications were ambitious and the deadline was tight, but the BBC wanted the machine to be ready as soon as possible. An article in the January 1982 edition of *Practical Computing* noted that the microcomputer should have some of the following features:

- A Basic high-level language, since Basic is easily understood by the beginner while allowing sophisticated techniques to be used. The Basic was to be as compatible as possible with existing Basics.
- A full keyboard, to include an additional row of keys capable of producing any code under software control.
- A Teletext extension to load software from Teletext transmissions.
- Medium-resolution colour graphics with good software support.
- A low price for the basic microcomputer, with the capability for expansion to a more powerful and flexible system.[3]

Not only was the machine to enable people to program at an entry level as well as to suit the more advanced user; the hardware specifications required a range of outputs, including Ultra High Frequency (UHF), com-posite (PAL) video in order to work in the home environment, and a genlocking (generator locking) facility for the micro to be used in a televi-sion studio for the broadcast of programs related to computer literacy. The machine also was to have a printer connection, expansion ports, and a network connection as standard, analog inputs for joysticks and for the monitoring of data such as temperature, and an input/output device that would allow programs to be loaded on to the machine by means of a cassette interface that would be controlled by the computer. Although many of these requirements were partially fulfilled by some of the machines currently on or about to come on to the market; the requirement that all these features be present in one machine was unheard of in micro-computer development in the 1980s. Yet the companies that the BBC had approached accepted the challenge. After hearing back from six companies with proposals in February 1981, the BBC decided that the bid from Acorn Computers was the strongest and "most attractive" of those they had received.[4]

From the Proton to the BBC Micro

Acorn Computers had experience in manufacturing microcomputers: Chris Curry, Hermann Hauser, Steve Furber, and Sophie Wilson all had been involved in kit computers before the company called Cambridge Processing Unit became Acorn Computers in 1979. Their journey into the world of developing commercial machines started with Curry's invention of the MK-14 kit, which he prototyped during his time at Science of Cambridge Ltd, a joint venture of Chris Curry and Clive Sinclair.[5] Furber showed Wilson the kit, and it inspired her to come up with the design of the Hawk, later to be developed into Acorn's System 1 machine.[6] The System 1 was also a kit computer. After developing these kit computers, Acorn released its Atom.

Released in March 1980, the Atom was available either in kit form or as an assembled machine. The Atom used the MOS Technology 6502 chip, ran its own version of BASIC, and had 2 kilobytes of random-access memory (expandable to 12 kilobytes) and 8 kilobytes of read-only memory (expandable to 12 kilobytes). After developing the Atom thoughts turned to Acorn's next machine, which would be called the Proton. Chris Curry, one of the founders of Acorn Computers, began working on that next machine with a dedicated team that included Hauser, Wilson, and Furber. Curry had worked for Sinclair Radionics/Research with Clive Sinclair, had always been fascinated by kit computers, and had spent his time research-ing and playing with various formations of machines during his time at the company.[7] As Furber noted in his recollections of that time, the members of the team were "hobbyists."[8]

When the proposal from the BBC came in, Acorn's Proton machine was not a fully formed piece of hardware and existed only as a series of discussions and in the minds of those wanting to develop it. Nonetheless, Curry called the BBC to invite representatives to come and see Acorn's latest prototype. As Sophie Wilson recalls, Curry "gloss[ed] over the fact that we hadn't made a prototype yet and we were still in the arguing stage of the Proton."[9] In a later oral-history interview about that period, Steve

Furber, one of the developers of the Micro, also recalls the week during which a prototype was constructed. Around April 1981, Hermann Hauser asked Sophie Wilson and Steve Furber whether they would be able to produce a prototype working five days later to show the BBC. Both Wilson and Furber were not sure if they could achieve making the prototype in time; however, Hauser managed to play them off one another, and the team began to build a prototype machine. Furber recalls:

[O]n the Monday … I tidied up the circuit diagram we'd been sketching for the Proton into something that was just about what we could build and we got Ramanuj Banerjee from the computer lab to come and wire up the prototype. And that took until about Wednesday, I think, and then from Wednesday to Friday we were trying to get it to work … . And we spent … all Wednesday night, Thursday night trying to get this thing to work and then on Friday morning there's the well documented final suggestion from Hermann about disconnecting this—I think it must have been a ground wire connecting an Acorn system rack, which we were using as the development host, and then a cable across to the prototype Proton board.[10]

As Sophie Wilson later recalled, the wire was in fact the "in-circuit emulator cable."[11] The 2009 television drama "Micro Men" shows members of the Acorn team working right up until an executive from the BBC walks into the room to see a working version of what they had proposed, and the cutting of the wire is depicted.[12] It was this research ethic that drove much of what Acorn Computers did, and it impressed the BBC team. As John Radcliffe and Robert Salkeld note in their overview of why Acorn was chosen for the project, Acorn "had a particularly strong in-house research and development team."[13] In turn, this strong research-and-development ethos would lead to the machine's specifications exceeding those that the BBC originally asked for, and would result in the delivery of a robust machine that would last for many years. It also took time, and thus the project was slightly behind schedule.

The BBC Microcomputer System was launched as two models: the Model A and the Model B. The Model A had 16 kilobytes of memory; the Model B had 32 kilobytes, but, as the service manual for both machines stated, "The Model A BBC Microcomputer can be expanded at any time to the Model B."[14] The prices, originally advertised as £235 for the Model A and £335 for the Model B, rose to £299 and £399 respectively as a result of increased costs of manufacturing. Fortunately, the Model A version (and eventually the Model B) had been chosen as one of the machines that would fall into the remit of schools being able to get 50 percent of the funding for the machine matched by the Department of Industry's Micros in Schools scheme. With the Model B computer costing about one month's average salary in the UK at the time, the machine was an investment for many home users and not necessarily within everyone's reach. This is further highlighted in a comparison between microcomputers in the first issue of the magazine *The Home Computer Course*, published in 1983, noting that two other contenders, the Oric and the Sinclair Spectrum, were priced at £130/£169 and £99/£125 respectively (depending on memory requirements).[15] Yet the summary of the BBC Micro in the same issue is most revealing when it states "this versatile machine can be easily upgraded to a powerful computing tool."

Hardware Specifications

In order to push forward with the Computer Literacy Project, the BBC recognized that it couldn't manufacture its own machine. This meant that a British manufacturer would have to be used—something that subsequently could be seen to tie in with the Conservative government's drive for entrepreneurship in the sector. The machine that emerged was the result of a partnership between the BBC and Acorn Computers. David Kitson, a senior engineer in the BBC's Engineering Designs Department, served as a direct liaison with Acorn. Richard Russell, one of the BBC Engineering team's designers, also contributed to the machine's design; among other things, he was responsible for some of the final details of BBC BASIC.[16]

The final specification of the machine was in line with what was initially envisioned by the BBC, except with a 6502 CPU running at 2 megahertz rather than the proposed Z80 chip that they had thought should be at the heart of the system. This was a continuation of Acorn's earlier Atom microcomputer. It ended up serving the system well in years to come despite the BBC's initial worries about the change in processor from the initial specification. In fact Acorn Computers managed to produce a machine that exceeded the BBC's extensive requirements. The final hardware specification as listed on the back of the BBC Microcomputer leaflet produced by the BBC's Continuing Education department states that the case is made of injection-molded thermoplastic, with a 240/115 fused mains input power supply with switched shrouded mains output.[17] The beige outer of the case and the sheer size of the machine also made it stand apart from other machines on the market at the time, looking slightly more "serious." The Micro was about four times the size of the Sinclair ZX

Spectrum because of the amount of hardware. The size of the Micro was also determined by the keyboard, which is listed as having a full QWERTY layout and an additional fifth row of ten user-programmable keys. Similarly, the specifications of the BBC Micro go on to state that the switches are of a sealed wafer type and are encased in a tough thermoplastic mounted in a steel panel within the case. A review of Model B in *The Home Computer Course* emphasizes these features: "The keyboard is a strong point of the BBC Model B, in terms of layout, facilities and quality of construction. The keys are properly sculptured, which means that even a touch typist would feel at home."[18] It was features such as these that made the Micro a robust machine, suitable for use and misuse in schools.

Although the BBC and Acorn Computers released the technical specifications in 1981, various parts were still being developed. Further specifications were released on March 31, 1982, and their requirements were eventually met. These specifications included the Teletext Adapter, the Prestel adapter, a single-drive 100K disk store, a dual-drive 800K disk store, a 6502 second-processor expansion, a Z80 second-processor expansion, and a CP/M-compatible disk system.[19] These features allowed for greater capability, especially in terms of migration between systems. The additional Z80 processor and CP/M compatible disk system could not only be used by audiences already adept with other microcomputers, but also extended the range of software options available to them. This expandability was made possible by the inclusion of the Tube, characterized in *The Home Computer Course* as "a sophisticated interface for connecting an alternative microprocessor, either to achieve faster computing, or to run software written for other machines."[20] Yet the magazine notes that "few users seem to have taken advantage of this feature."

One common feature that users did take advantage of, however, was loading software via the 7-pin DIN audio socket, which allowed the machine to be connected to a standard cassette recorder. Although that was a common way of loading and saving programs for many other microcomputers, the BBC Micro had the extended capability of being able to control the playback of the cassette player/recorder. Users had to rewind and play tapes, but during the loading phase, with a compatible lead, the cassette tape would stop at the correct moments. Many programs had on-screen prompts to tell the user to stop the tape after loading particular sections of a program, but the stop functionality built into the hardware of the Micro simplified this process for users by automatically stopping the tape and starting playback again once it was needed (again prompted by the user pressing particular keys related to the loading program on the screen).

As with other micros at the time, saving programs to a tape was a simple process. Using the *TAPE command would select the cassette filing system running at the default speed of 120 characters per second. Once a BASIC program had been written, the user would type SAVE "prog" ("prog" being the name of the save data they wanted to capture). The user would then be prompted to press the Record button on the tape recorder. A beep would signal the end of the save process. Loading files was similarly straightforward, with users typing in LOAD "prog" to load the program they had saved. However, the user of the Micro was not limited to cassette tapes. Floppy-disk drives were also compatible. On the underside of the Model B's case were a disk-drive port, a printer port, and a user port. Printers could be connected to the Micro via a parallel printer port (also known as a Centronics compatible port) or via a serial port (also referred to as an RS232 or V24 port). The command *FX5, 1 was input to signify the use of a parallel printer, the command *FX5, 2 to signify the use of a serial printer. The eight-bit user port also allowed for digital input/output alongside analog outputs via the "analogue in" port. Whereas the analogue port allowed joysticks to be connected or voltages to be measured, the digital input/output port allowed a range of devices to be connected. The output of the screen display was also unique to the Micro's capabilities in displaying various combinations of text, color, and graphical resolutions via its visual display unit (VDU) outputs. The Micro had eight modes, numbered from 0 to 7.

The graphics as listed in table 1.1 were the number of pixels on the screen (e.g., 640 pixels wide by 256 pixels high). Therefore, in text-only modes it was not possible to draw any high-resolution graphics, as only text characters could be displayed (although characters could be redesigned). The number of colors listed corresponded to how many

Table 1.1 The BBC Micro's display modes.

Mode	Graphics	Text	Colors	Memory	Model
0	640 × 256	80 × 32	2	20K	B
1	320 × 256	40 × 32	4	20K	B
2	160 × 256	20 × 32	16	20K	B
3	Text only	80 × 25	2	16K	B
4	320 × 256	40 × 32	2	10K	A&B
5	160 × 256	20 × 32	4	10K	A&B
6	Text only	40 × 25	2	8K	A&B
7	Teletext	40 × 25	16	1K	A&B

different colors the user could display on the screen at once, and the text numbers to how many columns and rows of text could be displayed on the screen in each mode setting. Together the graphics, text, and colors as listed in the table equated to the amount of memory needed for each mode to be displayed. Therefore, the choice of modes allowed for a compromise between memory usage, resolution, and amount of color displayed. As table 1.1 shows, the Model A, with its 16 kilobytes of memory, was capable of only four modes, whereas the Model B was capable of all eight modes. The Teletext mode (Mode 7) was especially important, as this mode was one of the key features listed in the original specification by the BBC.

Beyond these modes and the Micro's display specifications, the machine also had to be compatible with use in the television studio for filming of the various BBC programs produced to engage audiences with using the machine. In line with this requirement, two additional ports were needed. Those ports were highlighted in the television series *Making the Most of the Micro* even though the connections could be found inside every machine.[21] John Coll pointed out in the first episode of the series that "these two at the end are special connections so we can connect the studio equipment in and get a television picture from the computer."[22] Because the Micro was to be used in many different television series as part of the wider Computer Literacy Project remit, the additional ports were extremely important in a studio setting. Having this functionality allowed the computer's video output to be recorded and mixed into the other video captured footage within the programs. These ports were part of a system, known as "genlocking," in which all video equipment within the same environment could be synchronized. This system meant that there was no flicker from the Micro's monitor when recorded on a studio camera, as would usually be the case with CRT screens. A copy of the output from the BBC Micro was also fed into the studio mixing desk when examples of computer programming were displayed on the screen alongside footage of the presenters using the machine. The ability to show parts of BBC BASIC code for the examples discussed in the television programs was a major part of the Computer Literacy Project, and the genlocking facility helped the BBC achieve this. However, the genlocking feature was not only used in connection to recording the output of the Micro; it was also later used within the Domesday Project, as will be discussed in chapter 7.

Because these features were unique to the Micro, or worked differently than those of other microcomputing platforms that were available in the 1980s, the BBC Micro came with a Welcome Pack meant to help new users to navigate these characteristics of the hardware and to provide an introduction to using software with the machine.

Welcome to the BBC Micro

The Welcome Pack consisted of *Welcome: to the BBC Computer Literacy Project* (a booklet published by the British Broadcasting Corporation) and a cassette tape that contained software programs used to demonstrate some of the functionality of the machine. The first sentence of the Welcome booklet read "The computer you've bought is of advanced design and capable of doing a wide range of things—from making sounds (including music) to drawing pictures (in colour), dealing with words and numbers, and most of all, to responding to what you 'tell' it to do via the keyboard, providing you use the right instructions."[23] The purpose of the booklet was to begin to demystify the platform for users. In the first few pages, readers were shown how to plug their BBC Micro into a television set via a UHF lead.[24] In addition to written instructions, there were four black-and-white images to show users what they were reading about. Potential problems were covered, including the "snowstorm" that most people probably would see on their television screen. The first lines of text that should appear when all was working correctly after the user had plugged the Micro in and tuned the TV to the right channel (shown here in figure 1.1) were also shown.[25]

To alleviate the worries of even the most inexperienced user, there was a section titled "If you've never used a computer before." There was no assumption that everyone had had access to a computer before buying a BBC Microcomputer; it was this fact that drove the Computer Literacy Project in the first place. Even the language used within the

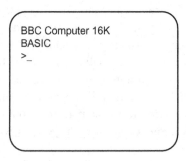

```
BBC Computer 16K
BASIC
>_
```

Figure 1.1 A representation of the BBC Micro Model A's start screen.

booklet could be equated to how people treat other people, and not necessarily machines. Partway through the introduction, even after the statement "remember that a computer is a tool," one encounters the statement "it is very difficult to actually hurt a computer—the BBC Microcomputer is designed to be robust."[26] The terminology had to be straightforward and accessible to all; thus, it alternates between machine-related words, such as "tool," and more human-related references, such as to not being able to "hurt" the computer. In contrast with the *Horizon* episode "Now the Chips Are Down," the language used throughout the Welcome booklet is simple and positive, setting forth the promise and the benefits of the machine rather than equating it to a complicated set of processes. Three and a half pages of the booklet are devoted to the keyboard alone.

As has already been mentioned, the Micro's beige case housed a full-sized keyboard with robust keys (see figure 1.2). In its layout and its responsiveness, it was somewhere between a typewriter and a keyboard such as those commonly used today. The Welcome booklet emphasized that by holding a key down one could cause a character to be repeated on the screen, whereas with a typewriter one had to press the same key again and again to get the same result. How the BBC Micro's keyboard responded was new to many people as they learned to understand its affordance.[27] "The computer keyboard," the Welcome booklet noted, "differs from the conventional keyboard in other ways as well. To begin with it has a set of red 'User-Definable' keys along the top. The programmer can use these keys to do anything he wants them to do ... ."[28]

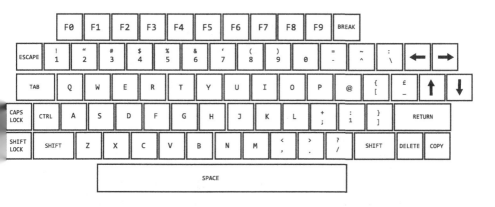

Figure 1.2 The layout of the BBC Micro's keyboard.

One thing that particularly had to be explained to new users was the purpose of the lights in the lower left corner of the Micro's keyboard. The light in the middle corresponded to a typewriter's CAPS LOCK key being on, the one on the right to a typewriter's SHIFT LOCK key being on. The light on the far left indicated that the cassette player was running. How to use the cassette player to load programs was explained a few pages later in the Welcome booklet. Before beginning to load programs from tapes, the new user was encouraged to learn how to use the keyboard, first by reading about how to use it and then by typing in particular commands so as to become more familiar with its layout and its responses.

The Welcome booklet encouraged readers to try programming a few lines of code before trying to access the programs on the cassette tape included with the pack. We can understand these coded practices as sites for shared expression, which was an important part of communication in creating content for the Micro. Being able to converse with others through known examples of BASIC, whether by loading a program or by being able to write a program, was an important part of the Computer Literacy Project. In his recent discussions of software and its effects on our culture and society, Lev Manovich states that "software has become our interface to the world, to others, to our memory and our imagination—a universal language through which the world speaks, and a universal engine on which the world runs."[29] When the BBC Micro was introduced, this was also true of learning to program one's own software so as to be able to easily access the machine, to share these processes, and to eliminate the fear once portrayed by the media when they first reported about the rise in micro-computing. As the Welcome booklet went on to explain the initial examples, it noted that "they may seem like gobbledegook but they produce an interesting result."[30] The booklet listed various draw commands, plot coordinates, and VDU changes to show a series of lines and colors appear on the screen, instead of starting the code from the now often expected example:

```
10 PRINT "HELLO WORLD!"
20 GOTO 10
RUN
```

The first lines of code are treated not as a program to be run, but as a series of individual commands that produce particular responses when typed and RETURN is pressed after each one (see figure 1.3). The commands include the following lines:

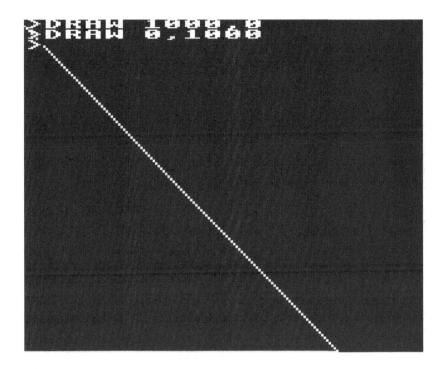

Figure 1.3 A screen shot of MODE 5 DRAW 1000,0 DRAW 0, 1000.

```
MODE 5 (changes the screen display mode)
DRAW 1000,0 (plots a line between the default
coordinate 0,0 to the coordinate 1000,0 across
the bottom of the screen)
DRAW 0,1000 (plots of line between 0 and 1000
and where the last line ended at 1000,0)
```

The reader is then asked to "try typing in a very short program of instructions which will be stored in the computer's memory" and told that "it is designed to produce a kaleidoscopic pattern on the screen."[31] This time, the program is laid out in a typical BASIC structure, with line numbers, as in the following example:

```
10 MODE 5
20 GCOL RND(7), RND(7)
30 PLOT 85, RND(1280), RND(1024)
40 GOTO 20
RUN
```

Figure 1.4 A screen shot of kaleidoscopic pattern code from the Welcome booklet (originally in color).

When the user presses RETURN after typing RUN, the program begins to display various lines and colors on the screen, as shown here in figure 1.4.

Although simple to type, the program included some complex statements that novice users would not necessarily have been able to understand immediately. However, the format of the program shows users some of the structures they will end up using, such as the 10, 20, 30, ... lines that are standard when programming with BASIC. The use of line numbers is documented in the introduction to BASIC written in the context of the 10 PRINT CHR$(205.5+RND(1));: GOTO 10 program on the Commodore 64. As Nick Montfort et al. note, "the interactive editing abilities that were based on line numbers were well represented even in very early versions of BASIC, including the first version of the BASIC that ran on the Dartmouth Time-Sharing System," and "line numbers thus represent not just an organizational scheme, but also an interactive affordance developed in a particular context."[32]

The convention of spacing the program 10 lines apart allowed a user to fill in extra lines as needed at 11, 12, 15, and so on, thus making BASIC flexible for users to manipulate further. It also allowed for editing up and down the program—once lines began to move off the top of the screen, the user had to list line numbers in order to get them back and re-edit any that needed changing. Therefore, the structure of BASIC gave users this freedom of being able to move around an otherwise fixed page, to acquire previously written data, and call particular lines through the known line numbers that were typed. Another command unique to the BBC Micro version of BASIC was the renumber function. This restructured any additional line numbers in a program into set increments determined by the user. For example, if extra line numbers were added at line 12 and line 14, then the renumber function could reorder the program into line numbers in increment of 10 again, and in doing so change GOTO commands that relied on the number lines.

The Welcome booklet directed a user who had become familiar with the Micro's keyboard, and had begun to understand the importance of typing in commands, to the Welcome cassette tape. The cassette tape contained 16 programs to help users explore more of the functionality of the Micro. The "modular" nature of splitting the programs into separate parts not only allowed programs to be accessed individually and repeatedly but also showed the user how to organize information on a cassette tape.[33] Much like present-day learning software packages, the Welcome Tape was organized into bite-sized chunks devoted to various capabilities of the machine. Each program on the Welcome cassette not only helped the user progress through the basic hardware capabilities of the system but also related them to features of the real world, such as clocks, memories, games, and telephone directories. Maintaining a familiar language as the user worked way through the programs became an important part of the way information was presented throughout the Computer Literacy Project.

Beginning with the first program, the Welcome cassette invites the new user to begin to get used to using the cassette player to load programs. The user is invited to press the space bar, the most prominent key on the bottom of the keyboard, to progress through the program and to determine whether it will be necessary to turn the cassette player on and off manually or whether the Micro will take over that control automatically. The Micro's ability to stop the cassette via the REMOTE control socket connected to the computer again helped the user to understand how much he or she would have to remember about running programs on the machine. Stopping the tape automatically took away some pressure from those users who could make use of the Micro's ability and allowed them to enjoy the programs as they were presented one by one.

After the initial welcome, the user was presented with the Welcome cassette's Index program. It listed all the other programs that were available on the cassette and allowed users to set the hours, minutes, and seconds of their own clocks. This command seemed redundant, in that nothing happened after numbers were entered, but the clock was revisited a few programs later to encourage the user to play with the inputting of commands. In the meantime, one could try pressing various keys so as to learn the layout of the Micro's keyboard.

The fourth program on the Welcome cassette, called Sketch, was introduced as being similar to Etch A Sketch (a popular toy that originated in the 1960s, when it was manufactured by the Ohio Art Company). Drawing on toys and popular-culture references showed how the Micro could appeal to a range of people, comforting users and allowing them to link up previously used processes in new ways through the machine. In a similar vein to learning to use the keyboard, some of the functionality of an Etch A Sketch is remediated via the software application, allowing users to recognize the tropes of older media forms and reframe them in terms of the new display that is offered rather than the material processes.[34] In their work on interaction design and computer technologies, Jay Bolter and Diane Gromala state that "the computer shaped the information it conveys and is shaped in turn by the physical and cultural worlds in which it functions."[35] In the example of Sketch, the Micro's keyboard becomes the interface of control rather than the two rotating knobs found on the Etch A Sketch product. The keyboard's functionality not only introduces new learning in terms of a new set of keys (again moving on from a typewriter approach) but also introduces the commands that make it possible to digitally draw on the screen. It is via this aspect of the program that the "User Definable" keys are introduced. The Welcome booklet explains:

In this program the User Definable keys work like this

f0 – makes the line appear red
f1 – makes the line appear green
f2 – makes the line appear yellow
f3 – makes the line appear blue
f4 – enables you to move the cursor without drawing anything
f9 – enables you to erase a line[36]

The familiarity of older technological processes repackaged in new forms continued with the Calculator program and the later Telephone program, both of which took everyday machines or lists of data and converts them into new structures through the Micro. Adding in multiple known conversions of common practices allowed the machine to be seen as a multi-purpose device and one that could be used for many other tasks that could improve a user's life without taking it over. This eased users into the possibilities of the machine without overwhelming them with unnecessarily complicated details.

The Clock program on the Welcome cassette may seem basic, but it helped users to learn about the hardware and the software. Clock made use of the notion of "memory," again emphasizing the perceived "intelligence" of the Micro in its recognition of earlier commands by the user but also linking the computer memory's with the user's memory. Warren Sack explores these differences and similarities of human and machine memory in his discussions of memory, in which he links the word "memory" with other words associated with the graphical user interface of the office, among them "file," "documents," and "trash."[37] Familiarizing users with a new term in relation to one already part of their knowledge base and constructing images of computer memory through making users remember their first interaction with the Clock program was intended to demystify the process of computing further and to build confidence in users' later explorations.

Other programs on the Welcome cassette also were intended to help make users aware of programming techniques without overtly labeling them as such. Alphasort is one example. It began by asking a user to list ten words of up to nine characters. Once the user had made a list, the Micro ordered it alphabetically. It performed that task so quickly that it then gave the user an option to view the list's construction in slow motion. If the user accepted that option, the words moved slowly across the screen and in and out of one another until the correct order was reached. This process displayed a "bubble sort" algorithm that worked by going through a list of items and comparing adjacent pairs of items, continually swapping them until they were in the right order. The end result of the sorting process is always found first, so the program continues to find the rest of the order through having to swap fewer and fewer results as it gets closer to find the correct solution.

The "bubble sort" algorithm was also reiterated in the Telephone program, which, according to the Welcome booklet, "shows in a very simple way just one use of the computer for ordering information in a regular manner" and adds that "later on, in the program called

TELEPHONE this will be demonstrated more completely."[38] Once again repetition through a variety of activities allowed this active reinforcement of processes. Yet instead of repeating the process in program after program, this learning was interrupted by other programs. At one point, the Welcome booklet promised "a little light relief." The "light relief" was an interactive poem providing a break from the serious ordering of information and the later calling on data sets provided by the search functionality of the Telephone program.

The poem had been provided by the Liverpool poet Roger McGough. According to the BBC's Poetry Season website, McGough, born in 1937, became part of Liverpool's "Mersey Beat scene" and "along with Mike McCartney and John Gorman, formed the comic group The Scaffold, which in 1968 reached No 1 with Lily the Pink."[39] After his poetry became successful through its inclusion in the Penguin Modern Poets collection, McGough became known for various works, including many poems for children. Therefore, the use of his poem in the BBC Micro Welcome pack appeared to make good sense. The poem was a playful experience for users as they navigated McGough's own playing with the possibilities of reordering the ways in which a poem could be read alongside the interplay of words and imagery.[40] Users who pressed the Return key were guided through variations of events as the poem was displayed. Occasionally a user was asked to enter his or her name and to indicate whether he or she wished to proceed with certain elements by responding either Y or N. The purpose of the poem was to expose more of the machine's capabilities: "Each time you come back to it, it will be different in some way. As well as being ingenious it illustrates, for example, how the computer can construct a verse (or anything) from random elements."[41] Choosing options throughout the rest of the poem moved the user toward a greater sense of what Janet Murray would call "agency" within interactive narratives defined as "the satisfying power to take meaningful action and see the result of our decisions and choices."[42]

Further examination and replaying of the poem revealed similar outcomes even if different combinations were selected. However, the element of choice made the experience feel personal to the user, as it related back to the overall learning encountered on using the Welcome cassette. The poem, as presented, reveals as much about McGough's encounters with making a poem for the Micro as it does about users accessing it and interacting with it. The choice of computing terms and the sarcastic nature of the poem's design reveal McGough's own perceptions of the world of computing and how these can be played with in a communicative manner through the medium of the narrative presented. The inclusion of the poem on the Welcome cassette tape also begins to show how the Micro could also be seen as a cross-disciplinary machine. The BBC Micro could be used just as much in English classes as in science and mathematics classes, allowing for Information Technology to be used in various lessons across the curriculum. Similarly, exploring the outcomes of McGough's poem hinted at the "encyclopedic" possibilities of the system in terms of multiple outcomes, storing segments of data to be called at different times and playing with the narrative of presented texts through interchanging data sets.[43]

These concepts were built on once again with the next program, Telephone; then some more light relief was provided by a game called Bat 'n' Ball. Unlike the version of Breakout that is part of the ZX Spectrum's Horizon tape (an equivalent tape to the Micro's Welcome tape), Bat 'n' Ball was represented by a basic set of line drawings. There were no bricks to break; instead, the "ceiling" of the game lowered at intervals throughout the game in order to make the game slightly harder. The game was also educational: in order to begin playing the game, one first had to construct it. The user did not have to type in the BASIC commands to make that happen, but he or she had to press the space bar between each line of commands that appeared pre-programmed on the screen. The BASIC program was accompanied by comments that showed the user what each sequence did:

CLG (clear graphics area)
MOVE 0,0 (move graphics cursor to 0,0)
DRAW 0, 800 (draw a line to 0,800)
DRAW 1272, 800 (draw top line)
DRAW 1272, 0 (draw side)
MOVE 4, 700 (move cursor)
DRAW 1268, 700 (draw wall)
MOVE 72, 50 (move cursor)
DRAW 192, 50 (draw bat)
PLOT 69, 80, 140 (draw a point at 80, 140)
(add three more to make a ball)

Then the game began, with the Z key used to move the bat to the left and the X key to move to it to the right. The Welcome booklet supported the ideas of game creation and playing ("Microprocessors are at the heart of all electronic games"; in turn, the modifying and cloning of arcade games such as *Pong!* and *Breakout* helped players to associate the Micro with other aspects of popular culture to which they might have already been exposed. This can be seen in the context of the possibilities of copying code in order to edit it or re-create a similar, known experience. "What happens in copying," Jussi Parikka writes, "is first the identification or framing of the object to be copied, followed by the reproduction of a similar object whose mode of existence is predicated upon its being distributed."[44] The description of the code used to construct the screen for the Bat 'n' Ball game and the visual association with other popular games began to build links between how the game software was created and also how the game was played. Whether users played the game or instead used the code as a starting point to create another version of a similar game, they were able to see a common reference point for the transference of ideas, processes, and outcomes.

Another game, the Yellow River Kingdom Game, was included on the Welcome tape in the form of the program KINGDOM. The program was a simulation in which the player decided how many villagers he or she should use to protect against flooding while growing enough rice, and protecting the village from thieves. The principles and rule structures within the simulation drew on the game of Hammurabi, which also was about strategy and resource allocation. In the case of Hammurabi (often cited as one of the earliest computer games), the "program was originally written in Focal at DEC ... [and then] David Ahl converted it to BASIC."[45] The original game consisted of just over 100 lines of code. By porting a similar game to the BBC Micro, this part of the Welcome tape once again opened up the possibilities of the BBC BASIC programming language by drawing on and modifying earlier examples, possibly with the hope of encouraging users to do the same.[46]

The playful nature of the Micro continued with the Music program, which drew on other audiences that might have played with electronic keyboards and wished to see how some of their music skills could be translated onto the BBC Micro. The top and middle rows of keys represented different notes. Users could begin to play their own variations of songs as they watched visual representations of blocks of color appear on screen. A mapping of musical notes to keyboard keys was provided in the Welcome booklet, with the proviso that users were encouraged to stick labels on the keys to help them remember what each key did when using them. These exercises show not only the adaptability of the hardware and software capabilities of the Micro but also how keys could be swapped in various programs and extensions.

This continuation of artistic references, drawing on a range of cultural influences, was seen once again in the PHOTO program listing where images of Marilyn Monroe are displayed in line drawings of changing colors. Here the intertextual references to the work of the pop artist Andy Warhol are clearly marked out by the four images that appear on the screen, which are changed by means of the color cycles that are generated by the program. Similarly, the PATTERNS program draws the user's attention to the user-definable keys again, pressing them in sequences to reveal randomly generated kaleidoscopic patterns, similar to those shown in the BASIC programming examples presented in the Welcome booklet itself. Covering these parts of the Micro shows not only its programming capabilities but also its graphical outputs as a way of showing off all of the functionality and presentation that the user should expect through interacting and making their own outputs with it.

The final full program on the Welcome cassette is that of Biorhythms. This charts the various physical, intellectual, and emotional cycles at the user's best and worst depending on their birth date and the day the rhythms are predicted for. Much like a horoscope, the data provided is to be interpreted by the user in their own way, whether they choose to believe what is presented to them or not. As the accompanying text states, "whether you believe in biorhythms or not, this program demonstrates the speed with which the computer can calculate (for example the number of days from your birth) and how it can be used to display graphical information." Here, the program provides a set of possibilities for further information gathering and graph plotting that the user could access, create and explore with their own programs, in the disguise of another popular-culture artifact of the biorhythms information. Situating learning about the Micro in the context of other 1980s artifacts was a major part in trying to make computer literacy appeal to as wide an audience as possible. This is reiterated in the final display of the cassette tape that mentioned how users can find out about further programs associated with the Computer Literacy Project. As with buying the Micro, the Welcome pack was just the start of the user's journey into how to think about, create, experiment, and produce content with the machine. One way this was achieved was through the range of television content produced by the BBC as it aimed to educate both home and school users about the Micro and other microcomputing machines.

The Computer Programme

As David Morley notes in his discussions of the role of the television in the home, television "should be seen, not in isolation, but as one of the number of information and communication technologies, occupying domestic time and space alongside the video-recorder, the computer and the telephone, as well as the Walkman, the answering machine, the stereo and the radio."[47] Although this statement was published a decade after the arrival on the BBC Microcomputer, it still resonates with what the Computer Literacy Project attempted to achieve at the time. Television was for many at the heart of everyday life, and activities were often scheduled around various programs in the television listings in people's leisure time.[48] Organizing more informal educational content via television programs was part of the remit of the BBC's own educational department. Therefore, in an attempt to remind audiences of the benefits of microcomputers beyond the doom and gloom of late-1970s documentaries that had focused on the downside of such machines, the Computer Literacy Project utilized home television as a way of introducing aspects of learning into both school and leisure time, starting with a series called *The Computer Programme* in 1982.

First aired on January 11, 1982, *The Computer Programme* was presented by two people: Chris Serle (who personified the inexperienced consumer learning about computing) and Ian "Mac" McNaught-Davis (the computer expert who would demystify the process). Computer processes were associated with objects in viewers' everyday lives, as when writing a computer program was compared to describing a set of instructions on how to operate a washing machine. Each week new concepts were explained, among them the "bubble sort" algorithm used in some computer programming techniques. Often a concept was explained away from the computer, after which Serle wrote the related computer program with the help of McNaught-Davis. In the second episode, titled "Just One Thing After Another," Serle is asked to sort metal weights of differing sizes from the heaviest to the lightest.[49] McNaught-Davis then explains the way in which he should approach the task. By comparing pairs of the metal weights next to each other on a table, Serle slowly moves each of the weights along the line so they eventually end up in the correct order. Instead of showing multiple lines of code on the screen, these real-world activities are then linked to typed programs on the computer, such as one that sorts names alphabetically using a similar process. Stripping back each command to something that everyday audiences could relate to meant that the programs could reach different demographics in order to capture the imagination of as many people as possible.

In his recollections about recording the series, published in the October 1982 issue of *Acorn User*, David Allen wrote that "in September

1981, we started with bare circuit boards and not even a cassette filing system. The first television series was produced with the most amazing 'lash up' (I think that's the engineering jargon)—and programs were fed into the machine through a specially devised interface from one of Acorn's System 3 computers."[50] Allen also recalls how even "the BBC disc drive shown in the studio was a fake, we even had a member of the team to operate its red light on cue." Despite such tricks (employed in order to get a program ready for airing on time), the series was successful enough to warrant a successor. The second series, *Making the Most of the Micro*, debuted in 1983. This coincided with the release of the BBC Buggy peripheral (as discussed in the next chapter) and the Teletext adapter (as discussed in chapter 6), and provided a more detailed insight into using microcomputers, again with the BBC Micro at the heart of the examples.

David Allen previewed details of *Making the Most of the Micro* in the first issue of *Acorn User*: "Whereas *The Computer Programme* provided a general introduction to computing, especially for those with no previous knowledge of experience, the new series will be aimed more at owners of machines, or those about to take a serious plunge into the world of personal computing."[51] "The next series," Allen went on to predict, "will look into 'how to' in more detail and more critically than the earlier series." Going into more detail than the first series, and exploring graphics, sound, how to utilize analog-to-digital conversion, and how to control other inputs connected to the micro, *Making the Most of the Micro* continued to use the BBC Micro to highlight some of the possibilities of microcomputing. At the end of the series, viewers were offered a chance to download a program specifically for the BBC Micro. The program was emitted as a sound at the end of episode 10, along with an image of a television transmitter aerial drawn on the Micro's screen to signify the start and end point of the transmission.[52] Viewers were then able to record this output directly to their Micros or record it on a cassette tape to be played back later. Once the program had been loaded, the following message (copied in part) from the presenter "Mac" and the production team was displayed:

If you've been watching *Making the Most of the Micro* we'd be glad to have your reactions, good or bad and an idea of the kind of things you'd like to see in future series. Drop us a line. ... And if you'd like to submit a question which might be answered in this live special programme in October, please send it on a postcard.[53]

Viewers were also asked if they wished be contacted to appear in the audience of the upcoming live program, or if they were willing to be phoned up during the transmission to ask their question. As much as the development of the platform was a collaborative effort of the BBC team and Acorn, the user base forming around using the machine and viewing the related television programs also helped to build up communities of people with shared interests in ways of developing possible uses further. A two-hour live special program was aired by the BBC under the title "Making the Most of the Micro Live" on Sunday, October 2, 1983. A series titled *Micro Live* aired in October 1984. *Micro Live*, a weekly live program, was hosted by Ian McNaught-Davis. Among the presenters were Lesley Judd, Fred Harris, and Connor Freff Cochran. Cochran was responsible for broadcasts from the US. John Coll, the author of the BBC Micro manual, appeared on both *Making the Most of the Micro* and "Making the Most of the Micro Live." Once again, the community of users helped to spread the learning of how to utilize the capabilities of the machine through more commonly found media outputs.

Linked Learning through Multiple Literacies

The linked approach to learning through the television series aired as part of the Computer Literacy Project meant that the BBC's project went beyond computer literacy to offer a general "media literacy" or "multi-literacies" as a way of exposing audiences to different avenues of learning.[54] As David Buckingham notes, "literacy today, it is argued, is inevitably and necessarily multimedia literacy; and to this extent traditional forms of literacy teaching are no longer adequate."[55] The idea of incorporating a multi-media approach not only via machine interaction but also literally in terms of multiple media outputs was a unique approach to solving what was seen to be a nationwide problem of general competencies within microcomputing.

Computer literacy in the 1980s could be situated in what Jussi Parikka defines as "knowledge work." According to Parikka, "knowledge work did not represent a uniform class, nor did work with computers have to be bound by nationality. Instead, 'the language' of computers enabled new forms of productive action that were not 'work' according to the old standards of the industrial era but yet represented the core of the knowledge economy and its thrust toward communication, cultural and social knowledge ... ."[56] However, in Britain the Computer Literacy Project was in many ways focused on nationality, evoking a sense of national pride for the British creators of computers and the resultant possibilities that being computer literate could provide for future work. This national approach was echoed in the opening pages of *The Computer Book*, released as part of the Computer Literacy Project's range of material that discusses computer literacy in line with other British literacies, including the Industrial Revolution.[57] Yet for some, what appeared to be a monopoly on British manufactured computers was not a good thing for the education system.

Janet Ainley, a mathematics teacher in the UK at that time, remembers:

It was a time when computers were first starting to come into schools and schools wanted to get hold of this new thing and ... "there is this very good ... offer." But what was on offer was only British-made computers ... . The motivation was nothing to do with education; it was actually about supporting the British computer industry.[58]

For Ainley the monopoly on British machines conveyed a sense that the educational aspects of the machine were exploited by political and thus industrial gains, whereas for others the strength of such initiatives were of benefit to British businesses as a way of positioning them within a global market. In a similar light, not only was the Conservative government pushing these platforms within the school system; the educational benefits of each platform were being promoted by how the machine was advertised, once again acting as a type of propaganda for a particular type of identification between the platform and "particular groups of consumers."[59] An advertisement for the BBC Microcomputer in the January 4, 1983 edition of *The Times* is headlined "See what they're teaching our kids these days."[60] A more detailed discussion of this advertisement by James Summer notes that "Acorn's strong and assured sales base in schools education led it to address much of its marketing to parents, continuing to promote the microcomputer as a learning device, while competitors increasingly stressed leisure or business advantages."[61] Yet other advertisements for the BBC Microcomputer, such as the one in the December 1982 issue of *Electronics and Computing Monthly*, are headlined "Broader Horizons." The latter advertisement states the multiple-use approach to the machine for business, education, science, control, or games applications, as the machine was able to "satisfy the needs of novice and expert alike."[62] Therefore, for some British audiences the approaches offered outside of the more formal school education system meant that computer literacies of many kinds were opened up to a much broader audience. In October 1983, reportedly, 25 percent of total sales were for use in education, 25 percent to home users, and 40 percent to business users.[63] In this respect, it is possible to see how situating the BBC Micro within a broader campaign focused on multiple literacies of related television series, books, correspondence courses, and radio programs enabled it to thrive within different contexts. By working across multiple outputs, the BBC was able to reach wider audiences for whom the more traditional literacies of reading and writing were not always assumed. Therefore these approaches provided multiple ways for people to learn how to use the system. This was particularly useful not only for software development but also for accessing and manipulating the hardware of the machine. As will be discussed in the next chapter, enabling users to go beyond the software-writing capabilities of the machine and encouraging them to tinker inside and outside of the Micro's beige case were additional ways of exposing the platform's hardware. The focus on learning to understand the hardware of the platform was also emphasized by going beyond the operating system and opening up the case of the machine.

The hobbyist phenomenon in microcomputing was nothing new. Hobbyists had already adopted many machines, notably the Altair and the
TRS-80 in the United States and various machines in Britain, Australia,
and Czechoslovakia.[1] However, the BBC Micro played a unique role in the
continuation of some aspects of the hobbyist ethos. Although the BBC
Micro was not a kit computer but a ready-made machine that could be
used right out of the box, the hobbyist roots of some members of the
Acorn team appeared to be evident in some of the internal and external
properties of the machine.[2] For that reason, the initial uses of the machine
as perceived by the BBC in developing the Computer Literacy Project
and the uses to which some owners put the machine were markedly
different.[3]

This chapter highlights how the Micro was expanded through user
need as well as designed experiences intended for users. In doing so, it
explores further connections to the hardware inside and outside of the
Micro's case through the modularity allowed by the system. The modular
nature of learning how to use the platform continued into how the hardware was manufactured.[4] The upgrade possibilities of the Micro were
unlike those of other micros on the market at the time, as were the input
and output functions that the machine offered. Thomas Lean recognizes
this modularity through his own tracing of the histories of Acorn
Computer's developments: "Although manufacturers made allowance for
expansion of their micros, this seems to have contributed to a pro-
nounced modular or systemic approach in Acorn's home computers."[5]

Lean then goes on to discuss this "modularity" of Acorn micros as emphasized in the Atom's 1980 advertising copy, and how it continued to be replicated in parts of later designs. Intentionally proposed add-ons were not only built into the original specification of the machine but also enabled users to extend this modularity in other ways. Similarly, the Micro's own version of BASIC played a role in how this modularity continued as people began to learn how to control various aspects of the machine. Learning how to use BBC BASIC to its full potential also allowed users to operate the Micro system in a variety of ways, including working with the various monitoring capabilities of the machine promoted on television programs such as those in the series *Making the Most of the Micro*. This aspect of using the machine was seen as a fundamental literacy for those wanting to interact with the machine beyond the commands given for loading information from cassette tapes or floppy disks.

BASIC Beginnings

The use of BASIC as a programming language was not unique to the Micro. As had been done with other machines, a modified version of the language was created for use with the Micro.

The Beginner's All-purpose Symbolic Instruction Code, which originated at Dartmouth College in 1964 as a result of work done by two professors, John Kennedy and Thomas Kurtz, was an evolution of other high-level languages, "building on some of what FORTRAN, Algol, and other languages had accomplished: greater portability across platforms along with keywords and syntax that facilitated understanding the language and writing programs."[6] BASIC has been modified, expanded on, and repurposed for various platforms, including many microcomputers of the 1980s.

In the original consultation for the BBC Micro, it was advised that BASIC should be used as a programming standard. The Micro's developers "were urged to use a well-designed and 'structured' BASIC, which would not only be powerful but encourage good practice in programming."[7] According to the User Guide, "The BBC Microcomputer includes a large and powerful operating system. This can be accessed from user-written machine-code routines or from BASIC."[8] For the majority of users, at least those who were not experienced with microcomputing, BBC BASIC was a way into controlling and creating programs for use with the machine. A command preceded by an asterisk allowed the user access to particular functions within the operating system, among them *TAPE (used to load tapes), *KEY (used to program a user-definable key), and *TELESOFT (used to select the Teletext filing system).

The developments that led to the version of BBC BASIC used with the Micro originated in the initial discussions between David Allen and John Coll. In 1980 the BBC sought advice from various groups, including the Local Education Authorities, the Council for Educational Technology, and the Science Policy Research Unit at the University of Sussex. It also approached John Coll, an educational advisor to the Micro Users in Secondary Education (MUSE) project. Coll was keen on using a "structured BASIC" that would appeal to beginners yet could support more complex programming by advanced users. David Allen had returned from a trip to Japan, where he had acquired a Sharp 1210 calculator. The calculator, which only had 896 bytes of random-access memory, could be used for mathematical functions but also could be used be used for programming in BASIC. Allen's use of the calculator confirmed that the BBC team wanted to use a version of BASIC with the microcomputer that would support the Computer Literacy Project. After further discussions with John Coll, they worked toward a version they called ABC, meaning Adopted BASIC for Computers.[9] In fact it was this version of BASIC that led to the Micro's being developed by Acorn—other companies did not particularly want to adapt their machines to run yet another version of BASIC. Sinclair already had Sinclair BASIC, and saw the proposed BBC BASIC not only as a threat but also as likely to tie users to a specific machine.[10]

However, the members of the team working on the specification for the BBC Micro continued to design their own version of the programming language. Initially developed by David Kitson (a senior engineer in the BBC's Engineering Designs Department) and Richard Russell (an expert on the BASIC language), a version of BASIC was created specifically for the Micro and implemented by the Acorn development team. That version of BASIC is widely credited to Sophie Wilson, who in a 2007 interview detailed how much of her own stamp she put on the final version of the language:

BBC BASIC is a compromise between my advanced interpreter of the day and the BBC's desire to keep the language "standard." Most of the time the advanced features managed to get included unchanged, so overall I was happy (the only significant loss I can remember is over labels vs line numbers—the BBC committee insisted on line numbers) … it felt significant at the time: a fast BASIC interpreter which was convenient to use (in ROM on all machines) with many advanced features.[11]

Although BBC BASIC was tied explicitly to the BBC Micro's processor and memory layout and therefore wasn't compatible with other computing platforms, this extra layer of BASIC as another platform allowed for transferrable skills across other machines. In a review of the Micro in *Electronics and Computing Monthly*, Harry Fairhead wrote:

The great thing about BBC BASIC is that it has all the advantages of BASIC—straightforwardness PLUS the advantages of a structured language such as PASCAL. Using its "procedures and functions" you can build up large programs from smaller routines. Once you've got used to this method of programming you find that it makes life much easier—especially when it comes to debugging, making modifications or adding extra routines.[12]

Because all characters were significant, there were no restrictions on the names of variables, strings, or arrays. BBC BASIC also had the capability of providing multi-line procedures and functions with any number of arguments. Another unique quality of BBC BASIC was its built-in assembler. Most other computers required a separate program to assemble machine code from assembly language programs. BBC BASIC allowed users to assemble machine code directly from within the BASIC program. This allowed for greater flexibility in being able to include machine-code routines within their BASIC programs, which would execute faster than they would if only BASIC was used.

Learning to use BBC BASIC made the Micro accessible to both inexperienced users and more advanced users as another a way of capturing a wider audience. To help users understand how to use BBC BASIC with the Micro, the BBC integrated a 30-hour BASIC course into the Computer Literacy Project in conjunction with the National Extension College. Potential users could teach themselves using course materials or take the course by correspondence. By the end of 1982, more than 100,000 copies had been sold.[13] The course booklet described many different examples, including examples of what a computer was capable of doing, at one end of the spectrum, and statement numbers, store locations, and arithmetic operators, at the other end. Short tests were provided at the end of each chapter, with the answers included at the back of the book. For those taking the correspondence version, longer assignments were included for users to send in and receive feedback on. *Me & My Micro*, a book published by the National Extension College Trust and released to accompany a Yorkshire Television series with the same title, included various programs written in BASIC for users to type in.[14] The differences between BBC BASIC and Sinclair's BASIC for the ZX Spectrum were explained at the beginning of each chapter, as these were the two main machines used to accompany the course.

In a similar move, BASIC was explained to audiences via the linked television programs that the BBC transmitted. During the second episode of *Making the Most of the Micro*, titled "Getting Down to BASIC," Ian McNaught-Davis explains the key concepts of BASIC primarily in terms of what he defines as the three principles of programming: sequence, decision (or branch), and loop.[15] To explain these concepts, there is a classroom scenario in which primary school students are asked multiplication questions. The teacher chooses two numbers, each between one and twelve, and the student is asked to provide an answer. If the answer is not known the teacher states it is wrong. Cutting back to the television studio, McNaught-Davis translates this into a simple program in BASIC for audiences to follow:

```
10  FIRST=RND(12)
20  SECOND=RND(12)
30  CORRECT = FIRST*SECOND
40  PRINT "What is " FIRST " times " SECOND
50  INPUT REPLY
60  IF REPLY=CORRECT THEN PRINT "Right" ELSE
PRINT "Wrong"
```

The program is then extended by showing the ability to add further lines of BASIC due to the listing being laid out in tens. McNaught-Davis explains other commands that can be added to allow for repeating the program until the answer is correct by adding

```
35  REPEAT
70  UNTIL REPLY=CORRECT
```

The final parts of the program are also changed to allow each user three tries to reach the correct answer and to allow 25 questions to be posed, one for each student in the classroom. The program is completed by adding the following lines:

```
32  TRY=0
55  TRY=TRY+1
```

```
70 UNTIL REPLY=CORRECT OR TRY=3
80 IF REPLY<> CORRECT THEN PRINT "The correct
answer is " CORRECT
```

and

```
5 FOR CHILD=1 TO 25
90 NEXT CHILD
```

The program is summed up by reiterating the three basic principles—sequence, branch, and loop—that were used in the simple BASIC code outlined above. Once again, the integration of examples with easy-to-follow, structured programs contributed to the literacies opened up to viewers and users alike. Much like the programming literacies presented in the Welcome booklet, the active use of BASIC programming examples in the television programs opened up the possibility for users to get a greater sense of control when using the machine. Wendy Chun recognizes this revelation faced by programmers when encountering the fundamental processes of software: "To enjoy this absolute power, the programmer must follow the rules of a programming language. Regardless, seeing his or her code produce visible and largely predictable results creates pleasure."[16] However, this pleasure and control over the Micro could be experienced in other ways, as users could go beyond programming.

Upgrading the machine

In contrast with a machine that had a solid molded-plastic case that hid the circuitry and the inner workings from the everyday user, accessibility was an important feature of Acorn's design for the BBC Micro. Whereas with some other computers only "insiders or experts [were] able to take the back off ... and play around with the electronics inside,"[17] the BBC Micro's case encouraged such investigation. Its outer case was easy to remove, with only four screws standing in the way of a user who wished to see the machine's inner workings. And the Micro could be modified, with implied consent and indeed assistance from its designers. As was noted in the preceding chapter, the Model A version of the BBC Micro could be upgraded to include many of the functions of the Model B, and the Model B also had the capabilities of adding extra processors to the machine as a way of increasing the 6502 chipset already present in its design. However, as much as the Micro's upgrades also needed to be purchased by keen consumers, the possibilities to examine the inside of the machine were made possible from the start. In many ways this process was encouraged, as beyond the case were further possibilities of expanding the machine, mainly in terms of adding additional read-only memory (ROMs), but also sideways RAM and ROM expansions that were developed later. This additional functionality, which allowed users easy access to components inside the machine, set the Micro apart from other microcomputers on the market in the early 1980s.

Alongside the BBC Micro User Guide, which could be purchased separately from Acorn Computers, users of the Micro could also request a circuit diagram of the machine's layout. This detailed map of the Micro's inner workings gave the user a chance to understand the connections, circuitry, and possibilities of the hardware beyond the more often pushed software literacy. This diagram came into play in circumstances such as installing a Speech facility on the machine. There were many variations of having computer-synthesized speech on the BBC Micro, from software packages such as Superior Software's *Speech!* to adding additional speech ROMs to the hardware of the machine.[18] The official Speech System upgrade from Acorn Computers was based on a Texas Instruments TMS5220 Voice Synthesis Processor, using a database of sounds held within a phrase ROM (or PHROM), part number TS6100, to store the sounds and the voice of the BBC newsreader Kenneth Kendall to pronounce the words to be spoken.

Like most microcomputers, the BBC has both read-only memory and random-access memory. Whereas ROM (read-only memory) allows for memory to be read by the machine to be used when needed, RAM (random-access memory) allows for read and write capabilities and is used for a wider range of processes. The Model B has 32 kilobytes of RAM available, of which some memory is reserved by the operating system for certain processes. Alongside this the Micro has two ROMs shipped with the basic hardware, one for the operating system (MOS ROM) and one for BBC BASIC (BASIC ROM). These are essential for the machine to boot up. If no ROMs are available besides the operating system ROM, the BBC will start up with the prompt "LANGUAGE?" in order to signify that it requires at least one language in order to operate in some way. The BBC BASIC ROM was not an essential component, as it would be possible to add other ROMs, such as one for Logo, to the machine. However, BBC BASIC was a fundamental component for the majority of users, and therefore one that would usually remain. Alongside these ROMs the Micro had further ROM expansion capabilities. The hardware could support four ROMs, and the operating system could to support up to sixteen ROMs. One of these ROM expansion sockets became useful for the Speech Upgrade system.

The introduction to the 1983 instruction manual for Acorn Computers' Speech Upgrade starts by outlining the various components of the main Printed Circuit Board (PCB), such as how to locate the issue number and how to navigate the board: "The edge further away from you (with the DIN sockets and modulator on it) is then *north*, to your right is *east*, to your left is *west* and nearest is *south.*"[19] Installing the Speech System required the user to manipulate particular parts of the circuit dependent on the issue of PCB the machine contained and was a process for the more experienced user to undertake. However, many users did not need access to the whole circuitry of the machine but instead needed to know how to upgrade particular aspects, including the other ROM expansions that were available without changing other parts of the internal circuitry. This was particularly important for users who wanted to upgrade some of the functionality of the machine in relation to the programs they wanted to run.

Nowadays we are used to computers having a certain amount of memory, which is more often than not sufficient to complete everyday tasks such as browsing the Web, using word processing software, playing computer games, and using 3D modeling packages. However, memory was limited in the 1980s and more often than not used for specific functions. Some programs required extra memory capacity to carry out tasks more efficiently. With that in mind, the BBC Micro's designers made sure there were extra ROM slots available. Whereas today users who wish to upgrade memory add another stick of compatible RAM, users of the BBC Micro would often use extra ROMs for particular programs. Those additions to the machine were both hardware-specific and software-specific. Acorn's retail price list of July 1986 lists particular ROMs under categories such as Upgrades and Interfaces, Languages, and Personal Productivity Tools. Many ROMs were priced around £50; many software programs were priced between £10 and £20.[20] Therefore, ROMs were an investment for users who required not only dedicated facilities but also the capability of installing the ROM in the first place.

Fitting ROM chips required the user to remove the cover of the machine and then remove the keyboard panel via another two screws on the inside panel. As the ROM fitting instructions note, "on the bottom right-hand side of the main circuit board there are five 28-pin sockets—for reference we shall label these A to E from left to right. The Operating

System is found in socket A and BASIC (serial number ending in B01 or B05) is usually found plugged into socket B."[21] This left the user with three extra ROM sockets to be used by other software packages. As defined by the ROM fitting instructions, these were usually categorized into either Language ROMs (including ROMs such as the ROM for BASIC, or word-processing packages such as Wordwise), or Service or Utility ROMs (including the Speech ROM that converted text to speech and utilities such as Printmaster that offered additional printer functionality). These distinctions were important for users to understand so that they knew how to structure where the ROMs should be placed. For language ROMs, the position determined the order in which the BBC Micro would access and find the ROM, giving priority to the slot with the earliest letter. For example, the BASIC ROM needed to be fitted in a higher priority socket to a language ROM to make sure that the Micro would boot up with BASIC functionality. This allowed the user to choose other programs that could be more easily accessed through calling them in the required language. However, Utility ROMs did not have to be placed in any particular order, as they would be called as and when needed, rather than immediately on starting up the machine.

The layout of the ROMs as detailed in the Watford Electronics ROM fitting instructions is shown here in figure 2.1. That diagram shows the spaces available to the user and what are listed as sideways ROM sockets for the BBC Model B. Similarly, the manual outlines techniques for handling ROMs to allow users to feel more confident with every stage of the installation process. As each ROM has a set of metal "legs" that are required to connect the ROM in places in the machine, it is possible for some of these to get bent when sold, in transit or when being fitted by the user. The manual suggests straightening these pins or legs by resting the

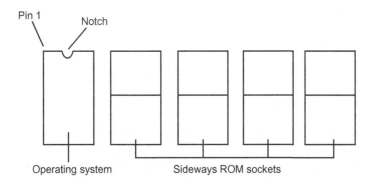

Figure 2.1 The ROM layout of the BBC Micro Model B.

ROM on a flat, nonconductive surface and gently rolling the legs along the surface so that they form a line at right angles with the chip. This allows for a more straightforward installation process for the user, as the legs should then go directly into the slots in the machine. The removal of ROMs is recommended with a common household flat-headed screwdriver to once again gently lift them out of place and move them. This process was remembered by Bridget Somekh in her recollections of the challenges teachers faced in learning to understand new technological processes through the introduction of the BBC Micro in the school where she worked: "On my first day at Netherhall I was asked by the Director, Rod Mulvey, to fit a Wordwise word processing chip into a BBC computer .... I knew that this required me to take the top off the machine. I had in my hand an open box with a small rectangular piece of metal, sitting on a bed of foam. If I had not known it was delicate, its packaging would have made this obvious."[22]

Learning to understand these processes was for many users an important part of understanding the full capabilities of the machine. As with memory slots on present-day computers, ROMs could be removed, changed, and re-used in different combinations depending on the languages and/or utilities that users wanted to use. However, the need for extra memory became more and more evident.

Although other machines (for example, Sinclair's ZX81) had allowed RAM expansion, the way the BBC Micro did so was markedly different. Various magazine articles heralded the use of sideways storage as a way of expanding the machine. Mike Rawlings summed this up in the March 1986 issue of *Acorn User*: "Extra memory provided by sideways RAM boards is useful not just for utilities, new commands or printer buffers but also for running longer programs. The dreaded 'No room' message can be cured by a second processor, but a cheaper answer is to move variables, text and even Basic subroutines into sideways RAM."[23] Therefore, having a ROM/RAM expansion board gave the user the ability to install extra ROM chips for extended program capabilities without having to exchange chips time and time again. The RAM chips also offered extra memory capabilities and the ability to load the ROM images from a disk or a tape.

By making use of the ROM addressing methods to access RAM chips, users could add memory for programs such as Word Processing Packages, Speech, and other utilities. Loading these programs into sideways RAM freed up the BBC Micro's initial RAM capabilities for other purposes. For example, when using a Word Processing Package, the ROM would contain the program itself, leaving the built-in RAM for the document that the user would create. Rather than loading the program into RAM (which would reduce the amount of space available for writing a document), loading the program into sideways RAM or ROM sockets meant that the memory could be used more efficiently, making it possible to run more processes without drawing as much on the Micro's main RAM capabilities. This is noted in the introduction to the ATPL (Advance Technology Products Limited) Sidewise User Manual in a paragraph titled "what are sideways roms?":

The BBC COMPUTER incorporates facilities whereby a number of applications programs may be resident in the machine in firmware, (e.g. ROM or EPROM memory) and which may be called upon by the user via the operating system to perform specific tasks such as word processing, floppy disc management and so on. The memory is organised in such a way that only one such SIDEWAYS ROM may be active at any instant in time and all communication between such ROMs must be performed via the operating system. ... SIDEWAYS ROMs therefore provide a convenient method of expanding the memory of the BBC COMPUTER.[24]

The flexibility of having access to extra ROM and RAM helped to extend the possibilities of the Micro, especially with software packages such as AMX Pagemaker. Conceived in 1984 by Alex Blok and Neil Lee, AMX Pagemaker was released by Advanced Memory Systems Ltd in October 1985 and was a desktop publishing application released for the BBC Micro. It allowed users to integrate both text and graphics to lay out newsletters and other documents, and could be used with the AMX mouse peripheral to allow for a more immediate interaction with what was happening on the screen instead of just using the standard keyboard. However, this functionality came at a cost to the user, who not only had to run the software off floppy disks but also had to install extra ROMs to enable the software to work. An advertisement for AMX PageMaker in the June 1986 edition of *Acorn User* states "It's a complete graphics design system and word processor rolled into one. AMX Pagemaker consists of two ROMs and two discs therefore it will work on a standard BBC. It has real time graphics with fast continuous scrolling up and down an A4 page and uses Mode 0, the highest graphics resolution on the BBC."[25] The two EPROM chips supplied with the package were seen as one of the drawbacks to the software, as along with realistically needing a twin disc drive to prevent the need to continuously swap disks these features were listed as meaning the package couldn't be "carried around in your pocket."[26] The need to add extra ROMs to the Micro in order for the software to run meant that many users would have to resort to ROM expansion boards to extend the number of ROMs the machine could handle, or else the user had to continually remove the case of the Micro to change ROMs depending on what package he or she wanted to use.

The need to change ROMs could be overcome by the option of installing a Zero Insertion Force (ZIF) socket on the left side of the key-board. The plastic case had a deliberate space left for the insertion of ROM cartridges at a later date, such as Acorn's original speech synthesis hardware; however, it was mainly used for the inclusion of the ZIF socket. The user had to push out the perforated, recessed plastic area in order to install the socket, and then connect the ribbon cable into a free internal sideways ROM socket. This additional socket then allowed the user to change ROMs more easily, without opening up the BBC Micro's case; it also reduced the risk of bending and breaking ROM pins. However, the ZIF socket allowed only one ROM to be added at a time, so an additional sideways RAM expansion board was often a preferred option for people needing extra ROM space.

The need to use ROMs in order to install particular software packages also meant that copying some of this software was slightly more difficult than it would have been if using ROMs hadn't been necessary. Copying software packages to tapes or to floppy disks was common practice in the 1980s, and, as John Chesterman and Andy Lipman noted, the "computer itself is a copying machine," as users were often advised to create back-up copies of their programs.[27] However, for programs that required extra ROMs, such as AMX PageMaker, the ROM chips also would also have to be copied. BBC Micro hobbyists could copy those chips by using dedicated ROM copying machines or by using the sideways ROM/RAM boards to copy the data into memory and onto writable ROMs. Copied ROMs were exchanged on school playgrounds and by teachers who couldn't afford to purchase new ROMs for use at home. Such activities were also discussed and shared in many computer clubs. As well as using the machine in the home or education environment, dedicated groups were set up around the particular platforms on offer for people to find out more about the machine and/or share common interests.

1980s Maker Culture

The year 2005 saw the introduction of two products that have since been associated with what has been termed "maker" or "DIY" culture: the mag-azine *Make* (published by Maker Media) and the Arduino microcontroller.[28]

Make and the associated website (makezine.com) claim to include among their subject matter DIY projects, how-tos, and inspiration from geeks, makers, and hackers. The emphasis is on "doing it yourself"—learning how to solder, to create electronic circuits, to remake, rewire, and modify old electronics, and to create new interfaces and projects with microcontrollers such as the Arduino. The Arduino microcontroller[29] and similar products have become accessible and affordable. Whether a user wants to monitor light and temperature, to create basic robotics, or to control other input and output procedures, it can be done with an Arduino and with a related language called Processing.

According to David Gauntlett, "*Make* magazine, and the associated Maker Faire events, ... showcase a huge range of DIY projects, which are often more to do with engineering and technology, but are driven by the same ethos, and often have an ecological dimension, by reusing former junk, or by producing or saving power."[30] This can be seen in kits sold by the company Technology Will Save Us, such as the DIY Thirsty Plant Kit.[31] Maker spaces, hack spaces, and various other ways for groups to gather and make "do-it-yourself" content have popped up around the world. For example, branches of TechShop have popped up in the United States as spaces for people to use equipment (such as laser cutters, woodworking tools, welding stations, and design software) that many people don't have in their homes.

According to Mark Hatch, CEO of TechShop, "a number of trends are coming together to push the Maker Movement forward. Cheap, powerful, and easy-to-use tools play an important role. Easier access to knowledge, capital, and markets also help to push the revolution. A renewed focus on community and local resources and a desire for more authentic and quality things, along with a renewed interest in how to make things, also contribute to the movement."[32]

Hatch's emphasis on the "renewed focus" hints at a past in which maker cultures were active. The "maker revolution" and DIY culture are often situated in previous independent movements, revolutions, and non-mainstream forms of production, such as the 'zine culture of the 1970s.[33] As was noted at the start of this chapter, hobbyist cultures surrounded kit computers in the 1970s and the early 1980s in the US and the UK. Though this waned somewhat in the US with the introduction of console-based game machines, in the UK much of this ethos was kept alive through the Computer Literacy Project and the range of microcomputers available for users to purchase. British microcomputers allowed for experimentation and extension that the more fixed hardware of console games did not allow for, and although office-based IBM and Apple II computers could allow for experimentation and extension they were often not marketed as doing so.

Whereas present-day discussions of maker culture and present-day DIY creations are often associated with the connectivity of online spaces, Internet communities, forums, and social media, the maker scene of the 1980s was one that resided in offline spaces of computer clubs, much like the TechShops that can be found in various states in the US.[34] In discussing the culture of 1980s hobbyist computing in Britain, David Skinner notes the importance of computer clubs, observing that the term "computer club" "encapsulates a wide range of organisations and activities" and that "some clubs were organised around particular makes of computers while others were location or work based."[35] However, it was via these computer clubs that users of micros could also seek help about how to use the machines or participate in the maker culture that was prevalent at the time. Much like the Maker Faires and TechShops of today, computer clubs allowed communities of like-minded Micro owners to congregate, to make, to learn, and to explore the possibilities of the machine.

Computer clubs helped to build a wider network of support for users to dip in and out of, and communities to be a part of. Lean notes these distinctions in his discussions of computer clubs in the 1980s: "Compared to the millions spent by the government and the millions reached by the BBC, the efforts of individual computer clubs may seem small, but they offered a human touch and hands-on advice which many people sorely wanted ... ."[36]

The clubs were complemented by magazines that encouraged the production of extra peripherals that could be used with various micro-computers. David Skinner notes that "magazines played an important role in the growth of interest in computing."[37] This was a DIY culture that was actively promoted through a monthly section in *The Micro User* titled "Do-It-Yourself." The February 1984 issue contained a detailed explanation of how a user could make a "DIY sideways ROM board" so as to have up to "16 sideways ROMs in your micro, simply and cheaply."[38] Mark Hatch's slogan "Make, Share, Give, Learn, Tool Up, Play, Partici-pate, Support, and Change"[39] was already prevalent, and these articles encouraged users to create peripherals such as controllers for micros as cheap alternatives to those on the market. Generic books such as *How To Make Computer-Controlled Robots and Computer Model Controllers* (published in 1984 in the Usborne Electronic Workshop series) also provided users with instructions on how to control and create robots on computers such as the Commodore 64, the Vic 20, the Spectrum, and the BBC Micro. In addition to discussing basic components (including light-emitting diodes, resistors, and transistors), the aforementioned book also listed other materials that would be needed and provided test programs and the variations of the languages used to program and run them on each platform. Maker culture was encouraged in the 1980s in Britain by these books and magazines, which allowed users to draw on cheap and accessible resources, much as was done in the maker movements of the mid 2000s and later. Yet the BBC Micro differed from other microcomputers of the time in that its built-in interface allowed for this functionality without requiring an extra interfacing kit to be purchased separately.

Monitoring Inputs and Making Things Move

The BBC Micro came with multiple input and output ports, as shown in figure 2.2. Whereas with other popular British systems such as the ZX Spectrum users had to buy manufactured expansions, the Micro was developed so that the ports were instantly available to users. As was noted in the preceding chapter, the Micro had an RS423 (a serial communications port), a cassette port, and an "analogue in" port at the back of the machine. Underneath were ports for a disk drive and a printer, a digital input/output "user" port, and ports labeled 1Mhz Bus and Tube. The 1Mhz Bus port was mainly for hard disks and sound synthesizers allowing for input and output capabilities; the Tube was for secondary processor modules such as the Z-80 or the 6502. Not all of these ports were standard on other microcomputers at the time. The operating-system ROM for the Micro was 16 kilobytes in size; however, 768 bytes of this couldn't be accessed, as it was used specifically to access the input and output devices on the circuit. Owing to the method that was called memory mapping, the input and output capabilities of the machine were immediately accessible by reading and writing memory; one didn't have to go through a separate interface. This allowed for more direct processes to take place, as each input and each output was self-contained within its own circuit. In the BBC User Guide, the circuits for the inputs and outputs were illustrated in an appendix titled "Memory map and memory map assignments."[40] Each address range was listed with a hexadecimal address and a description of its purpose. In terms of input and outputs, three specific ranges were used:

FE00 to FEFF Internal memory mapped input/output (SHEILA)
FD00 to FDFF External memory mapped input/output (JIM)
FC00 to FCFF External memory mapped input/output (FRED)

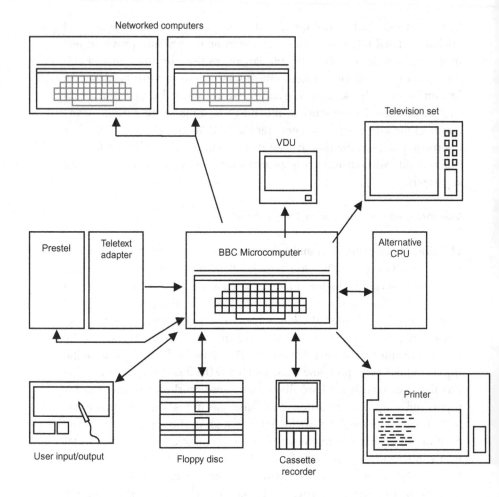

Networked computers

Television set

VDU

Prestel

Teletext adapter

BBC Microcomputer

Alternative CPU

User input/output

Floppy disc

Cassette recorder

Printer

Figure 2.2   An illustration of how the BBC Micro was to be connected up.

The name SHEILA was used for the input and output ports related to video, cassette, sound, and interrupts. JIM was used for the 1-MHz bus or paged RAM. FRED was another name used for the 1-MHz bus.

Whereas most other microcomputers had digital input ports for the use of game controllers, the BBC Micro's "analogue in" port could also used for these peripherals. The VIC 20, the Commodore 64, the Amiga, and the ZX Spectrum used joystick adapters with the Atari 2600 joystick pinout (a digital controller that had five switches: one for up, one for down, one for left, one for right, and one for fire). However, the user port on the BBC Micro contained a four-channel analog-to-digital converter that allowed for two joysticks to be connected and also supported a Light Pen (discussed below). This meant that companies such as Kempston (which manufactured a range of Atari female 9-pin D-type joysticks for other platforms) had to manufacture BBC-Micro-specific joysticks with a male 15-pin D-type connector using analog sticks rather than digital ones to work with the platform. The analog-to-digital converter also allowed for other uses, as was noted in the March 1983 issue of *The Micro User*: "The analogue to digital converter on the BBC microcomputer provides a rather simple way to connect, or interface, the computer to the outside world. This means that you can fit the micro with joysticks for games programs, or use it to received information from temperature sensors, light detectors, laboratory instruments, etc."[41] Subsequently, users could make their own games paddles in order to measure x-axis or y-axis control on the Micro through the change in voltage recorded.[42]

The difference between analog and digital inputs was explained to viewers of the *Making the Most of the Micro* series in the eighth episode, titled "Everything Under Control."[43] Hosts Ian McNaught-Davis and John Coll demonstrated the digital input functions of the machine by using a joystick connected to the "analogue in" on the Micro. Pins 10 and 13 on the Micro's "analogue-to-digital converter" allowed a switch on a games controller (or a fire button) to be recognized as being on or off. John Coll demonstrated those actions by using a digital output device connected to the Micro to turn on a series of lights in several different sequences. Another BBC BASIC command was also introduced to users in the form of PEEK and POKE. Whereas in other versions of BASIC the command PEEK would be used to read information at a particular address on the memory map and POKE would be used to set information into an address, on the BBC the command ? was used instead to read or write from memory. With a BBC Micro one could read the digital inputs and set the digital outputs with ease from BASIC by using the particular memory map addresses that equated to the ports.

In order to show how an analog input device produced a varying signal, McNaught-Davis was asked to move the joystick controller, the movement of which was represented on the screen by a wiggly line. Instead of being composed of on and off signals, the voltages from the analog signal were recorded at timed intervals depending on the accuracy of the information required. If the signals were recorded less frequently, the image displayed would be blockier, as there wasn't enough information to record the joystick component being moved. This information was then translated into further practical examples, such as fading lights in and out using analog outputs instead of digital ones that would normally mean the lights would be either on or off, as well as inputting sound from a microphone to be registered as a voltage conversion into patterns on the screen display attached to the BBC Micro. The examples provided by the television program verbalized and visualized these processes to help the audience comprehend the computed tasks in a more coherent way and make sense of the processes. Combined with magazine articles explaining how to process other inputs (such as biofeedback programs generated by electrodes attached to the skin via Velcro straps to act as a Lie Detector[44]), the translation of computing processes to everyday language helped to once again situate the Micro in a wider spectrum of literacies for people as they began to enter an increasingly computerized age. The emphasis on making sure that the general public was made aware of how processes worked both inside and outside of the machine had the potential to open up the platform beyond a purely "hobbyist" audience.

This emphasis on how computers worked and could be used continued as a range of other peripherals were released for use with the platform. In addition to measuring various voltages from a range of devices, the "analogue in" port on the BBC Micro was compatible with the Light Pens that were manufactured for the machine. The manual for the R H Electronics Light Pen stated: "There are a number of devices which enable the user to interact with a computer. The standard ASCII keyboard is the most common of these devices with Light Pens probably a close second."[45] The R H Electronics Light Pen was to be used with the BBC Microcomputer and with raster scan displays (such as color or black and white televisions or high-resolution monitors). The pen sent a video strobe pulse (VSP) back to the computer when the on-screen pixel beneath the pen was redrawn, which in turn allowed the computer to locate the position of the pen on the screen. Much like a mouse, the Light Pen allowed for ease of selection on the screen. It came equipped with programs that enabled people to use it to draw shapes, and to play games such as Drafts by pointing and clicking rather than using only the keyboard as an input device. The "analogue in" port in these instances allowed for a further extension of the interfaces through which the user could interact with the machine. As Alexander Galloway notes, "an interface is not something that appears before you but rather is a gateway that opens up and allows passage to some place beyond," and when discussed in terms of the science of cybernetics "is the place where flesh meets metal."[46] This was certainly true of the materiality of external peripherals available for the machine—particularly the BBC Buggy, which not only allowed for interaction but also once again brought out the DIY culture inherent in using some of the additional equipment for the platform.

Turtles, Buggies, and Construction

In 1983, only a year after the BBC Micro's initial release, a company called Economatics launched a product called the BBC Buggy. It claimed to be the first computer-controlled buggy for the machine, yet it was released at a time when Logo-inspired turtles, such as the Edinburgh Turtle, were being developed and marketed.[47] However, unlike the turtles that became associated with the Logo language and the turtle graphics, the BBC Buggy initially came in kit form. Made from fischertecnik parts and sold with a step-by-step instruction construction guide, the BBC Buggy drew on earlier BBC Micro references to toy culture, hobbyist cultures, electronics, and construction. Once again the kit was "the fruit of a collaboration"—this time, Simon Beesley wrote, between "the BBC Computer Literacy Project and the Microelectronics Education Programmme."[48] "After discussing ideas for the BBC's *Making the Most of the Micro* series with producer David Allen," Beesley continued, "Mike Bostock, Technology Manager for the MEP, built a prototype Buggy using Lego Bricks."

Whereas changing ROM chips and constructing game paddles were aimed at a slightly older audience, the fischertechnik aesthetic, with its links to Lego, made the Buggy more accessible to younger people. Similarly, much like the Logo turtles, fischertechnik kits were seen as educational, as they offered ways of teaching people about motorized processes and mechanisms through the inclusion of electric motors and gears. It was thinking about the use of gears and about the cause-and-effect relationships involved in rotating linked circular objects that led Seymour Papert (one of the creators of the programming language Logo) to begin thinking about mathematical processes and exploratory learning.

Computational thinking and computer-based educational techniques existed long before the BBC Micro and had a line of predecessors that ventured into using machines to teach some form of literacy. Logo was one of those programs. As Mike Cook noted in a comparison of the BBC Buggy and the Edinburgh Turtle, "Logo is a language that has taken off in schools, especially primary schools, where it is used to teach children about geometry and problem solving in a stimulating and exciting way."[49] Conceived in 1967 by Seymour Papert and Wallace Feurzeig, Logo was devised as a way of teaching programming concepts but is now remembered for its connections with teaching mathematical logic and artificial intelligence and for "turtle graphics." In his 1980 book *Mindstorms*, Papert characterized "the Turtle" as "a computer-controlled cybernetic animal [that] exists within the cognitive mini-cultures of the 'Logo environment,' Logo being the computer language in which communication with the Turtle takes place. The Turtle serves no other purpose than of being good to program and good to think with. Some Turtles are abstract objects that live on computer screens. Others, like the floor Turtles … are physical objects that can be picked up like any mechanical toy."[50]

The combination of the Turtle and the Logo programming language provided an environment in which to teach children simple programming concepts through the use of basic words such as "square" and "triangle." Building upon those concepts enabled a child to draw shapes on a screen or (if a Turtle had a pen attached to it and a sheet of paper underneath it) across a floor. The aim of Logo was to put the child in control of the learning process and also in control of the machine and its outputs. Wallace Feurzeig, the leader of Logo's initial development team at BBN, recalled:

Initially the interest was not only mathematics. I named it 'Logo' from the Greek [logos] which means a word, a thought, the idea, but word is very prominent. And the notion was that computers were not just for doing science or math technical kinds of things; they could be used for language, for music, for all kinds of things, that computers would be interesting to people in various ways. We were interested not only in mathematics but other areas, too.[51]

In the 1980s, after the publication of Papert's book *Mindstorms: Children, Computers, and Powerful Ideas*, Logo was introduced into schools in both the UK and the US. Logo was not unique to the BBC Micro; for example, a version of Logo was developed for the Apple II computer. In the July/August issue of *Acorn User*, an Acorn version of Logo was announced as being in development, with the Massachusetts Institute of Technology providing the 6502 source code and overseeing the conversion of the code to run on the BBC Micro. "Expected to be a very complete and powerful implementation," the Acornsoft version of Logo was subsequently released with three manuals, a reference card, and two 16-kilobyte ROMs.[52] The Acorn version of Logo was one of several developed for the Micro. Other versions of Logo released for the BBC Micro were developed by educators and by various companies that wanted to bring the ideas of navigation and mathematical problem-solving techniques into the classroom by using screen-based or floor-based turtles. The ease with which BASIC could be learned enabled educators to use it to create new programs that translated some of ideas inherent in Logo. Much of how these concepts could be taught embodied approaches that also were facilitated by the BBC Micro, including the ability to move beyond BASIC and to encounter other aspects found outside of the machine. As had been demonstrated in the TV series *Making the Most of the Micro*, music, language, and gaming as well as traditional mathematics and science were all discussed in relation to how people could use the platform. The ability for users to connect robots, to learn visually, and to be in control of the machine meant that other technologies were also manufactured for the BBC Micro in the hope of continuing some of this "hands-on" ethos. The BBC Buggy was an example.

By becoming an interface between programming the Micro and seeing the results of a physical output in the space outside of the screen, the Buggy enabled users to become literate both in constructing the machine and in controlling it. Subsequently, the extra interface between the Micro and the user and the processes involved in constructing the final product acted as another layer of learning and interrogation for the user. This was encouraged in the opening paragraphs of the assembly instructions for the BBC Buggy: "For those Buggy owners who have not used fischertechnik before, it is recommended to experiment a little with fitting various parts together before starting actual assembly of the Buggy."[53] The Buggy came with building blocks, gear wheels, hinges, axles, building plates, a circuit board, an interface board, a bar-code reader, a power supply, and a 5-meter 20-way ribbon cable to be connected to a Micro. Assembling a Buggy required nothing more than a screwdriver and an M4 spanner.

The kit also included a cassette tape of thirteen programs that could be used with the hardware. These included "test facilities," a simple program for direct computer control, a "memory switch" program that demonstrated how computer memory worked, and some programs that demonstrated the learning or "artificial intelligence" aspects of the Buggy. A program called Snail was used to plan screen routes. One called Explore for Wall showed the Buggy mapping out boundaries. One called Explore for Object enabled the Buggy to seek out an object or objects, define shapes, and then return to the start position. A program called Line made the Buggy follow a line that had been laid out on the floor (usually with black tape) and map the route on the Micro's screen. A program called Sunseeker enabled the Buggy to seek out a light while negotiating obstructions in its path, much as light-based sensors available for the Arduino microcontroller units do today. These programs were similar in quality to the BBC Micro's own Welcome Tape as a way to give users a taste of the potential of the product and to demystify the process of users potentially creating their own devices or programs. The Buggy was also introduced in an episode of *Making the Most of the Micro* as a way of promoting its use to a wider audience and situating it within a wider context of input and output devices with which the BBC Micro could be used.[54]

In the eighth episode of *Making the Most of the Micro*, the BBC Buggy was situated in a context of car-bomb detectors and other navigational machines. The technology was placed in a socio-cultural context that drew on the IRA bombings that were occurring during the 1980s in Great Britain and in Northern Ireland. These real-world uses of the technology served as stepping stones for the simpler machines attached to the Micro itself, all the while showing the possibilities that the learning encountered could lead to. Various tracking controls and search techniques were then placed in the context of programming, in this case using loop functions, emphasizing the connected learning of past computer literacy television programs. It was then demonstrated how the BBC Buggy could be programmed to find its way around a maze and to learn a route by displaying on the Micro's screen the parts of the maze it has already visited. The four sensors (two digital and two analog) were discussed. The two digital sensors were explained in terms of the buffers found on the sides of the Buggy that detected other physical objects the machine might collide with. There was also an analog light sensor, which allowed the program to search for the bright light by detecting differences in light values in conjunction with an attached infrared light. The light was reflected from a nearby surface, and this allowed the Buggy to follow a line. If the sensor detected a level of light above a pre-determined value, the line was detected as white; otherwise, the line was detected as black. This enabled the Buggy to find out what parts of the maze it was on. At the end of the program, the Buggy was shown having to find its way out of the maze once it had found and registered the dead ends it had encountered. These processes served to show a broad audience both how the machine worked and its memory capabilities of storing routes it had previously found.

As with other external components, the combination of physical artifacts connected to the BBC Micro and the machine's ability to display various inputs related to the object allowed the user to experience various input/output relationships beyond purely relying on software functionality. The materiality of these objects not only aided another form of learning but also once again emphasized the "modularity" of the BBC Micro as seen in Acorn's earlier hobbyist constructions. The "bricolage" approach to learning—the approach of constructing new tools and engaging with making and material processes in the construction of new objects—allowed the user to be a hobbyist too, albeit under the guidance of initial instructions and software tests.[55] From inputting and removing ROMs in order to change the internal capabilities of the Micro to constructing a BBC Buggy and programming it to follow commands, the user had to learn, at least on a basic level, how each of the individual components would affect the machine and any possible inputs or outputs. This also was true of constructing the BBC Buggy or making other DIY hardware components for the BBC Micro, in that users were encouraged to engage with new types of learning to understand the machine's possibilities. The extendable nature of the Micro enabled users to feel another type of agency beyond software commands and actively allowed for another type of experimentation through hardware-related material literacies linked to software literacies.

However, these literacies were not always available to all. Although the Buggy was promoted to a wider audience through programs such as those connected to the Computer Literacy Project, its uses were also highlighted as a teaching aid in both school and industry and an example of more complex systems used in the industry at the time. In reality the BBC Buggy was mainly used in schools alongside other navigational systems, such as Logo. The price of the Buggy, £160, was just under half the price of the already expensive BBC Micro machine and therefore was more suitable for educational settings than for homes. This was confirmed by the note within the Buggy's instructions that it was compatible with a supplementary pen kit available for Logo use. Once again the school was often at the heart of the BBC Micro's use, and so the role of the teacher became central to further software development within this field.

Making and Playing Games

[II]

I would hate to see computers just used for playing games. It's degrading.

The Computer Programme (BBC television series), episode 1, January 11, 1982

As much as the words of Ian McNaught-Davis in the first episode of *The Computer Programme* attempt to downplay the use of the BBC Micro purely for game playing, that was a major use of the platform for many people. Digital game culture was a key part of microcomputing developments in Britain during the 1980s, on the BBC Micro as well as on other systems such as the ZX Spectrum. However, in part because of its associations with the Computer Literacy Project and education more generally, and in part because of its price, the BBC Micro was not always seen to be a major contender in the computer game market.

One scene in *Micro Men*, a television drama aired in 2009, depicts the development of the BBC Micro in parallel to Clive Sinclair's efforts with his competing machine.[1] The actor playing the role of Chris Curry walks into a WHSmith store that carries a variety of computer games.[2] One of the store's assistants is explaining to a potential customer how to use a ZX Spectrum. She asks if there are games for it, and the store assistant replies that there are indeed many games for it. At this point Chris Curry asks "Do you have any games for the BBC Micro?" The assistant replies, with an air of distance, "Er ... yeah ... somewhere we do." The camera then pans across the store to a shelf displaying a small section of BBC Micro games next to rows and rows of ZX Spectrum games.

While the ZX Spectrum was seen as a cheaper gaming machine, the BBC Micro was also a platform for developing a range of fundamental games in Britain that have later been recognized globally. Similarly, the machine's links to more formal educational contexts and programs meant that it was an ideal platform for developing educational games.

In April 1981, Minister for Trade and Industry and Information Technology Kenneth Baker launched the Micros in Schools initiative, starting with a provision for secondary schools.[3] In what Baker later called "the most significant programme" that he introduced during his time in office, the government identified two computers, the Acorn BBC Micro and the Research Machines 380Z, to be used in the initiative. "If schools bought either of these," Baker wrote in 1993, "then we would meet 50 percent of the cost. It was an offer they couldn't refuse."[4] This scheme was then offered to primary schools from October 1982 on, with the range of subsided platforms extended to include the Research Machines 480Z, the BBC Micro, and the Sinclair ZX Spectrum.[5] Baker's Micros in Schools initiative did what it had set out to do, and subsequently there was a noticeable rise in the availability of microcomputers in schools. Indeed, Neil Selwyn notes, "Whereas in 1980 there were only around 700 micro-computers in UK schools, by 1982 over 4000 secondary schools had ordered microcomputers. For schools, at least, microcomputing had fast become a matter for attention."[6] This attention meant that the development of software was undertaken not only by software developers but also by teachers.

Using microcomputers in education was actively promoted in a variety of media. The second episode of *Making the Most of the Micro* showed a group of primary school children sitting around a single machine and working together to solve problems proposed by a game.[7] *Acorn User* and other magazines published articles with titles such as "Teaching Toddlers." Contributors to microcomputing magazines interviewed people who were working to get the BBC Micro introduced into schools, such as Robert Chantry-Price, Director of the North West Regional Centre for the Microelectronics Education Programme, who talked about how people could "introduce the computer into a variety of educational contexts—not as something artificial that has been grafted on, but as a vital part of the curriculum."[8] *The Micro User* had a dedicated column about schools using BBC Micros in their classrooms, such as Hollingwood Lane First School in Bradford, where using a Micro was said to have "become an integral part of daily life, with children from the youngest child upwards using the Micro as naturally as they would a book or crayons."[9] Alongside such articles and columns the magazines would run include advertisements for the BBC Micro. One such advertisement, headlined "The BBC Micro can now give your children a private education," lists a range of educational programs that could be purchased for the machine for users "from children who are getting to grips with the alphabet, to adults who want a gentle but intensive introduction to the complex world of computing."[10] These advertisements often contained listings for educational software and games that used quizzes or rote learning to teaching word usage or number usage.

Although the Micros in Schools initiative helped to bring microcomputers into the classroom, it did not necessarily call for one machine per child. Indeed, often there was only one machine per classroom or one for an entire school. Disappointment with limited access was evident in the results a survey of BBC Micro users conducted for a legacy report in 2012. One respondent commented "The BBC micro, if you were lucky you got ½–1 hour a week to do 'something' with it. Usually that was to play 'Lemonade' or write programs. I, alas, was unlucky, and got maybe two sessions a year … ."[11]

In 1983, Mike Matson, then a Deputy Headteacher at a school in Devon, convinced the local Parent-Teacher Association that the school should invest in a computer for classroom use. A BBC Micro was ordered, despite concerns about its price. Matson also bought his own BBC Micro and set about seeing what software was available. His disappointment with the software on offer led him to create his own educational game—in his words, "something more exciting."[12] The game was titled *Granny's Garden*.

Matson and his friend Neil Souch then set up a software-development house they called 4Mation. 4Mation went on to develop and release other educational programs, among them *Flowers of Crystal*, *Dragon World*, and *Box of Treasures*. However, out all of these titles it was *Granny's Garden* that became the standout educational game for those who had access to a BBC Micro either at school or at home.

The development, the design, and the uses of *Granny's Garden* illustrate how the BBC Micro could be discussed as a multi-literacy machine, and how the uses of the platform went beyond what the hardware and the BBC's Computer Literacy Project had initially set out to achieve. By situating *Granny's Garden* in a wider context of games and education in 1980s Britain and by comparing it with other games that were then being developed in the United States, we can begin to see how the BBC Micro as a platform enabled a certain kind of creativity to emerge among groups of educators.

In the United States, according to Martin Campbell-Kelly, "by the end of 1983 there were estimated to be 35,000 different personal computer software products from about 3,000 vendors, an increase of 50 percent from the previous year."[13] Campbell-Kelly goes on to note how software was classified by the personal computer software industry into "productivity" software (including spreadsheets and word processors), "industry" software with specific industrial uses, and "consumer and educational" software (including games). The opportunities provided by microcomputers also allowed teachers to create their own content.

Teachers writing educational programs was nothing new in the 1970s or in the 1980s, either in the UK or elsewhere. Mitzuko Ito notes the rise of "edutainment" programs in the 1980s in the United States, with games such as *Where in the World Is Carmen Sandiego?* being used in classrooms. Ito classifies education software as "academic," "entertainment," or "construction" depending on the approaches central to a title's design, use, and reception.[14] Although in many ways *Granny's Garden* would fit into the "academic" category, in other ways it is closer to "entertainment." In the United States during the 1980s, "entertainment" titles were generally developed by the commercial software industry. In terms of its content, *Granny's Garden* was an entertainment-based program with exploration and discovery at the heart of the experience. Instead of mapping educational concepts onto the game, Matson was aware of how the game would be used in relation to the whole classroom experience, and of the game's potential usefulness in a range of subject areas.

In fact, in contrast to the mainly academic content of educational games produced in the US, the games developed by teachers for the BBC Micro were the ones that became the most successful in a sea of generic software that tried to map traditional learning via a computer, such as the *French Tutor* and *Maths Tutor* (developed by Salmander Software) and *Fun Academy* (developed by SHARDS Software Ltd). However, *L—A Mathemagical Adventure*, a game created by the Association of Teachers of Mathematics, was based on solving puzzles in order to learn about arithmetic and logical pattern matching. Instead of presenting sums on the screen to be solved, *L* created a story world for its users to enter, providing descriptions of areas, introducing characters, and integrating the characters into the general gameplay. The *Mary Rose* game, released by Ginn in 1983, was also seen as "the type of program that should show the way forward to prospective programmers of educational software."[15] One of the strengths of *Mary Rose* discussed in the January 1984 issue of *The Micro User* was that children could further their work away from the Micro by researching themes found within the game. This ability to "diversify" the curriculum and activities, along with the possibilities of extending the narrative of the game in variety of ways, could also been seen to play a part in the success of *Granny's Garden*.

Teachers such as Matson already had a framework for how classrooms would work in terms of one machine per group of up to 30 children. The software and platform in itself were not enough to maintain learning for classroom sessions; therefore the story at the heart of the game was in many ways the starting point to the experience, and other means of learning were often delivered in parallel as the microcomputer was shared among the students in the classroom. Instead of focusing games purely on earlier arcade-game principles of time and reward, these examples took game design in other directions by taking into consideration the reality of how the platform would actually be used in the classroom. If consumers of the BBC Micro had not taken the production of software into their own hands, the culture of educational software for the platform would have been very different. Although *Granny's Garden* was devised for educational environments, it was also an adventure game, a genre that had inspired Matson early in his own explorations of computing. However, creating games for the classroom was no quick or easy task. Matson spent 250 hours programming *Granny's Garden* in BBC BASIC as an easily accessible language promoted to be used with the machine. The limited memory and graphical capabilities meant that much of the story world presented was in text form, yet images and some basic animations were provided during the game, usually to introduce new characters. The combination of characters and text helped to aid the further possibilities of the game by providing ways to discuss how these characteristics of the game shaped further meaning for teachers and children in the classroom.

Granny's Garden: Beginning the Adventure

Granny's Garden was first and foremost an adventure game. Mike Matson had come to computing as a result of his having experienced the game of *Adventure* while using a friend's computer on a weekend in the early 1980s.[16] Therefore, the adventure-game genre seemed appropriate for an educational game. In his writings about early adventure games, Nick Montfort recognized the pleasures of what he defined as "interactive fictions" in terms of both narrative components and the "interactor's" sense of exploring the spaces of the world.[17] The limited graphical display of *Granny's Garden* emulated some of those original narrative forms from the

1970s, as some of these structures could be found in 1980s computer games. It is these elements of narrative and exploration that define the use of *Granny's Garden* in classrooms and that made it memorable for those using it at the time and for those who remember it today.

Upon loading *Granny's Garden*, the user is presented with a red title screen listing *Granny's Garden* Part 1 and *Granny's Garden* Part 2 under the heading of the software publisher, 4Mation Educational Resources. As has already been noted, the game was programmed in BASIC; thus, the program itself took up much of the available memory, each part taking more than 20 kilobytes. Therefore, it was not possible to have both parts of the program in memory at the same time, as only about 22 kilobytes of memory were available in a 32-kilobyte Model B BBC Micro. Using Mode 7 graphics meant that only 1 kilobyte of screen memory was allocated to this part of the program, allowing more memory for the BASIC program, but this still wasn't enough to allow for the game to exist in one program to be run. However, dividing the program up also allowed for the second part to be accessed more easily once the game was loaded, something that was important because of the complexity of some parts of the game and how they could be solved.

After a player selected Part 1 or Part 2 of the game, the first screen to greet the users was "Ready to start?' The user would then type either Y or N. These commands, although at the time criticized by some for not encouraging written-language literacy among children, were standard for use in the adventure-game genre.[18] However, on entering the next screen, other literacies came into play, such as the ability to work out coordinates to get past the "magic tree" puzzle. This was the first real challenge to face the player. The player was confronted with twelve trees on the screen, four along the bottom in columns (listed as a, b, c, and d) and three along the side in lines numbered 1, 2, and 3.

Various combinations, such as A1 or D3, would have to be entered, each followed by a space bar, before the correct tree was chosen that matched up to the random number generated by the program when the game was loaded. There was no fixed solution for the player on this screen, as choosing the magic tree to enable the player to get to the next screen was a random task. After multiple plays of the game, various cheats or Easter eggs were found by players, such as the ability to type T instead of Y at the initial "Ready to start?" screen, which would then mean that the magic tree was always A1 on the next screen.[19] These hints were important for players because of later consequences in the game that could result in the "magic tree" screen's being seen over and over.

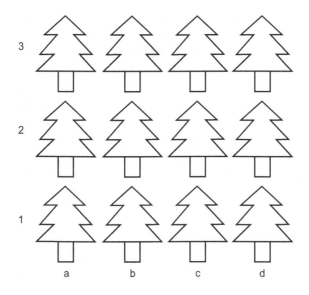

Figure 3.1 The layout of the tree puzzle in *Granny's Garden*.

However, once the "magic tree" screen was successfully passed, the player was welcomed into the "Kingdom of the Mountains." Matson's geography specialism is seemingly present throughout the game, on this screen and through later maps provided, but so too is his love of adventure games. The Kingdom of the Mountains provides a path into a secret cave, reminiscent of the cave analogy attached to the original *Adventure* game by Crowther and Woods.[20] This section acts as a starting point to the background story and to basic interaction with the game. The player is faced with a series of questions such as "Do you see a cave?" and "Do you want to go into the cave?"—both of which request Y or N answers. Choosing N does nothing more than tell the player that he doesn't want to go into the cave, showing that the initial narrative has a fixed outcome. The player must agree to the first set of choices in order to progress. The game text addresses the player as "you" throughout, bringing the identity of the child playing the game into the narrative. Here the child is pitched as an adventurer, and the child's problem-solving capabilities are projected into the game, as are the child's real-world identity and his or her ability to solve the problems.[21] Encountering further non-playable characters in the gameworld maintains the player-as-adventurer role. This is a key component of keeping the game both enjoyable and engaging enough so that players want to progress the narrative, which is empha-sized once the initial screens depicting the interaction with the game end and the narrative begins. Once inside the cave section of the game, the narrative progresses, telling the player that the King and Queen of the mountains have been locked away by a wicked witch and that their six children have been taken away. Now the player's objective is to find and rescue the children while avoiding the witch.

Although the game is titled *Granny's Garden*, it is the witch that is at the center of the narrative. Upon finding the witch at certain moments in the game as a result of entering an incorrect action, the animated witch character appears, accompanied by menacing music blasting out of the BBC Micro. With her blue face, yellow eye, purple hat, and green hair, the witch was a frightening character for some primary school children at the time. Fairy tale and story references to Snow White, Hansel and Gretel, and Grotbags (a witch in a popular British children's television show of the 1980s) all sprang to mind when the screen popped up.[22] Similarly, not only was the first sight of the witch alarming, so too was the resultant action. If the witch was found, the player would be put back to the begin-ning screen after the words "Ha ha! Now I've got you! I will send you home at once" were displayed. In the case of the first part of the game this meant that the players were taken back to the "Choose the magic tree" screen. This punishment or failure within the game would act as a means for players to want to continue, particularly as the game was often played in groups due to lack of computer access in the school environment.[23] However, before failure can occur the player has to find his or her way further into the narrative to rescue the first child, Esther, by tackling a series of events related to various problem-solving activities.

Problems to be solved within *Granny's Garden* are generally divided into puzzles and riddles. There are word-based riddles asking the player to solve a problem presented on the screen or to solve more spatially driven puzzles that revolve around buildings or areas found within the program. Using concepts including remembering narrative events through teams of players working together, or by drawing on the indi-vidual player's knowledge of how games might work, each set of puzzles or riddles generally leads to finding one of the characters and subse-quently completing that section of the narrative. Puzzles and riddles have been associated with games and with interactive fictions, respec-tively. *Granny's Garden*, as an educational piece of software, similarly bridges the gap between what has been defined as a game and what we can see as an interactive fiction. Katie Salen and Eric Zimmerman state one definition of games as "a system in which players engage in an artificial conflict, defined by rules, that results in a quantifiable outcome."[24] Within this definition they also count puzzles as existing within the category of games even though they reference the counterargument of puzzle and game design as being contradictory using Scott Kim's writing about how "puzzles are different from games because puzzles have a correct answer or outcome."[25] Although this is true of both the puzzle and riddle elements found within *Granny's Garden*, the puzzles found within the gameworld help to progress the narrative fiction and engage the player in solving problems. Together, these elements help with the learning inherent in educational software. The user has to know that he or she is providing the right answer in order to learn and feel a sense of agency in doing so, and to enjoy the learning. The combination of random events from the initial "magic tree" scenario allows rules, outcomes, and some artificial conflict in solving and achieving these outcomes to filter through various elements. However, the puzzle-solving components of the game are by far the strongest means of progressing the narrative and forming communities of participation through the learners in order to succeed.

One of the first word-based puzzles within the game is situated in the opening section. The player is eased into the activity of finding the first child, Esther, by the relatively easy nature of the task and by prompts that are given to any player who doesn't understand what the correct answer might be. Upon being shown a picture of a house on the screen, the letters F, I, and G can be found depicted in bright blue against the white walls, the purple window frame, and the yellow roof of the building. After being welcomed to the woodcutter's house, a question is posed on screen. It is here that the player is asked "There is a secret word on the house. What is it?" If the clue of the writing clearly shown on the house isn't entirely obvious, there are significant hints to help the player along.

Learning the right combination of actions becomes part of the "reflective learning" process of the game that is built into the puzzles and riddles throughout *Granny's Garden*. According to James Paul Gee, "reflective learning" through video games can be discussed in terms of a four-step process: "probe, hypothesis, reprobe, rethink."[26] In order to understand and recognize particular patterns that become synonymous with solving the puzzles and riddles within *Granny's Garden*, players are in many ways presented with this four-step process to work together. First, what is presented on the screen is probed by the player by answering Yes or No or by typing other words that may or may not be recognized by the system. Once this probing phase has been conducted, the player can begin to hypothesize about the next set of actions he or she might want to use. This reflection is based on actions committed earlier and the outcomes associated with those. In the case of FIG written on the house, the player may only have initially spotted the F and the I, and may thus have formed an incorrect answer in his or her mind. Once the world is reprobed by using the first wrong answer to hypothesize about another potentially correct answer, the next set of words are entered into the machine. This leads to a feedback loop of either a correct answer being rewarded by the next stage of the narrative unfolding, or another incorrect answer being registered and a further clue offered to help the player. This stage allows the player to rethink his or her actions, and it may help with further word-based puzzles both inside and outside of the game-world, in this game or in later puzzles presented in other media. This crossover of skill is important in educational games that were used to encourage a wide range of thinking in other activities once the game or sections of the game were completed. These skills can be found in the range of spatial puzzles built into *Granny's Garden* found at various stages within the program.

It is upon entering the house that collecting objects start to be built into the game as well as sets of directions, such as go upstairs, go to the kitchen, or go to the backroom. These objects help with later clues and are a way to get the player to remember what they have taken and how it could be used. By playing the game in small groups around one computer screen, the collective memory of the group also becomes important as students can work together in order to solve later problems. Teamwork is built in through the realization that this is how the game might be played and also through help built into the game itself when hints are given if the wrong word is entered. On this occasion an apple is offered to the player and they can choose to take it along with a stick offered at a later prompt. Whereas the apple becomes important in killing a snake, the stick serves no purpose, although this is learned only upon completing this section. In each room there is another object presented, such as a cooking pot in the kitchen that if, looked into when prompted, summons the witch to take the player back to the start screen. Learning the layout of areas is another one of the key skills learned in the adventure game format, as later on a map is presented to players where a similar task of place negotiation and object collection is presented but in a different graphical form. Upon finding the correct layout in both scenarios, the rescued children are depicted on the screen as crude stick figures, in line with the graphical possibilities offered by the BBC Micro and the BBC BASIC programming skills of Matson. Finding the children also unlocks passwords reminiscent of other games of the time. As the game could not be saved during play, the passwords provided an alternative way for players to save their progress. In this instance the password allowed the player to type in the found word (e.g., snow or river) so as to progress to the next section without having to replay the game from the start.

On entering "Yes" to having a password, the player is asked "Are you sure you have a password?" Because the game often was played by teams of people huddled around the computer screen, the emphasis on the second question to make sure the player was not cheating and had genuinely earned the right to progress through gaining the earlier knowledge to acquire the password acted as another moral questioning for the player. This was reiterated in the manual for the program: "passwords should be kept secret."[27] Once again the program was speaking back to the player in a voice of authority, echoing the initial comments displayed on first playing the game encouraging the player that they could see the cave and they did indeed want to help the King and Queen find their children. Ensuring the player seemingly influenced the narrative yet was really constrained by the design of the interaction and flow of subsequent events both helped aid the illusion of this new type of program within the classroom. However, the inclusion of puzzles within the game also helped with the problem-solving components needed by the game in order to further the narrative experience. This is seen in another puzzle-based activity in the game when the player is presented with the Talking Toadstool to find the character of Tom. Here the player is presented with various creatures that can help them across the other side of the Giant's garden leading to the rescue of Tom. The words "worm," "bee," "snail," "spider," and "butterfly" are listed on the screen, and various scenarios are presented to the user in which a choice of each creature could be entered. The creatures are only listed once, again reiterating how the collective memory of the team was an important part of the activity when more than one child was playing the game on a Micro. The second part of the puzzle involves the player working out which creature was best suited to each task, from getting the player-character across a pond to protecting the player-character from being hit by nuts falling from a tree. Once the correct solution is found, the player is rewarded with a picture of the successful creature displayed on the screen accompanied by some text that helps to progress the narrative. The language of the narrative again draws the player into the game allowing the player to become a direct part of the story in the expansion of the fictional world into the player's space. Most of the puzzles are quite short and easy to complete; however, a riddle included in the game and the final mapped quest are more difficult. Both the riddle and the mapped quest involve saving two children at once rather than just one child, therefore the level of difficulty appears to increase with the end reward.

Whereas riddles can be classified as a type of puzzle, Nick Montfort traces riddles back to written texts before interactive fictions emerged: "Although the riddle is a literary form of great antiquity, it is often dismissed as nothing more than a diversion for children."[28] In the case of *Granny's Garden* this can be seen to be true because of the game's audience of children and young people, yet the nature of the game changes the purpose of the riddle once again. In Part 2 of the game the player is faced with finding two new children, Clare and Anna. This part of the game is set in the City of Dragons and is accompanied by what appears to be a mock-up of the Great Wall of China and by a character named Ah-Choo. Before entering the city, the player is asked to name his or her favorite food. This is not part of the riddle; it is another way of drawing the player into the fictional space of the game before the riddle begins. Once inside the city, the player finds Anna, who the player is told to take to meet the dragons. The next screen depicts four baby dragons that have been left behind to guard Clare. The player's role is to find the foods that the dragons like in order to separate the dragons and place a magic collar on each one that will tame it. A player has three bags of chips, three oranges, three lollipops, and three buns to feed to the dragons as a way of luring them out in the hope of putting a magic collar on them. Upon typing the word "buns" as the first food to try with the dragons, the player is presented with a riddle:

The red dragon loves buns
The green dragons sometimes eats them
The blue dragon sometimes eats them
The yellow dragon hates them.

At a first glance the player can easily decode "love" and "hate." By loving a food offered, the dragon of that color will be drawn on screen. However, if on the second food offering that dragon sometimes eats the next food item, such as chips, then that dragon will remain on the screen. This means that the dragon cannot be collared, and the puzzle becomes harder to solve— more dragons means more variables on the screen to confuse the player. The nature of the riddle therefore involves calling out dragons one at a time that love but then hate a particular food type in order to make them go away again. This is a particularly challenging aspect of the riddle due to the word usage of the player being able to decode the meaning of sometimes eats and then planning the right combination of foods to input in order to remove other dragons from the screen. Matson reveals years later that this puzzle "stumped everyone" although it was his "favourite part: just because it was the most difficult section to get working."[29] Therefore, for Matson, his own computer literacy related to executing this particular puzzle was successful, but the played experience was not as rewarding for those who struggled to interpret the meaning behind collaring the dragons. However, for those who managed to master this section of the game, not only were they rewarded with saving Anna and Clare, they were also treated to the final part of the narrative and the final puzzle to be solved, a mapped area to be negotiated, traversed, and overcome in the hope of finding the remaining two children, Daniel and Jessica.

This final section goes back to a geographical puzzle layout, much like when the player first enters the house in Part 1 of the game, except this time the map is shown on the screen rather than depicted in text-based description of the rooms. The map is located in the Land of Mystery, and it is here that the player must decide which path to take, as represented in figure 3.2. Going to each area reveals either a piece of information to remember to use in another area or an object; for example, going to the cottage means that the player finds a key, and going to the forest reveals that the trees are called Pompom trees. Once again the player has to navigate the paths of the map in the correct order to gain the right items in order to get the final rewards of finding Daniel and Jessica while trying

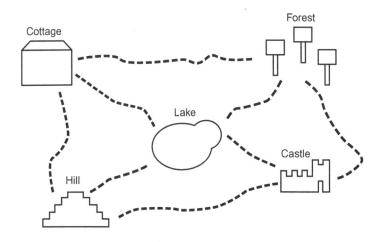

Figure 3.2 The layout of the Land of Mystery map in *Granny's Garden*.

not to find the witch character in one of the locations and risk being sent back to the beginning of this part of the game. Matson notes his geography background emerging in this final section where he states that the map is his "tribute to that old Adventure game I played. Because I was a geography specialist, I had to get a map in there somewhere."[30] However, beyond this specialism it is in the final parts of the game that shows how the creator was influenced by microcomputing culture around him at the time and the magazines that were available in order to help people create content. Using the key to open the castle door leads the player to the Castle of Dreams, with the accompanying text "Everything is strange in here." The character of Ah-Choo is presented once again to the player followed by other intertwined characters such as the other female characters found in Part 1 of the game, images of the Great Wall of China associated with the previously played section of the game, "City of Dragons," along with the dragon characters layered in multiple colors tiling across the screen. Matson recognizes this obscure setting in a later interview about the game: "I probably read an article in a magazine about how to create these wonderful effects, so I just threw them in. I'm a child of the '60s, too, so you've got to have your psychedelic stuff."[31]

After these images it is revealed that you have found Daniel. Completing the final parts of the map then leads to finding the last character of Jessica. It is at this stage that the game ends, and Granny is revealed for the first time, not as a graphic but in a piece of text with the final words "And Granny says it's time for tea." Although this is where the game program ended on the BBC Micro, for others this is also where parts of the narrative began. In line with the multiple outputs produced for the Computer Literacy Project and the emphasis on multiple types of learning via the machine as explored in earlier chapters, *Granny's Garden* was no different. In fact for many classrooms it was the additional material that played a larger part of their learning practice, something intentionally built into the program's packaging as it recognized the limited use of the Micro in some school settings.

Beyond the Garden

The flexibility of the microcomputer, its apparent value for a vast variety of purposes across the curriculum and its capacity for extension and improvement make it a potentially forceful agent in educational change.

Clive Baker, "The Microcomputer and the Curriculum: A Critique," Journal of Curriculum Studies 17, no. 4 (1985): 449–451

In a telephone interview with Thomas Lean, Matson noted that he saw *Granny's Garden* being used in discussions of a variety of classroom settings, including science, mathematics, and English.[32] This was also noted by Smith and Segger, who stated in their discussion of using *Granny's Garden* with children with severe learning difficulties that "a major strength of programs like [*Granny's Garden*] is that they can generate huge amounts of classroom activity away from the computer—for example in drama, creative writing, plastic creativity, drawing etc."[33] The multi-curriculum approach of *Granny's Garden* not only helped with the limited amount of micros that were in schools and encouraging equality of use among classrooms but also helped to justify the cost of the machine. The game was deliberately designed to be used for 15–20 minutes by groups of children. In this instance *Granny's Garden* sums up the part of what Katie Salen called the "ecology of games," including going "beyond the game" as a site of enquiry in terms of understanding the literacies and other related activities that are presented or could be used in conjunction with or alongside the game experience.[34]

The manual accompanying *Granny's Garden* had a section on "Using the program" (if it is to be used in the home with individual users) and a section titled "In the Classroom." The "In the Classroom" section reiterates earlier discussions of classroom use, stating that "one of the great features of the micro is its ability to stimulate purposeful discussion."[35] The design of *Granny's Garden* itself adds to this discussion. By creating the program in Mode 7, which allowed for a character-based screen instead of a bitmap screen, Matson could create blocky characters that were memorable and that provided the initial basis for further narrative discussions. Rather than having a single pixel on the screen, the memory of the Micro in Mode 7 was used to refer to a sets of pixels defined elsewhere in memory.[36] This enabled the program to make more effective use of the available memory in that particular display mode, as well as adding various effects, such as flashing graphics and control codes to change the color of backgrounds, characters, and text by means of single-character commands. Therefore, although the characters and images displayed were not very detailed, and were animated in some instances but not in others, the overall story of the program could be projected through the instances in which the images were depicted with text. This gave the player a reference point for further discussions.

In the *Granny's Garden* manual, Matson characterized certain components of the story as possible starting points for further work in the classroom:

1. The twelve trees—grids, co-ordinates, 'battleships'
2. Land of Mystery—plans, maps
3. Castle of Dreams—what are dreams?, dreams in stories
4. Castles/Cottages—what differences are there?
5. Insects—friends or foes?
6. Forest—trees, litter, fire
7. Dragons
8. Witches—history and literature
9. Giants
10. Snake/Apple—Adam and Eve, are snakes always nasty
11. Toadstools etc—Invent our own characters
12. Computers—clever or stupid?

By reading the manual accompanying the program, users could gain further insight into Matson's backstory to the game about a granny who has hurt her leg and is unable to play with the children, thus allowing them the freedom to have their own adventures in her garden.[37] All of these activities allow for an extension of the gameworld or particular narratives found in the gameworld by the users exploring their own possibilities. This exploration also occurs through the intertextual references (discussed earlier) that are inherent throughout the program including commonly found fairytale and folktale tropes found in stories introduced to similar age groups, such as Snow White and Hansel and Gretel. "Children in this age group [6–7 years]," David Whitebread noted, "are, of course, very excited about fairy stories with witches and dragons and elves, and the program tapped into this area of interest very effectively."[38]

Drawing on these references allowed for other creative outputs, which are, once again, encouraged in the "additional ideas" section of the manual for *Granny's Garden*. Here, Matson presents a range of suggestions that could result in follow on activities, such as creating a *Granny's Garden* board game for other people to play, producing a map of the Kingdom of the Mountains to show the locations of scenes in the adventure, extending the game into a performance using music and drama, producing pixelated computer graphics in an art sessions, or even writing their own adventure game. In doing so, users are inspired to compare their own abilities with those of the Micro, and think about what the computer can and can't do in relation to themselves. These activities situate computer literacy in a context of other media literacies, using approaches across disciplines to extend classroom time and the gameworld while other students have access to the Micro. This type of media literacy can be seen in David

Buckingham's discussions of how these approaches enable reflection, critique, and analysis by linking media forms, common themes and characters from different media platforms rather than learning how to use media purely as a mode of production.[39] The Micro facilitates these discussions by being the platform that displays the content, yet by understanding how to interpret this content and extend it in other forms, the children are then able to work across various modes to foster their own learning and interpretations of the adventure world presented to them. These multiple factors became one of the core themes inherent in other 4Mation software as Matson decided to continue making educational programs after the success of *Granny's Garden*.

4mation: The Adventure Continues

Unconvinced by publishers of BBC Micro games at the time, Matson and Souch went on to form 4Mation as a company that would develop and sell *Granny's Garden* and other programs they had written. The other programs included *Dragon World* and *Box of Treasures*, both released in 1985, which came embedded with the cross-curriculum multi-literacy approach to computing as identified by using *Granny's Garden*. Each program came not only with the tape or disk to be used on the BBC Micro but also a range of extra material including a user guide, a book of ideas, a short story book accompanying the program's narrative as well guides for creating your own cut-out dragon. These all came in multiple booklets unlike the *Granny's Garden* manual, which incorporated all of these components in far fewer pages. Within the book of ideas for using *Dragon World* in the classroom, Matson notes that the computer should in fact be left in the cupboard or untouched in the classroom in the early stages of using the program. Instead the story should be read first in order to get the children excited and engaged with the process that follows, as well as build up the confidence in the teacher's ability to see the project through. This type of instruction also helps to build up a base of users taking them from what Sonia Livingstone would define as "traditionalists" who spend very little time using computers to "specialists" who spend more than an average amount of time with a particular medium.[40] Although national computer literacy was at the forefront of the BBC Micro campaign, this did not mean that all teachers or students were initially educated in using the Micro; therefore, accustoming the teacher to bringing the computer into the classroom and the students to the machine was part of this process.

By providing cross-curricular activities, Matson was also able to empower teachers by allowing them to feel comfortable within their particular disciplines and to begin to use the computer as a means of providing additional content for their classrooms. The computer program provided a talking point for these cross-curricular projects as well as subject-specific examples across Art, Dance/Drama, Environment, Language, Logic, Mathematics, Music, Physical Education, and Science. Instead of seeing the Micro as a way of teaching computing, the program was used in the same way as a piece of text allowing for a concept or an activity to be used in various subjects as a starting point to a conversation and learning process. The *Box of Treasures* program took these concepts further and included a book in the software package that showed the work of children at other schools when they used certain parts of the program. Matson worked with various schools, some of them in Australia, to help test the software, allowing 4Mation to document aspects of this when selling their products in the hope of inspiring other institutions about the wide range of possibilities the software enabled. Although the *Box of Treasures* software package placed more emphasis on the program in the first instance, through playing the Adventure, using the Blank program to print a range of forms and the Create program to write and edit stories, as well as create static and moving pictures to add to the stories, these could still be used to extend what was on the screen to off-screen tasks. This software package helped to show multiple approaches to learning and provided a means for students to explore their own uses for the machine.

It was these experiences with the machine that led to the popularity of *Granny's Garden* in both schools and homes. The witch came to symbolize fear and failure in parts of the game. In a 2011 article in the magazine *PC Gamer*, nostalgia for the game is apparent as the author, Richard Cobbett, takes readers though the game's history and though how the BBC Micro was used in schools at the time.[41] Although the game was ported to other platforms, such as the Commodore 64 and ZX Spectrum, it is the BBC Micro version that is most fondly remembered. Thanks to the success of 4Mation, which was based on the releases of the *Granny's Garden*, *Dragon World*, and *Flowers of Crystal*, the company still exists and distributes educational titles today. Even though Matson has long since departed from the company and gone on to be involved in other projects, *Granny's Garden* still lives on in a PC version, purchasable with single-user and network licenses.[42] The game's graphics have been updated, but the six missing children and the City of Dragons have been preserved as in the initial structure of the original game. Once again other classroom activities are emphasized as a way of expanding the use of computers in education rather than teaching purely through using the machine itself.

In hindsight, the lessons learned through educational games played on the BBC Micro, such as *Granny's Garden*, were learned not only by the children playing them but also by the games' creators. Although the games were written on and for the BBC Micro, memory restrictions and lack of machines in the classroom had to be built into the subsequent use of the educational programs provided by those seeking to enable a mode of delivery enhanced by but not centered on the machine. The additional material produced and sold with *Granny's Garden* and the subsequent 4Mation releases emulate the strategy of the BBC's Computer Literacy Project as a way of providing multiple avenues of learning with the machine at the heart of the process. That approach set the platform apart from other microcomputing platforms of its time and was, in many ways, the reason for the machine's success and existence. Therefore, to trace these similarities through into a piece of software remembered with the same fondness shows the reach of the platform beyond its hardware.

However, an awareness of the possibilities and restraints of the platform were also important in this decision making behind these programs. "Developers of software for the early Beebs [BBC Micro]," Mike Matson recalled in a 2007 interview with Thomas Lean, "were frustrated by the lack of memory. There were many occasions when finding a spare couple of bytes was a cause for celebration .... The only way to get the most of the limited memory (and to get the speed) was to write in assembler."[43] Beyond BBC BASIC, which was used to write the original *Granny's Garden*, writing in assembly was one way of being able to create more efficient content for use on the machine. As the games industry surrounding the BBC Micro continued to grow in the 1980s, learning to write platform-specific content for the machine became more and more important.

Many histories of the computer games of the 1980s are written from American and Japanese perspectives and use "pre-crash" and "post-crash" developments in the United States to contextualize the global gaming scene.[1] (Here "crash" refers to the crash of the North American video-game industry in 1983.) Similarly, collective nostalgia for particular games mean that they are often discussed in contexts beyond their original platforms and inceptions. These initial developments often get lost as the last iteration of a game's platform, publisher, or developer is remembered and are discussed more frequently than the original products. However, from a UK perspective the market for games "held up in 1982–5 because … the home computer was already, before the US crash, the preferred platform for playing games."[2]

Despite this recognition, dominant histories of the British game-development scene are often placed in the context of the games played and developed on the ZX Spectrum and the Commodore 64, with the BBC Micro often left unmentioned because it is so often thought about as being a machine for educational purposes and not for playing computer games.[3] Yet, as these histories reveal, the platform emerged at a time of innovation within the British home computing scene. This innovation spread beyond engineering the platforms on offer, and could also be seen in a range of software, including computer games, being developed by various people for the growing range of microcomputers on the market. Although the BBC Micro was not always seen as a home computer for playing computer games on, many people did write games for the platform, and many of the magazines focusing on the BBC Micro encouraged game creation as a form of learning how to program either in the version of BASIC available on the machine, or in machine code.[4] The magazines were read by many Micro users. For example, Tim Tyler, the creator of the game *Repton*, later recalled having "consumed a fair number of computer magazines from the era[:] *Your Computer* (I bought the second one), *Personal Computer World*, *Computer and Video Games*—and later on, *Acorn User*, *Beebug*, *A&B Computing*, and *BBC Micro User*."[5]

Not only was writing code from scratch encouraged as a way for people to become computer literate, but code was freely available via a variety of outputs for users to copy, manipulate, and use to create their own modifications of games.[6] These games may not have ended up on the shelves of the stores that sold them, but they were created by people eager to learn more about the platforms and how to program for them. "Whether or not you find games enjoyable," a section on programming in the first issue of *Acorn User* proclaimed, "programming a Micro to play them is one of the fastest and most rewarding ways of learning how BASIC works. Moreover, since the BBC computer is still in its infancy, there isn't much software available off the shelf—all the more reason to get down to writing your own programs and dumping them on tape!"[7]

The growing need for games programmers was constantly advertised in various magazines. Not only did games offer users a way to learn to program; users also began to push the boundaries of the platforms they were creating them for, with machine-code games being pushed more and more by companies as they allowed for quicker outputs and more detailed gameworlds than those programmed in BASIC. *The Micro User* and other magazines ran regular columns in each issue to gradually introduce readers and users to programming in machine code as a way of making games. These factors, along with the sales of home computers in the 1980s, "had the curious effects of making [the] country the locus of a vibrant 'cottage industry' in games production."[8] In recent discussions about the rise of independent game creation, Jesper Juul and others note that the term "independent game" was in use before the "indie game" movement began.[9]

The BBC Micro played a role in the development of numerous games, including Philip and Andrew Oliver's first efforts and Superior Software's *Repton* series. *Elite* was one of the more notable games written on and for the BBC Micro platform. According to Aphra Kerr's discussion of the early British gaming industry, "David Braben and Ian Bell's computer game *Elite* put the British industry on the map when it was released in 1984 and sold 150,000 copies."[10] Subsequent histories, however, often fail to trace the game back to nuances of the Micro that led to certain design decisions that were enforced and encountered when Braben and Bell were developing and programming *Elite*. In *Supercade*, Nick Sweeney briefly discusses *Elite* and the BBC Micro in the chapter on the ZX Spectrum but the BBC Micro does not have its own chapter in the book. Sweeney calls *Elite* "the stand-out classic of the starfield genre."[11] *Elite* is also included in lists such as IGN's 2000 Top 25 PC Games of All Time.[12] Because of variations in copies of the game, its publication is often credited to Firebird rather than to Acornsoft. The recognition of Acornsoft as the first publisher of *Elite*, in many ways, starts to unfold the true origins of the game on the BBC Micro, which was manufactured by Acorn Computers. Although many other popular titles were released for the BBC Micro, it is *Elite* that shows the depth and the possibilities of the hardware, the chipset, and the develop-ment opportunities for those willing to try hard enough to achieve their aims in creating games in the 1980s. It is by examining the histories related to the original game and the limitations brought about by develop-ing the game on the BBC Micro, before the possibilities of porting to other systems could even be conceived, that we can see why *Elite* was such an important game not only for the BBC Micro platform but also for game development in the 1980s.

Acornsoft was the software division of Acorn Computers. Located in Cambridge near the Acorn offices, and founded in 1980, Acornsoft was headed up by its managing director, David Johnson-Davies, and its co-founders, Hermann Hauser and Chris Curry; later they were joined by Chris Jordan as the publications editor and Tim Dobson as one of the programmers.[13] Johnson-Davies had written *Moon Lander* for the Sinclair Research MK-14, and also had written a manual titled *Atomic Theory and Practice* for the Acorn Atom.[14] In its early days, Acornsoft released a series of Games Packs for the Atom, each including a few games (for example, Games Pack 1 had *Asteroids*, *Sub Hunt*, and *Breakout*). The company went on to release numerous titles for the BBC Micro and for the subsequent Acorn Electron. Because the Acorn Electron was cheaper than the Micro, it helped to drive sales of the company's games, including those distrib-uted by Acornsoft.

Acornsoft's games included the Oliver twins' *Black Box* and *Gambit*, released together in April 1984 for the BBC Model B. *Gambit* was the twins' entry in a Design a Game competition held by a Saturday-morning televi-sion show.[15] The twins' entry—the only one that was fully functional—had been programmed on a BBC Micro and submitted on a cassette tape.

The twins had first wanted to write an arcade game for the Design a Game competition, but at the time they were still developing their knowledge of assembly programming and they didn't think they had necessary skills. However, lessons in creating games often meant that previous game genres or titles were referenced as a way of sparking potential programmers' interest. These often built upon the arcade culture that had already emerged. This was true of many of the early games released by Acornsoft, including *Snapper* (a *Pac-Man* clone), *Hopper* (a *Frogger* clone), and *Planetoid!* (a *Defender* clone). *Snapper*, written by Jonathan Griffiths and released by Acornsoft in 1982 for the BBC Micro, was subject to some attention after its release because of its similarities to *Pac-Man*. According to a blog entry at http://www.retrogamer.net, it was so close to the original *Pac-Man* game that "Namco took offence, and later versions of the game replaced Pac Man with a sort of grapefruit, and the ghosts with generic monsters."[16] Alongside these arcade clones and related controversies, Acornsoft also released educational titles and other non-gaming programs (such as ViewSheet, a spreadsheet utility written by Mark Cotton, released in 1984) and published books (including Jonathan Griffiths' *Creative Assembler*). Jonathan Griffiths, an author of various Acornsoft titles, contributed articles to *Acorn User* in which he gave advice on how to write games for the BBC Micro and for the Acorn Electron.[17] However, it was Acornsoft's role as a publisher of computer games that saw the development of some of Britain's well-known games programmers from the 1980s, including not only David Braben and Ian Bell, but also Geoff Crammond, the author of *Revs*.

Crammond, having purchased one of the first BBC Micros, began writing games for the platform, initially using BBC BASIC and then teaching himself 6502 assembly language. In a later interview, he told Magnus Anderson and Rebecca Levene that he "realized that [he] would be able to program *Space Invaders*, which was very current, and have it run like it did in pubs and arcades."[18] After thinking about publishing options, Crammond came across a leaflet for Acornsoft's catalog of games. This game Crammond programmed became *Super Invaders*, a *Space Invaders* clone. After Acornsoft published *Super Invaders*, Crammond started work on *Aviator*, a 3D game that simulated piloting a Spitfire. However, it was Crammond's next game, *Revs*, that was the "turning point" in his game-development career; it allowed him to leave his job at the British telecommunications and engineering company Marconi and work on games full time.[19] As Crammond recalled in a later *Retro Gamer* interview, "*Revs* came about because Acorn Computers were sponsoring a Formula 3 racing driver by the name of David Hunt—the younger brother of the ex-F1 champion James Hunt. After the launch of *Aviator*, Acornsoft asked me if I could do a Formula 3 racing game given that I would have access to David and his team, who were, at that time, Eddie Jordan based at Silverstone. This sounded great, so naturally I agreed." Putting *Revs* in the same class of difficulty as Crammond's *Aviator* and Braben and Bell's *Elite*, a reviewer in the July 1985 issue of *Acorn User* praises the game's attention to details, including "things like the rear-view mirror's revealing other racers coming up behind, and the thump-thump as the car runs on the corner curbs."[20] *Revs* was later ported to the Commodore 64, and Crammond went on to develop games for other platforms (among them *Stunt Car Racer* and *Formula One Grand Prix*), but it was the initial connection to Acornsoft that allowed him to develop his career in the games industry. And much the same was true of David Braben and Ian Bell, the creators of *Elite*.

Developing *Elite*

Even now, just a week after its launch, *Elite* has already firmly established itself as a cult game for the Beeb that seems to create its own self perpetuating fame.

David Fell, "*Elite*—An Outstanding New Game from Acornsoft," *Beebug*, November 1984

The BBC Micro as a potential site for game creation created a bond between David Braben and Ian Bell. A chance meeting at Cambridge University and a shared interest in Acorn's microcomputing platforms led the duo to create *Elite*, one of the best-known games for the Micro.[21] Braben, unable to afford a Micro at the time, had to use his personally modified Acorn Atom. "The only other low cost machine at that time," he later noted, "was the Sinclair ZX80. It was nowhere near as good and not dramatically cheaper (the starting price for an Acorn Atom was £120, whereas for a ZX80 it was £99)."[22] The Atom and David Johnson-Davies' book *Atomic Theory and Practice* gave Braben his first tastes of programming. The book, he recalled, "was very helpful in learning to program in BASIC."[23] Therefore, even though Braben didn't own a BBC Micro at the time, he was already acquainted with the fundamental principles of how to develop a game for that machine as a result of his experiences with other Acorn hardware. In a time of game creation where many releases were built on arcade game clones, Braben started to think about other potential game projects.[24] "I played some games on arcade machines—for example in a local chip shop," he recalled, "but there were relatively few games around (on any platform) that weren't arcade games or arcade game clones."[25] However, Braben wasn't interested in arcade-style games or in the ports that were available on the BBC Micro. He wanted a longer game experience, the chance for players to explore larger worlds and not just gain points from shooting or collecting things. The idea that points only equated to extra lives was also something he was not fond of, and subsequently he wanted to think about other ways of creating game content. It was this drive, along with meeting Ian Bell, that led to the creation of *Elite*.

Histories of gaming often cite *Elite* as the "first three-dimensional game." "In the same way that Cyan had plenty of previous experience to prepare them for producing *Myst*," Andrew Hutchison writes, "id Software had released *Hovertank 3D* in 1991 with the claim that it was the first ever personal computer game with 3D elements (id Software, 2005). This claim has been contested, and the game *Elite* (Braben Bell, 1984) has been presented as an earlier example (Wikipedia, 2005)."[26] However, some discussions of what were earlier three-dimensional games go back to *Battlezone* in 1980 and *3D Monster Maze* in 1981.[27] Whereas *3D Monster Maze* (programmed for the Sinclair ZX81) had raster graphics, *Battlezone* had vector graphics. Braben and Bell used vector graphics for *Elite*. In an interview conducted in 2012, the BBC news presenter Rory Cellan-Jones stated that *Elite* was three-dimensional in "a way that had never been seen before"; David Braben responded that he felt it was the "first true 3D game using wireframe graphics."[28] Although 3D graphics had been experimented with and commercialized before the creation of *Elite*, the ability to move around and explore space that *Elite* offered was unlike anything players had seen before on the Micro.

It was not only the three-dimensional graphics that set *Elite* apart. *Elite* is now commonly described as a space-trading game. The three-dimensional graphics were fundamental to its design, as the purpose was to make the player feel as though he or she could traverse an expansive universe (see figure 4.1). The player controlling the Cobra Mark III spaceship could find planets and trade goods with them in the hope of gaining the exclusive Elite rating. However, other spacecraft, other traders, and police (Vipers) were also present within the gameworld to stop the player from succeeding. To develop the game's three-dimensional graphics and to create a sense of explorable space, Braben and Bell had to consider how to use the BBC Micro to its full advantage. The first hurdle they faced for was the limited memory available to them—the BBC Micro Model B only had 32 kilobytes. As Anderson and Levene note, "the image used on screen took up a vast chunk of [memory]; a third, or two thirds for really high-resolution two-colour mode, which immediately bumped their

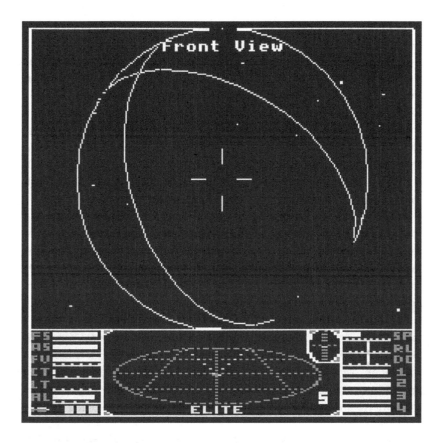

Figure 4.1 A screenshot showing the front view of *Elite*.

available memory down to 22 kilobytes."[29] The constraints on memory presented a challenge to Braben and Bell: how could they represent space with multiple galaxies and yet still have the game be playable within the restrictions imposed by the platform? Although the BBC Micro allowed for its read-only memory to be expanded, usually that was done for word-processor packages, as was discussed in chapter 2. Because of the cost of the additional external ROM it would require, expanding the ROM was not a preferred option for the gaming market. By using techniques that pushed the boundaries the platform, as will be detailed throughout this chapter, Bell and Braben managed to develop a game that had eight galaxies for players to explore and hundreds of stars. That led to the creation of what is commonly said to have been the first "open-world" or "open-ended" game.

The first layer to be stripped away in using the machine was to program the game solely with assembly language directly accessing the 6502 processor, and not the BBC BASIC programming language that was widely advertised as the way for new users to learn how to program on the Micro. As was noted in earlier chapters, for most users BASIC was the interface between the user and the machine, allowing people to type in simple commands, load games or software, and create simple games, shapes, and animations. However, running BASIC took up memory and ran slowly (each command had to be interpreted before it was executed). By using assembly language, as many other BBC Micro games did, Braben and Bell were able to gain more memory and therefore more freedom to include further events, namely how the three-dimensional world would be generated and displayed to the player. Although there were books, magazines, and television series devoted to using the BBC Micro and to creating small programs for the machine, those basic skills were only the starting point to future game development. To create larger, more sophisticated games, users had to develop their own learning and had to continue to "hack away" at learning to program more and more assembly language.[30] Yet books were still on hand for times when programmers needed extra help or understanding of the machine. One such book—*The Advanced User Guide to the BBC Micro* by Bray, Dickens, and Holme—was cited as "excellent, invaluable in fact for details of the BBC Micro" by Braben in his own recollections of developing for the machine.[31]

These creative programming techniques were subsequently referred to as "silver bullets" by Braben in his 2011 Game Developers Conference post-mortem of the game.[32] Another "silver bullet" was to use the on-screen display to its full capacity, a feat that was subsequently accomplished in two ways. In the first instance Braben developed a memory-saving technique by creating a "special display mode [that] reduced the resolution to 256 × 256 pixels."[33] Using that exact boundary meant that all screen coordinates would fit into one byte of memory. According to Braben, that "meant that in the calculations while drawing lines, it would never need to check the 'carry' flag—it stayed within 8 'bits' so it went much faster."[34] The specialist screen display allowed Braben to use what he called "lazy evaluation" in his line-drawing algorithm.[35] That "display also used less memory" and allowed for the graphics to be redrawn as and when they were required rather than being drawn over and over again in order to display the right lines.[36] By freeing up space to perform other functions, the technique gave the illusion of a greater sense of three-dimensionality through the use of hidden line removal.

Hidden line removal is a technique whereby any edges of wireframe objects that face away from the viewer are not drawn. In light of this, another "silver bullet" was described with reference to Braben and Bell manipulating the screen's display. Here, the duo showed innovation in using the platform by manipulating the black and white and color aspects of the display to affect how the graphics were shown. Braben designed a method of changing the graphics from being in black and white on the top two-thirds of the screen to color in the bottom third by changing the display mode part of the way down the screen. "One problem," Braben recalled in a later interview, "is it was black and white, so at the top of the display we started a timer and switched to a lower resolution colour mode by changing the display settings at that point, then changing them back again once it reached the bottom."[37]

That technique was unheard of in the BBC development team. Sophie Wilson and Steve Furber agreed, the former calling *Elite* "the program that couldn't have been written" and the latter commenting that "what David Braben managed to do with a computer with no memory and no computer power—*Elite* had the BBC design team staggered." "It was," he continued, "one of the most outstanding games."[38] What were seen by many as technological limitations had been challenged by Braben and Bell, who were determined to see through their extensive design decisions for the game, and thus see them slowly come to life. The resultant 3D graphics of *Elite* allowed for what felt to players like an expansive universe, traversing the seemingly limitless possibilities of space. This expansive universe was attributed to yet another one of Braben's post-mortem "silver bullets." Bell and Braben used Fibonacci number sequences in order to generate a vast array of galaxies and to make the *Elite* universe feel "huge."[39]

In his book *Backroom Boys*, Francis Spufford discusses Bell and Braben's use of the Fibonacci sequence at great length, revealing that "experiments had shown them they could squash a solar system into just twelve digits, as long as they were digits in Base 16, so that would be their starting point: a single number in hexadecimal notation, twelve digits long."[40] Spufford goes on to document how this allowed Braben and Bell to generate a series of galaxies based on these iterations in the sequence; some of the digits controlled physical specifications of the systems, some created the names of the galaxies, some were responsible for stock-market information about the galaxy, and some generated a description of the galaxy. However, owing to the way the galaxies were generated , Braben and Bell had to go in and moderate the information that was produced, as some of it led to inappropriately named planets or caused the cluster of the galaxy to look different than the programmers envisaged. Despite having to edit some of what was produced, it was by using this technique that the space of *Elite* could be as large as it ended up being, with eight galaxies containing 256 planets, a cut-down version of the original attempt to create 2^{48} galaxies.[41]

This expansive universe, a far cry from the arcade-game remakes and clones that were available for the BBC Micro at the time, was noted in the original reviews of the game. A 1984 review in *Beebug* characterized *Elite* as "the first in a new generation of 3-D space games featuring interstellar travel in a distant cluster of galaxies."[42] It was this innovation that also saw *Elite* take a step further in terms of its design, compared to other games such as *Battlezone*. The movement in *Elite* was seen to be more versatile allowing the player to speed up and slow down the spaceship thus creating a range of motion and endless possibilities. In playing the game, "space combat was more fluid and free form, and excitingly mimicked the dogfights seen in the *Star Wars* films."[43] *Battlezone* can in many ways be seen as one of the first three-dimensional games, appearing a few years before *Elite*. However, *Elite* was seen as an extension from this as the "first three-dimensional" space game, before being discussed as an "open world" or "open ended" game, and also as a "space-trading game" or even a "role-playing game." In a global context, the nature of game development in the 1980s Britain meant that the creation of "firsts" in some of these instances would have felt to be legitimately the case to Braben and Bell during this time, even if we can see them in a greater combination of historical innovations in retrospect. In his global histories of game development and consumption, Tristan Donovan writes that "the idea of a being a space-age trucker had already been explored in a few trading games, such as 1974's *Star Traders*—a text game for mainframe computers—and 1980's *Galactic Trader* on the Apple II, but neither Bell or Braben knew of their existence."[44] What was happening in the United States was known in Great Britain only if it was documented in one of the many computing and platform-specific magazines. Similarly, many home users did not have access to expensive machines such as the Apple II.

Once again, the notion of "firsts" in game history begins to become skewed and harder to define as further examinations beyond the mainstream press and more common histories reveal other sides to the development of such games that are not always unique to gaming, but often unique to the specific platform of creation. Isolating a game to its production values, as well as the culture and background of the programmers at the time starts to reveal common themes. Beyond the analysis of the platform and game creation, further histories can also be provided through the histories of the game's reception, and the additional commentary related to the game as found in print and online archives from its time of release. It is by recognizing the BBC Micro as the first platform the game was made both on and for that we can start to find player responses to *Elite* in the numerous platform-specific game magazines that were sold during its release.

The Reception of *Elite*

As has already been noted, when playing *Elite* the player is able to switch among front, side, and back views in order to explore the universe as the spaceship is moving through the galaxies. In doing so, these spaces allowed for "z-axis movement into and out of the frame" showing passing planets and spaceships from different angles, rather than fixing the viewpoint all within one screen or perspective.[45] Not only does this make the universe to appear to be more expansive, it also shifts the user's perspective. Allowing for a shift in the viewpoint helped with the open-ended nature of the gameworld, which matched up with the mapped viewed of seeing different planets to potentially land on to and trade items from. This was one of the key points about *Elite*. It was not a point-collecting game that could be played repetitively in short bursts. *Elite* was time-consuming. It involved exploration, "leveling up" your ship and captain with various weapons and items that could be used to trade with other ships it may encounter. These items could also help players get their ships out of compromising situations in order to prolong play and try not to be faced with the dreaded "Game Over" screen. At the time *Elite* could be seen as an endurance test, a completely new type of game that was not experienced much in digital game-playing scenarios at the time. "From the start, there were no tutorials, no obvious path and no helpful assistant; the player was delivered into an unforgiving universe and allowed to reach the ultimate goal of being ranked "Elite" through whatever means—moral and physical—he deemed appropriate."[46]

Examining the archives of letters pages from BBC Micro focused magazines sold at the time reveals other stories about the game's initial reception. Far from being a big hit with every player, a game that must be played, the title caused frustration for groups of players due to its new styles of gameplay. While it is easy to draw relationships between games, such as the links to *Eve Online* as a possible development from *Elite*, the initial reception of the game from a player perspective shows the reality of how *Elite* was not always seen by all as ground-breaking, innovative, or a welcomed break from the stability of arcade-style games at the time. In the January 1985 issue of *The Micro User*, two letters describing readers' frustration with *Elite* were published. The first (from Paul R. Lemon of Aintree, Merseyside) begins: "As soon as I saw the adverts I bought *Elite*, from Acornsoft. Having been a fan of Atari's *Star Raiders* for years I couldn't resist."[47] However, the next paragraph goes on to reveal that the reader is less than excited about the game since he began playing it: "Today I am selling *Elite*! At 26 I'm reasonably coordinated and until now have had no problems with any computer game but *Elite* is beyond me. It's infuriating and potentially dangerous for computers as I've never felt more like taking an axe to the keyboard." The reader goes on to list his reasons for disliking the game, blaming the poor quality of the controls and commenting that, although the game is graphically superior to other titles, the overall gameplay lets the game down, as the combat sequences prove to be too difficult for the reader to continually overcome. This frustration is echoed by the second reader, A.M.D. from Exeter, Devon, whose main complaint is the difficulty of the game from the start: "To get to even a friendly Corporate State planet on your first try you are besieged by countless enemy ships which eliminate you before you can even find them, never mind identify them."

Because of its long playing hours, its open-ended possibilities, and its space-trading nature, *Elite* is often seen as an innovative starting point in the creation of different game genres. To move from Harmless to Mostly Harmless to Poor to Average to Above Average to Competent to Dangerous to Deadly and finally Elite takes time and investment from the player. This resulted in failure for quite a few players, a consequence of games as recognized by Jesper Juul in *The Art of Failure*: "Players tend to prefer games that are somewhat challenging, and for a moment it can sound as if this explains the paradox—players like to fail, but not too much."[48] *Elite* was not balanced enough for all players. This factor, combined with the fact that *Elite* offered a different style of gaming from point collection and quick play times, meant that not all players could adapt to the experience as easily as others. As the reader A.M.D. concluded in the closing sentences of a letter about *Elite* in the January 1985 issue of *The Micro User*, "a game is only a game if it allows you a chance of winning. Continual failure is very depressing and I have quickly developed an anti-game attitude."

The two letters cited above caused such a debate among other readers that the entire letters section of the April 1985 issue of *The Micro User*

("Micro Mail") was dedicated to letters from other players of *Elite*.[49] Their comments ranged from similar voices of frustration. One reader complained about "being attacked and watching your energy decrease every second," another that "*Elite* is for the macho among us."

The January and February 1986 issues of *The Micro User* had a pull-out guide that explained how to get the most out of *Elite* and cheat codes that could enable a player to start with better weapons and more money by manipulating the *Elite* game file (on either tape or disc). Part 1 of the guide details game-playing tactics that are needed to succeed in the game with a proviso: "We hope this guide will help you to get to *Elite*. But remember, the Order of Elite is a fighting quality far beyond courage, macho and cool precision. Select wisely in battle and be strong." At the bottom of the page is a preview promising that part 2 of the guide offers "a secret weapon to help you achieve victory." Whereas in today's gaming culture cheat guides and walkthroughs are released nearly simultaneously with the games, the cheat guide in *The Micro User* appeared nearly four years after the release of the original game.

Beyond these examples of the paradoxical nature of player views of the game, there were also distinct successes among the game-playing community. The news section of the May 1985 issue of *The Micro User* contained an article on the National *Elite* Championships that were scheduled to take play on May 9 of that year in the Westminster district of London. The article noted that the competition had been entered by "more than 5,000 of the cult game's diehard followers" and that six finalists had been chosen to "fight it out for the opportunity to win equipment and software to the value of £1,000."[50] The two-day tournament, held on a weekend, had coincided with the players having access to a "new second processor version of the game—all colour and with faster graphics—for the final." The article in *The Micro User* went on to mention that the game was so popular that it had been shortlisted for the Home Computer Software of the Year category in the British Microcomputing Awards 1985, and that it was "certainly the most successful game ever for the BBC Micro in that one in every four home users has now bought one." It was this popularity of the game that sees its initial platform development histories become lost in future listings of the game, with the company Firebird publishing the Commodore 64 and ZX Spectrum versions. Future versions of the game saw it also ported to the Apple II, as well as the NES console and other platforms, although each release of the game was slightly different dependent on the capabilities of each platform release. "The BBC version," Acorn announced in 1985, "will still be the best around because of the speed of graphics."[51]

However, one part of the game's release that did continue between each platform was the additional material that came boxed with the game. This was yet another way of setting the game apart from other titles on offer, showing how the game could be seen as a new entity among the waves of arcade clone titles that continued to be released, and justifying its slightly higher price tag relative to other game releases.

Expanding the Universe

The release of *Elite* in September 1984 was carefully planned, including a press launch at Thorpe Park (a theme park in Surrey, UK). The game was also boxed slightly differently than other Acornsoft titles, and was packaged with the Space Trader's Flight Training Manual, a quick-start-style user guide with control listings and ship identification images, a pull-out poster featuring the game's logo and ship identification, and a novella by the fantasy author Robert Holdstock. Because *Elite* was such a shift in gameplay from other games for the BBC Micro, the extensive manual was a much-needed starting point to the experience. Retaining the qualities of the game, placing the player as a space trader in the fictional universe of the *Elite* gameworld, the flight-training manual starts by situating the player in the Cobra Mk III space craft in which the reader would begin the game. A detailed discussion of the interior of the ship served to create a fictional world that couldn't be offered by the on-screen game graphics. Not only was the expansive world envisioned by creative programming techniques within the playable game; the world was further continued in the training manual, in the ship-identification chart, and in the novella released with the game.

Titled *The Dark Wheel*, the novella was packaged with the manual and the game tape as a way of showing the expanse of the universe and extending the "fictional spaces" of the gameworld for the player.[52] Although *Elite* offered a screen display far beyond what was expected of the Micro, it was still limited in its representation of the world. The novella created an additional world for the player to become lost in. Far outweighing the art on the box in which the game came and the poster and the manual that accompanied the game, the novella provided an extra way for the player to identify with or position himself as Alex Ryder, the character introduced in the narrative. In his writing about box art, Raiford Guins draws on Paul Gilroy's discussions of the jackets of LP records as "functional/expressive surfaces."[53] The box art of various video games can be seen as a way of exploring a narrative space of the gameworld not afforded by the technical screen outputs of the time, with the case of the box art for *Elite* demonstrating this as it depicts a three-dimensional ship complete with engines glowing as it portrays a sense of movement into the rest of the drawn universe. Yet the box art alone was not enough, and the world continues to expand through this extra material released with the game. It is possible to see how this links to the multi-platform, convergent nature of the BBC Micro as a computing experience. Not only was the BBC Micro about distinct hardware and computer literacy skills; the Computer Literacy Project connected to the BBC Micro created content across a range of media forms for users to access. The BBC Micro's success and functionality relied on multiple sources being used for learning, such as the television and radio shows, magazines, and TV tie-in games. Actively engaging users within games through associated storytelling (as was shown in the previous chapter in relation to *Granny's Garden*) was therefore often a common element of the BBC Micro game-playing experience.

The involvement of the novella within the game pack once again lent itself to an early "transmedia" experience.[54] The product was not just the playing of the game, but exploring the universe created around the design of the game as highlighted by the tagline on the back of the novella, "read the novel/play the game." Playing *Elite* the game with reading the additional material allowed the user to find a way into his own fictional world, but thanks to the much-needed initial game manual the player had more of an idea what to do and what possible dangers lay in front of him. *The Dark Wheel* was not essential reading before the game but it was a helpful addition to understanding more of the gameworld for those that read it. *The Dark Wheel* was very much an additional part of the overall game narrative for the player, showing another side of the *Elite* fiction and along with it creating various talking points for further discussion by players when they were not playing the game. In a pre–World Wide Web world this was an interesting add-on. It had not been explored much by others until the point of release, and once again it shows the ingenuity that this new genre of game provided at the time. However, the innovation did not end there.

The Legacy and the Future of *Elite*

Braben also did something else innovative during the development of *Elite*: he "negotiated a non-exclusive license which would allow them to develop and market versions for other machines after the versions for the Acorn machines were finished."[55] Therefore, *Elite* went on to be released for other platforms after being released for the BBC Micro. It was also this initial success that lead Braben to continue with game creation and eventually go on to set up Frontier Developments. Braben's ethos also continues through two principles stated by that company: "We get our games into customers' hands by: i) working with a number of top publishers, with whom we have developed long term relationships, and ii) a growing number of self-published titles using digital distribution channels on the major gaming platforms."[56] The ability to self-publish titles also led to the creation of the successor to *Elite*. On November 5, 2012, Frontier Developments launched a Kickstarter campaign for a game called *Elite: Dangerous*.[57] According to the front page of the Kickstarter site for the project, "*Elite: Dangerous'* is the latest installment of a long series of epic space games, starting with '*Elite*'—one of the most successful games of the 1980s." The Kickstarter project's ambitious target of £1.25 million was met 48 hours before the 60-day deadline, showing not only the growth of what Henry Jenkins, Sam Ford, and Joshua Green term to be "spreadable media" but also a recognition that fans of the franchise wanted to play a role in financing another *Elite* game.[58]

Not only was Frontier mentioned as part of the "Cambridge Phenomenon"; so too was Jagex in relation to its success with the game *Runescape*, which allowed the company to hire more than 450 people by the beginning of 2011.[59] Today, Cambridge Science Park is home to these and other video-game companies, including Sony and Ninja Theory. Therefore, not only does the success of *Elite* remain in Cambridge through one of the developer's companies; the technology industries of the 1980s continue to make Cambridge a site of innovation where companies formed from or in relation to Acorn or Sinclair Computers offer a wide variety of services beyond the games industry. However, Cambridge was not the only site of game-related content in the 1980s. As we will see in the next chapter, other places and publishers in the UK also figured in the development of games for the BBC Micro.

In addition to the games published by Acornsoft, the BBC Micro saw a range of other game titles being developed for and published on the platform. As was the case with other microcomputing platforms, game developers self-published some games but also set up their own publishing companies targeted at a range of platforms, including the BBC Micro. A company called Level 9 was well known for releasing adventure games, some of them made for the BBC Micro and for Nascom computers.[1] Other companies, such as Aardvark, were run by one person and developed games primarily for the BBC Micro. Going under the name of Orlando, Nick Pelling was both the developer and the publisher of games for Aardvark, most notably the game *Frak!* (released in 1984). A platform game in which players control a caveman character called Trogg, *Frak!* was praised for the way it utilized the characteristics of BBC Micro platform. According to a review in the September 1984 issue of *Acorn User*, "the outstanding thing about [*Frak!*] is the graphics," "the characters could have stepped right out of a Disney movie from the good old cartoon days," and "*Frak!* represents one of the new wave of BBC games that are at last living up to the machine."[2]

Alongside one-person publishers there were other companies that also focused on the BBC Micro as their platform of choice, among them Micro Power and Superior Software. Micro Power started out under the name of Program Power and while some of their games were ported to other platforms, their focus on the BBC Micro and Acorn Electron saw them release a range of arcade clones, much like some of the earlier titles released by Acornsoft that were discussed in the preceding chapter. However, their title *Doctor Who and the Mines of Terror* was far from an arcade clone and ended up requiring its own ROM chip for the game to run with the cassette tape or floppy disk it came packaged with. The additional 16 kilobytes of ROM were needed in order for the Micro to have enough available memory to run the game, and once again exposed the possibilities of upgrading the platform to allow for technical work-arounds to be made.

It was this recognition of the strengths of the BBC Micro platform that also saw the development of one of the largest software producers and publishers for the BBC Micro; Superior Software. It is in this chapter that we will look at Superior Software and its role in game publishing for the BBC Micro in more detail, as well as examining one of their best known titles, that of *Repton*. Charting the development of *Repton* not only exposes the possibilities posed by the BBC Micro platform for game development, but also the innovation of the game series' different developers. This innovation went beyond the initial game title offered and showed how later iterations of the game enabled users to edit levels and use a dedicated scripting language to modify some in-game behaviors. These features show how present-day discussions about the ability to modify and share computer games can be seen in light of the histories of *Repton* and some of the similar features it offered in the 1980s.

Superior Software

After Acornsoft, the BBC Micro's biggest publisher was Superior Software ... .

Magnus Anderson and Rebecca Levene, *Grand Thieves & Tomb Raiders: How British Videogames Conquered the World* (Aurum, 2012)

Superior Software was founded in 1982 by Richard Hanson and John Dyson, both of whom had published games with Micro Power. In a tale similar to that of David Braben, Hanson remembers how he bought his first home computer, an Acorn Atom, while he was at university in Leeds.[3] Hanson notes that he "wrote some games and other software for the Acorn Atom using Basic and a 6502 assembler, and 17 of my games and utilities were published by a Leeds-based software publisher called Program Power, which subsequently became known as Micro Power." "Later," he writes, "I bought one of the first BBC Micros and wrote some games and utility software for that computer."[4] After writing the first four games for Superior Software, starting with a budget of £100, the duo started selling their software via advertisements in a few magazines. Their catalog of games then grew after inviting other programmers to send them their software to potentially distribute and market. In 1986, Superior Software even released a booklet titled *Top Tips for Games Authors* introduced by Christopher Payne, the company's marketing consultant. The opening pages detail how to select a target computer for your game stating how "the Spectrum marketplace is quite overcrowded with many software houses preferring to concentrate on the Commodore 64 and Amstrad markets. Very few companies support the Atari (300,000 computers sold), but rather more release programs for the BBC Micro (500,000 computers sold) and the Electron (300,000 computers sold)."[5] Payne goes on to note that the Spectrum and Commodore games markets at the time had relativity short product life-cycle compared to the BBC and Electron which can have games that go on "selling well for months." Obviously, Superior Software favored the Acorn machines as they were the platforms the company released their games on, but, as the booklet suggests, Superior was also aware of the market and the increased competition for game titles in an ever-growing software industry. Knowing their competition was key, not only for the release platforms but also in terms of the other publishing companies they were up against.

In his discussions of Superior Software's main publishing competitors at the time, Hanson cites Acornsoft, Micro Power, and Software Invasion and writes that all these companies "pushed against the technical capabilities of the BBC Micro." "Each company," he notes, "would regularly bring out new landmark games."[6] Hanson goes on to note that "Gallup produced a weekly software chart and one memorable week in January 1987 Superior Software's games were placed at positions 1, 2, 3 and 9 in the BBC Micro software chart; the top slot was filled by *Repton 3*, which held the number 1 position for 12 weeks, finally being overtaken by *Ravenskull*."[7] *Ravenskull*, developed by Martin Edmonson and Nicholas Chamberlain, was released in 1986. As with many of the early programmers, Edmondson received a BBC Micro for Christmas and, with Chamberlain, began to program games for the machine, one of which ended up being *Ravenskull*. As well as *Ravenskull*, Superior Software produced titles such as *Stryker's Run* (a 2D side-scrolling game designed by Chris Roberts and Philip Meller), *Grand Prix Construction Set* (a simulation of Formula 1 racing that enabled players to create their own tracks), and *Repton*.

Although not as widely discussed as *Elite* in more mainstream game histories, *Repton* also worked with the characteristics of the BBC Micro platform.

Repton in the Beginning

After *Elite*, [*Repton* is] probably the best-known game ever to be released for the BBC family of home computers. Its 15-year old creator earned telephone-number royalties from its publication, and that of its sequel.

Edge Staff, "The Making of: *Repton*," July 23, 2009 (http://www.edge -online.com/features/making-repton/)

Released in 1985, *Repton* was created by Tim Tyler in a month on his BBC Micro and subsequently published by Superior Software. Although *Repton* has been compared to *Boulderdash*, Tyler has been quoted as saying that he never played that game.[8] In fact, according to Tyler his history with programming games began before he even had access to a machine:

I learned to program before having a computer from an article about writing adventure games in *Which* magazine. Then, my friends got computers. I saw how cool the games were and it was obvious that these were new and cool gadgets—and I wanted one for myself. I persuaded my relatives that computers were "educational"—they put up 200 pounds, I put up 200 pounds, and soon I had a BBC model B. I fairly quickly got the hang of programming it. It was fun—and seemed like a possible source of profit. Eventually that worked out for me.[9]

Beyond fitting in with the rhetoric of the BBC Micro as an educational platform as a means for gaining the money to purchase the machine, Tyler also bought a BBC Model B "partly because that's what my friends had—and it seemed to offer the best quality at the time at a reasonable price. The proper keyboard was a definite attraction."[10] Utilizing the specific properties of the BBC Micro, beyond the full-size keyboard, allowed Tyler to create what turned out to be an extremely successful game.

Repton involves the player controlling a reptile-like character around a two-dimensional mapped view to collect diamonds. The player has to control the character to push boulders onto the monsters in its way during each of the twelve levels. The game's seemingly large side-scrolling spaces allow the player to move around in what seems to be an expansive space. To achieve this, while still having the game run quickly, Tyler learned how to make full use of the 6845 CRTC chip, which, he noted, "allowed manipulation of its registers to achieve hardware scrolling—which was pretty cool." "One of my first machine code programs," he continued, "poked values into this chip to make the screen scroll sideways."[11] This method of using the CRTC (cathode-ray-tube controller) on the BBC Micro allowed Tyler to use the machine more efficiently, as redrawing the screen didn't require as much effort from the CPU (central processing unit) when scrolling, thus creating smoother overall gameplay. "Almost all of my games," Tyler comments, "later used this technique to provide gaming areas larger than the screen"—and those games included *Repton*.

Aside from the way the game was programmed, its release also saw further incentives for players in purchasing the title, beyond completing the game for their own personal reward. When all twelve levels were complete, a congratulatory message was displayed on the screen. The first person to send Superior Software a photograph of the congratulatory screen won £100, as was noted in advertisements for the game in 1985. Therefore, not only was the game successful in its own right, the reward for quick completion also helped to incentivize players to buy it and work their way through the levels. However, beyond the prize involved, the game also received complementary reviews in both *The Micro User* and *Acorn User* with statements such as "this is an astounding game reaching new heights in BBC arcade adventures" and "for my money the best arcade game for the Beeb and Electron yet!"[12]

Three months after the success of the game among BBC Micro players, Superior Software asked Tyler to create a sequel. *Repton 2* was released in time for Christmas in 1985. In *Repton 2*, the player had to contend with warp zones that took the player-character to various screens. Although technically one large level, the warp zones divided the game up into the equivalent of eighteen screens. To complete the game, players had to collect all of the puzzle pieces, with the final piece opening up the special character on the first screen. Unlike *Repton*, there are no passwords for the levels in *Repton 2*, which made it substantially harder to complete. Despite this, the game was initially released to positive reviews in both *The Micro User* and *Acorn User*. One reviewere wrote: "I haven't completed even 10 per cent of this adventure, but I relish the prospect of finding my way further into it."[13] *Repton 2* was voted BBC Micro Game of the Year in 1985, but Tyler's interest in the series waned. After his success with the first two games, Tyler sold the *Repton* series.

Despite Tyler's departure from the series, Superior Software decided to continue the *Repton* titles. *Repton 3* was programmed by Matthew Atkinson. However, Tyler didn't walk away completely. He contributed a few of the level designs to this version even though he didn't program the game. The game was similar to the first *Repton* game, and bought back the concept of having a password revealed at the end of each completed level so that players had access to the level directly at a later stage. In a later article titled "The Making of *Repton*," Chris Payne, the marketing manager at Superior Software, is credited for the inclusion of both the password facility and the map facility in the original game.[14] Although *Repton 3*, like the first *Repton* game, involved collecting diamonds, it introduced an additional timer feature: a time bomb. In addition to collecting the diamonds, the player had to diffuse the bomb at the end of each level. Yet, as with the first game, players had to complete the game within the time limit; otherwise the character would be killed. Building on a similar formula to the first two titles, *Repton 3* was "the best-selling game for the BBC from its launch in November 1986 until mid-February 1987."[15] However, *Repton 3* wasn't just successful in its reception among players. It now serves as an important example of how level editors were integrated into games in the 1980s. *Repton 3* was very much a BBC Micro game in its design and its capabilities. Players could now also modify the character of Repton, and new levels could be created and then shared.

Attempts have been made to recognize how histories of level editing can be traced back to games before *Doom*. James Newman, in particular, notes how this "lineage may, in fact be traced back further still to games such as Electronic Arts' Pinball Construction Set (1983), Adventure Construction Set (1985), Racing Destruction Set (1985) or Sensible Software's 1987 title Shoot Em Up Construction Kit."[16] Newman sees these kits not as games but as "resources with which to make games." In this instance the construction kit is seen as separate component to the games available, not necessarily allowing for a seamless synergy between playing the game and creating game content in the form of already designed levels. Although the various construction kits on offer allowed for a variety of levels to be created for distinct genres of games, they were not built into particular games themselves. Thus, they became generic toolkits for those wishing to build on a particular genre.

As was noted earlier, Superior Software also released the *Grand Prix Construction Set*, which, like the other construction sets mentioned above, allowed for levels to be built while not necessarily being a part of a particular game. Yet *Repton 3*'s built-in level editor drew on earlier concepts, such as the game *Lode Runner*, released by Brøderbund in 1983 and often cited as one of the first games to include a level editor.[17] The menu system of *Lode Runner* gives the user not only a play option but also a "Game Generator" that allows the user to edit, test, and move content he or she is modifying. While editing the game, the user is able to construct new walls, to add poles that can be climbed, and to re-position enemies and rewards. On completion, levels can be saved and shared on the many microcomputing platforms for which the game was available, including the Apple II, the VIC-20, the ZX Spectrum, the BBC Micro, and the Commodore 64. This was emphasized in a review of the BBC Micro version of the game in the November 1985 issue of *The Micro User*: "Should [the levels] be insufficient you can use the game's in-built screen editor to create your own. These can be saved to tape and re-loaded at a later date."[18]

Similarly, *Impact!* and various other games released in the 1980s included level editing capabilities within the game itself. Although *Impact!* was a simple game (similar to the game *Breakout*) in which the player had to hit a ball across the screen to destroy colored blocks, the player could change the levels, insert different rewards, and re-structure and re-purpose the game. The player, referred to as the "designer" on the game's menu screen, was presented with a limited range of actions, including the ability to draw levels while changing the positioning of laser reflectors, indestructible blocks, and bonus blocks, but this additional functionality extended the possibilities of the gameworld and created the potential for more level designs that players could encounter. In these instances the platform determined the output, the game format, and the type of save files generated, but users with the same game copy and the same platform could then swap information. Although not unique in their capabilities for file sharing through saving content to cassette tapes or floppy disks, the cultures of British microcomputing games allowed for content to be shared more easily than in games developed for video game consoles as used predominantly in the United States in the earlier half of the 1980s. Alex Wade recognizes these differences in each of these industries:

US consumers were more inclined towards using what they were being sold—hardwired into the process of consumption—whereas the UK was as flexible as the Spectrum's rubber keyboard, flouting copyright and established trade practices to integrate production and consumption seamlessly, a genuine precursor to the user network societies generated today by participatory media culture, and "Web 2.0" applications where the consumer is fully and willingly complicit in the production process.[19]

The properties of the platform became paramount in players' and creators' understandings of how software could be written, played, and shared, and this included the abilities of level editing. The *Repton 3* level editor offered players a range of options from designing their own levels to redesigning the characters in the game. Upon opening this part of the game disk, the player, now titled "The Editor," was presented with a blank screen and was then able to click on a variety of options by moving a cursor over the menu items. These options included creating maps by placing walls, diamonds, and paths, but also changing some of these components, including the Repton character. A basic range of colors was available for new sprites to be created and placed in these player-defined levels. Levels could then be saved to cassette tape or floppy disk and shared with other players, a concept that was mentioned in many of the *Repton 3* reviews found in magazines from the time. However, as is evident from the following reviews from these magazines, this detail is often not as prominent as the game play elements that are still the main discussion point of the articles. We can see that the level editor as a point of discussion is a relatively new factor in magazine reviews of *Repton 3*, and that not as much page space is dedicated to this part of the game, which more generally relies on the player's understanding of other game-related concepts, including graphics and playability.

In the January 1987 issue of *Acorn User*, David Lawrence opened an article with a discussion of *Repton 3*'s playability and graphical competencies. "To be fair," he writes, "*Repton 3* is very good, the graphics are large and colourful, the tune almost bearable and the scrolling acceptable. The basic idea is exactly the same as its forebears: diamonds still have to be collected, boulder puzzles solved and monsters killed."[20] However, later in the review a few sentences are dedicated to the "main facility of *Repton 3*: its "screen and character designer." "This," Lawrence goes on to inform the reader, "enables you to redefine totally all the characters and screens used in the game. Screens are designed in sets of eight and three sets are provided." Yet beyond this description little is made of the level-editing feature within the review, and instead the fact the game is the third in a series becomes the focal point of the discussion.

Similarly, a review in the December 1986 issue of *The Micro User* also focuses on the gameplay and the similarities or differences to the other *Repton* titles. Throughout the review, the game space of *Repton 3* is referred to as a maze, with comments such as "each level is laid out like a maze" and "your route through the maze must be carefully planned."[21] It is not until the last few sentences of the review that the level editor is discussed, and then only in limited detail. The reviewer, James Riddell, comments: "Not only does Superior Software give you one of the best games of 1986 it also supplies a maze-editing utility. You can design your own fiendish mazes, save them to cassette or disc, and pass them on to your friends for them to solve." Yet despite its lack of a full mention in some of the reviews, the level and character editor were sophisticated enough for Superior Software to release further commercial versions of the game: *Repton Thru Time, The Life of Repton,* and *Around the World in 40 Screens.* According to "The Making of *Repton,*" these were produced in house, "using the same tools they shipped with the game ... and running on the same code of the original."[22] Advertisements for the titles start with comments about *Repton* fans wanting further levels of the game, with Superior Software keeping up the demand with these later releases. This also appealed to players who might have had a different platform than their friends, as the levels made by players were platform specific. Whereas the BBC Micro versions weren't compatible with the Acorn Electron *Repton 3* editor, the commercial releases were compatible across platforms.

In addition, these new games allowed players to see other possibilities of maps or characters that they could create, thus extending the life cycle of *Repton 3* even further and opening up the possibility of expansion packs for games made by both companies and players. Although commonplace with games today, expansion packs were an innovative idea on the part of Superior Software. This model of expansion also filtered down into player-created levels with the ability for players to define their own passwords for their levels so that other players had to complete them in the same way they would one of the Superior Software levels. Similarly, another feature of the editor meant that you could only edit one of the predefined screens once you had acquired the appropriate edit code by completing the level. Here game play and design went hand in hand as players attempted their own development skills. The game-design competitions that were frequently advertised in magazines weren't based on the *Repton* game specifically but were based on the culture of game creation that was emerging through various outlets at the time. In fact a challenge issued in the April 1987 issue of *Micro User* called for readers to design the most original character: "What about a spaceman, robot or werewolf in place of Repton? Who can design the most fiendishly difficult screens? And what about a jungle, spaceship or plan view of the city streets instead of the present underground scenes?"[23] The editor within *Repton 3* was a big hit with players, who now didn't have to learn to program their own games on the Micro but could still take part in the wave of game creation occurring in the UK as the software scene continued to grow. In fact, the editor was so popular that Superior Software built on this concept further with its last release for the Micro, *Repton Infinity*.

Maps, Graphics, and Code

Repton Infinity was written by David Acton and David Lawrence for Superior Software and was released in 1988. Not only did it have a level editor; it also had its own language built into the editor, going under the name of Reptol. The back of game box sums up these features: "Repton Infinity is the ultimate Repton program. You can completely redesign all of the game characters and game screens. But more than this, you can now also create a wide range of diversely different games using a special game-creating language."

A closer look at the advertisements for *Repton Infinity*, its box art, and its manual reveals how Superior Software tried to sell the game as both a playable product and one that could be extended through other features in a way that was accessible to game-playing audiences. To help players get started with using the editor, *Repton Infinity* came with four designed games, titled *Repton 3—Take 2*, *Repton 4*, *Robbo*, and *Trakker*. As was noted in the instruction manual for the game, one of the main differences between *Repton Infinity* games and *Repton 3* was the removal of a time limit for completing a screen. Instead there was a minimum score that players had to reach before being able to continue to the next level.

The tag line on the box emphasizes the creative aspects offered by the game: "You control the behaviour of the creatures. ... You determine the rules of the game. ... You create the whole scenario!" The decision to start the games with *Repton 3* and build on the players' prior knowledge of the series or introduce new players to its mechanics helped to familiarize them with the type of gameplay inherent in the game series as a means to build on it in their own creations. The additional features in the game are marketed in a similar way, drawing on known conventions in popular culture and in technical product creation as a way of appealing to different knowledge bases of potential audiences. The character designer is named the "filmstrip." Although it served a different purpose than a traditional film strip, it provided a platform for not only designing characters but animating them in a way akin to a timeline format offered by the filmstrip. Using familiar terms aided the transition from player to content creator by drawing on other popular media forms to which players would have had access. In this instance the game creator, in which the player could use the unique Reptol language to generate new relationships between assets in the game, was called "Blueprint." As a recognizable term for setting the foundations and planning, Blueprint can be interpreted by those that may not be as familiar with programming terminology or do not see themselves as capable of programming in the same way that the BBC Micro would have afforded with creating their own programs in BBC BASIC or machine code. Using Blueprint once again seeks to open up an audience not necessarily fluent in programming languages but might be drawn into tinkering with one provided within the game editing functions.

In the *Repton Infinity* manual, the Reptol language is introduced with reference to showing players how to design their own set of characters. The manual continues as follows:

A character definition in Repton Infinity consists of three major sections: these are called TYPE, ACTION and HITS and are introduced by the keyword DEFINE. For example, DEFINE TYPE. The TYPE section is used for setting the "system" and "user" flags for each character (Flags are simply pieces of information that tell us something about a character—for examples, whether it can be squashed by a rock or not). The ACTION section describes how each character moves or behaves. Finally, the HITS section is used to decide what happens when one character hits another.[24]

After defining the properties of characters, such as whether they are "solid" so that the Repton character can push them during the game or "deadly" for characters that will kill Repton, players can begin to create If … Then statements for various parts of the game in order to create a set of actions that are executed at particular moments in the gameplay. Much like the original BBC Micro manual and Welcome Pack, the *Repton Infinity* manual provides players with simple examples to help them form their own action statements. Events in the game are broken down into sentences for players to understand before being translated into If … Then statements in the Reptol language.

These tutorials for using the editor also flow through how the player can use the "Land Scape" screen designer to create their level designs for their games as well as the File Link function, which is the final stage in the *Repton Infinity* game design process. In an advertisement for the game the File Link option is highlighted with a screen shot of the game depicting a flow diagram linking up the landscape, blueprint, and filmstrip options that come together to create the final game file, much like what is depicted in the user manual. Users of the BBC Micro had to use the File Link option to test and share their game with others as a way of compiling the separate components created in the editing tools. In this instance the interplay of technological and non-technological terms running throughout the editor may have helped to attract audiences who had not thought about creating their own games before, and separates the processes out from those that once relied on users being able to generate their own code or modify other people's code. However, because the game was released at a time when the BBC Micro was beginning to decline and other 16-bit machines were coming onto the market, the game did not receive as much praise as it could have warranted. Similarly, the ability to share files was restricted to users of the platform, and relied on swapping physical media with the correct files on it, as the game was released at a time when online file sharing was not as prevalent as it is today.

Whether the ease of use of the editor and the familiarity of the terms used to describe its component parts did draw in new audiences of people who wanted to make games is not clear. Searching issues of magazines related to the BBC Micro does not provide many clues to games made by others in *Repton Infinity*, although a "design a screen competition" flyer could be found in the boxed game. Fortunately, thanks to the archives of player material that have been uploaded by fans of the BBC Micro platform and of the *Repton* series, some of these levels created have since emerged on various webpages dedicated to showcasing them. The Repton Continuum site has tried to compile a list of levels (old or newly created) made in *Repton 3* or *Repton Infinity*.[25] Although the levels are downloadable and potentially playable on an emulation platform for the Acorn Electron or BBC Micro, the website also displays screen shots of levels that have been uploaded to the site. Levels created for *Repton 3* and *Repton Infinity* feature symbols mapping the game's landscape, football themes, and even attempts to create a top-down-perspective version of the game. Alongside these are anecdotes about some of the level creation. For example, one of Dave Jeffrey's levels, Farmdat, was based on the farm on which the author lived. Under images of the levels, Jeffrey writes: "All the levels were done between 1986 and 1991. There is a level called 'TIMOTHY' on the set 'SET1' which is the first I ever designed for *Repton 3* back on Christmas day

1986." Once again, what these images and the development of such software during the 1980s show is that player-created content and the abilities
to change, adapt, and play other people's levels associated with gaming
practices on microcomputers were prevalent before the World Wide Web,
downloadable content, and online connectivity. However, it is these technologies that have subsequently enabled the content to be archived, found,
and potentially played again.

The Legacy of *Repton* and Superior Software

Histories of games from the 1980s often discuss playing games via the
console, or game playing and game creation via the microcomputer, yet
the level editor as a tool partway between these two cultures is rarely
mentioned. Whereas player creativity and level creation are mentioned as
growing phenomena from the 1990s on through often-cited examples of
Doom and *Little Big Planet*, we can see how these cultures of player as producer of content predate this. As well as allowing a player to play various
levels, *Little Big Planet* comes equipped with a level editor containing
tutorial voiceovers in a style similar to that of the main game. That part of
Little Big Planet allows players to use what Hanna Wirman calls "tools" of
level creation, adding to the co-creativity of the gameworld.[26] Not only is
the content generated in the game; it is also shared by players and users
of the *Little Big Planet* community through the Playstation Network system.
What we might call the "*Little Big Planet* effect" (the ability to "Play. Create.
Share," as the game's advertising puts it) can also be seen in offline games
offered by microcomputing cultures in Britain in the 1980s. As Melanie
Swalwell notes in reference to that period in the context of Australian
microcomputing cultures, there is the "historical amnesia of those who
think that user productivity began with the age of broadband."[27] *Repton
Infinity*, in particular, offered a series of tools that not only merged playing
and content creation through changing the content of levels and graphics
but also provided functionality through its own programming language.
This reveals yet another layer of technical experimentation during this
time beyond players having to create their own games from scratch.

   Similarly, Superior Software's commitment to publishing games
for the BBC Micro and for the Acorn Electron continued even after the
Acorn Archimedes and other machines came on the market. Superior
Software made sure that owners of the Micro still had access to game
software without the need to update their machines quickly in order to
get new releases. Because of this practice, some of Superior Software's

titles, along with the BBC Micro, often get lost in retellings of game histories. However, Superior Software was responsible for many innovative titles, including *Exile*, developed by Peter Irvin and Jeremy Smith and released in 1988. As Anderson and Levene later noted, *Exile* "came out at the tail end of the 8-bit era, on a computer that had lost its momentum as a gaming machine."[28] Although it received mixed reviews, much like *Elite* it managed to push the possibilities of the BBC Micro to create a game with a complete physics engine in it, a feat hardly heard of at the time.

Knowledge of the BBC Micro and of other Acorn platforms was one of the main reasons for Superior Software's success in the 1980s. "We've dabbled with software for Amstrad, Commodore, Spectrum and Amiga machines," Richard Hanson of Superior Software wrote in the February 1989 issue of *Electron User*, "but the Acorn market remains the best for us."[29] In 1986, the company came to an agreement with Acorn to take over publication of Acornsoft game titles, including *Elite* and *Revs*. Some of these titles were released in Superior Software's Play It Again Sam compilations along with *Ravenskull* and *Stryker's Run*. In fact, relationships with developers who had published with Acornsoft were also continued. Superior Software's first game for the Acorn Archimedes was *Zarch*, developed by David Braben.

After continuing to publish games for the Acorn platforms into the early 1990s, Superior Software, under the name Superior Interactive, also managed to keep some of these games alive on other platforms, including titles for Windows PC and versions of *Repton* and *Repton 3* for the iPhone.[30] Converting these games once again shows Superior Software's commitment to the fans of these titles from their original release and those that have been able to experience them more recently. The dedication to the fans and to their love of the BBC Micro and subsequent Acorn platforms shows how the BBC Micro, so often thought of as a computer used in schools, had a wider user base in other markets and also stood the test of time in the 1980s microcomputing games software market, managing to compete alongside other, cheaper microcomputers. The robust nature of the Micro allowed for its continued use in the software market and for innovative use of additional hardware.

Extending the Platform

III

We currently live in an age of set-top boxes, TiVO, and "smart televisions" containing downloadable applications such as games and Web browsers. Networks, email, and the Internet are discussed by both Manuel Castells and Jan van Dijk in relation to what they discuss as the "network society," seen as coming of age in the 1990s with the Web and the birth of URLs creating more accessible connections.[1] However, microcomputers of the 1980s also used networked technologies to allow users to connect with other services. Email, bulletin-board systems, and local networks such as Acorn's Econet were all used as methods for transmitting data between machines and were systems and services that the Computer Literacy Project was keen to make users aware of. This connectivity was extended by other purposefully designed add-ons for the BBC Micro, including the Teletext adapter.

Alongside using telephone networks as a means for communication of data, the possibilities of having "interactive" or "smart" televisions was being increasingly explored during the late 1970s in Britain. These practices continued in the development of extra hardware for the BBC Microcomputer, including the Teletext adapter and the use of telesoftware. Built into the original specification for the BBC Micro, the Teletext adapter was designed to work with another one of the BBC's services so that users could connect to content in a variety of ways. The BBC had already been involved in developing Teletext systems decades earlier. Utilizing Teletext as another way to distribute content appeared to fit in with the multiple-media approach. Beyond the television's role of allowing viewers to watch broadcast content, it was also used as a medium to connect the BBC Micro to a visual display, extending the use of the screen through the other possibilities offered by the microcomputing system. The possibilities of connecting the machine to other resources by using the Teletext adapter was yet another way that the Micro could act as a hub for the dissemination of information from the Teletext service and of related telesoftware downloads that became available. The BBC Microcomputer, in light of these examples, can once again be seen to be at the heart of converging technologies. The attached television or monitor as a display, along with the Teletext adapter, allowed this ethos of the machine to be explored in new, innovative ways. In the remainder of this chapter, it is through an exploration of the histories of Teletext and the development of the Teletext adapter that these technologies will be situated in light of the other networked possibilities offered by the BBC Micro in a period when other microcomputing platforms were also being connected to email systems, to bulletin-board systems, and to Prestel.

Viewdata: Teletext and Prestel

Television content in Britain was already advanced in terms of the types of information it displayed beyond the broadcast programs on offer. From the 1930s to the early 1980s there were only three major terrestrial television channels in the UK: BBC One, BBC Two, and ITV (Independent Television). A fourth channel was established in 1982, and a fifth in 1997. However, it was the British Broadcasting Corporation and the Independent Television stations that were at the heart of initial developments in television communications. Beyond the capability to watch television broadcasts, both corporations were interested in extending this reach, initially thinking about access for the hard-of-hearing and deaf communities, and in finding ways to transform the television so that users could start to find additional information without having to rely on an external microcomputer. The decreasing cost of silicon chips allowed for the development of new television peripherals and services, including a new service under the name of Teletext.

The development of Teletext began in the late 1960s, when engineers in the BBC's Designs Department began to explore the possibilities of having text-based systems related to television content.[2] According to the winter 1983–84 edition of *Eng Inf: The Quarterly for BBC Engineering Staff*, "It was Peter Rainger who, as Head of Designs Department, first laid the framework of the Teletext system in 1970 and became one of its co-patentees in 1972."[3] That work was later taken over by John

Chambers, head of the Special Projects section, who had written the Teletext technical specification that had been published in 1976.[4] After the BBC's initial prototyping of the Teletext system, it was decided in 1972 that further consultation with industry and support from the Independent Television (ITV) stations would help with any future success of the project. According to Richard Veith, "a committee comprised of representatives from the BBC, ITV, the semiconductor industry, and the television manufacturing industry was established to design a suitable system standard."[5] After these discussions, the BBC developed a Teletext system called Ceefax ("see facts") and the Independent Television stations developed a version called Oracle (Optional Reception of Announcements by Coded Line Electronics). Teletext, referred to by Paul Gregg in 1994 as an "electronic book, where pages can be called up on the television screen,"[6] was finally approved by the government in late 1974. The rise of Teletext services in the 1970s allowed people to view databases of content in text form, as well as basic character-based graphics. These databases included football scores, flight arrival times, and stock prices as well as television listings. Teletext pages were broadcast using the standard television signal, but otherwise unused scan lines were used to deliver extra data through the aerial. In Britain there are 625 scan lines in a television picture. (In the United States there are 525.) Teletext could, in theory occupy lines 7 to 22 and lines 320 to 335, but in practice only a few of those lines were used.

Teletext enabled users to interact with their television set by calling up page numbers they had entered while in Teletext mode; however, this interaction did not occur instantly. The Teletext system was essentially a database of information, structured by indexes, sub-indexes, branches, and linked pages of information, much like present-day hypertext systems or Web pages. Using the word "page" helped people understand the structure of the system in relation to other non-digital media such as magazines and books, drawing on past concepts to explain the new technological domain that was emerging. This reusing of terms also followed through into other terminology used within the system—for example, pages were "numbered in groups of 100, called magazines," with a total of eight magazines available for each broadcast channel.[7] In order to work over a broadcast signal, all Teletext pages were broadcast in a constant cycle. Therefore, a user who dialed up page 10 would have to wait for that page to come round in the cycle before it displayed on the television screen. However, Teletext pages would cycle every 22 to 25 seconds per 100 pages, depending on the amount of time it took for data to displayed in each magazine. Pages were not necessarily cycled in numerical order; therefore, the most popular pages in were broadcast more frequently to allow them to be accessed more quickly. As well as Teletext offering pages of information, the system also allowed for subtitling capabilities in some television shows. Initially developed as a separate service in parallel to the original Teletext specification, the ability to include subtitles and captions for a range of programs was soon built into the final design. Using the same Teletext decoder for both operations seemed advantageous, since both operations were based on similar Teletext techniques.

The potential offered by Teletext saw the demand for decoders for televisions (or televisions with built-in decoders) rise from 5,000 between 1974 and 1978 to more than 500,000 in 1982.[8] The rise of Teletext was often associated with the fact that many British consumers preferred to lease or rent a television set rather than buying one outright. Both Ceefax and Oracle succeeded in allowing viewers to interact with the television to find out the latest sports and news headlines, extending the possibilities of the broadcasters capabilities in an age before on-demand viewing and 24-hour news channels. However, Teletext was not the only communication system being developed. The British Post Office was developing a separate videotex system under the name of Prestel. Unlike the Teletext service, Prestel worked with a telephone connection rather than an aerial signal to offer two-way communication between the home television set and a computer.

Originally developed under the name "Viewdata," Prestel was designed as a way for people to use computing technologies without having to rely on command-line inputs or to learn how to use a different interface. Instead the navigation was standardized and behaved in a similar way to the Teletext format.[9] However, instead of being labeled "pages," as in Teletext's terminology, Prestel was organized into "frames" that could be "stepped through in either direction" or "tagged so that important frames [could] be returned to without having to remember the frame number."[10] This differed from how pages were accessed by using Teletext, which relied on the sequencing of rolling set of pages. Although both systems delivered information in varying ways, Prestel was also organized as a database of information, albeit one available to consumers and businesses depending on their need and the services they paid for. In his book *The Language of New Media*, Lev Manovich discusses the database as an important feature of new media content, and this structure was an important part of both systems as to the way they were developed.[11] Although developed separately, the desire to have comparable standards meant that the Post Office agreed that Prestel should "adopt the Teletext specifications for format, colours, character sets, and display features."[12]

Because both the Prestel and Teletext systems were standardized, their later integration with the BBC Microcomputer was seen in one of the display modes built into the platform: that of Mode 7. However, the costs of running Prestel and the low uptake by companies using the system meant that it did not take off as significantly as Teletext systems at the time. Various pricing models were put in place, including some that allowed companies using the system to have their own databases to access information (for example, travel agents could book flights directly with an airline).

Yet the emergence of Teletext data through the aerial and the development of Prestel by using telephone networks facilitated the possibilities of even further interaction with both the television and telephone. According to the March 1985 issue of *The Micro User*, "Originally, when launched in the late Seventies, [Prestel] was seen as a method by which home and business users could get information quickly. What is now happening is that users are becoming accustomed to *interactivity*—the watchword of the current comms explosion."[13] One way in which this explosion in interactivity continued with both Teletext and Prestel services on the BBC Micro was seen in the development of using telesoftware with the machine. Although the possibilities of downloadable content by using cable networks had been explored through Intellivision's Playcable system in 1981, this was a subscription-based service. It proved to be too expensive, and therefore its user base was limited. By utilizing the Teletext service as a content provider already known to the public, the BBC could allow people to download software for free using telesoftware services via the Teletext adapter available for the BBC Micro.

The Teletext Adapter

As was noted in earlier chapters, the Teletext adapter was one of the components written into the original specifications intended for the BBC Micro. However, Acorn did not release it when the Micro was rolled out. It was released in April 1983. An article in the July 1983 issue of *The Micro User* reported that "three thousand orders have been received for Acorn's Teletext adapter, which is designed to enable the BBC Micro to download pages transmitted over the air by Ceefax and Oracle."[14]

Examples of the initial hype surrounding the adapter can be seen in numerous magazine articles that preceded its release. One such article in the second issue of the *Acorn User*, written by David Allen, begins by telling readers that "an exciting new use for the broadcasting television signal is the transmission of programs on Ceefax which can immediately be received by a decoder and immediately 'run' at home on a BBC Micro" and that "telesoftware could provide broadcasters with the chance to provide viewers with interactive material to back up a television series."[15] Allen goes on to note that the "domestic decoder" had been developed by Acorn Computers working alongside the BBC's design and research departments, and that the resultant product can be connected to a user's current television aerial in order to detect Ceefax pages. Once again, in line with the Computer Literacy Project, the implied simplicity of connecting up existing, known technologies allowed the Teletext adapter to be used more easily as users were already familiar with both the BBC Micro and using the Ceefax or Oracle services through their television sets.

Housed in a beige box with an angled front, the Teletext adapter extended the look and feel of the computer to which it was attached. Priced at £149, the adapter was expensive add-on, yet whereas a modem used a telephone line to download and access information the Teletext service was free through the television aerial.[16] An article in the May 1987 issue of *The Micro User* noted that other services relying on telephone lines for the distribution of data were expensive in other ways: "The telesoftware service available via the telephone network has the disadvantage that even the free software has hidden costs such as telephone connection charges and the software has been indirectly paid for. For example, *The Micro User* monthly listing can be downloaded from MicroLink for just the connection charge, but if you want to download all the listings it can cost almost as much as buying the listings cassette."[17]

However, the Teletext adapter offered an alternative way of downloading telesoftware to the machine. Teletext transmission was not a two-way updatable system, as its modem-based counterparts were, but it did allow for a new line of distribution and a new platform for people to explore. The adapter transformed the BBC Micro further and as such continued its role as a convergent machine—one that enabled convergence through multiple learning platforms and one that now also enabled a type of convergence focused around distribution of information and software. In fact, this concept of "convergence" in relation to the "convergence of telecommunications and computer technology" was acknowledged in a book by Jerome Aumente in 1987, long before we began to speak to technological convergence as is so often used in the media today.[18] Similarly, the modularity associated with the Micro continued to be seen in the component parts needed to run the Teletext adapter package. Aside from the adapter itself, the system required a Teletext ROM (or TELEROM) to be fitted and required connecting a ribbon cable; it also required connecting a coaxial cable to the television receiver or video monitor.

The instruction manual that accompanied the adapter emphasized that the existing aerial lead could be used. As with other BBC Micro manuals, the connection to existing and known technologies to ease the process for new users was important in the wording. Once the TELEROM was fitted into an available ROM slot in the machine, the Teletext adapter was connected by the 34-way socket on the Teletext adapter by using a ribbon cable to the plug labeled "1MHz BUS" on the computer. An aerial lead was then connected to the Teletext adapter's aerial socket, and other peripherals (such as a storage device, either disk or cassette) were connected so that any data received through the adapter could be saved. After turning on the adapter and then the BBC Micro, the user was shown the following display screen to indicate that the TELEROM is connected and that the adapter was functioning:

BBC Computer 32K
Acorn TFS
BASIC
>_

If "Acorn TFS no power" appeared instead, either the adapter hadn't been connected properly or the adapter hadn't been turned on. (The adapter could be turned off after use to free up memory space so that larger programs could be run later without the user's having to unplug the adapter from the machine each time.)

After connecting up the system, the user had to tune the adapter to receive Teletext from one of the BBC channels or from ITV. The adapter came equipped with four channels that enabled a user to store and tune in more than one broadcasting channel. The manual recommended storing channels as follows:

Channel 1 – BBC1
Channel 2 – BBC 2
Channel 3 – ITV
Channel 4 – ITV2

Selecting the channels relied on BASIC inputs into the system, starting commands with *TELETEXT and then pressing the correct function key. The red functions keys on the top of the BBC Micro keyboard were also used as commands with the Teletext adapter as a way of quickly entering and accessing the correct parts of the system. Although Teletext adapters for other microcomputers were also released after the BBC Micro's adapter, such as the TTX 2000 adapter for the ZX Spectrum and the Microtext Teletext Adapter for the Commodore 64, the foresight of the BBC and of Acorn in integrating the possibilities of the system with the BBC Micro's initial design was evident in the Micro's Mode 7.

Mode 7

One of the most useful features of the BBC Micro is mode 7, the Teletext mode. This is the one the micro enters automatically when you switch it on or press the Break key. It's unlike any of the other modes of the micro and is in fact controlled by a special chip used only for Teletext.

Nigel Peters, "Graphics A La Mode 7," *The Micro User*, August 1984

As has already been mentioned, the BBC Micro had eight display modes. Upon turning on the machine, users would see the display in Mode 7 as the default setting. Although associated with Teletext and being able to display Ceefax and Oracle pages in line with the universal layouts developed for these systems, Mode 7 was also the most common mode that many people on the BBC Micro would have experienced without knowing. Different modes on the Micro could be called up by typing in the mode command and then the related number in order to change the screen display and the characteristics determined by that mode, as was noted in chapter 1 above. Mode 7 was the most efficient of the modes, taking up only 1 kilobyte of memory by using its unique ways of displaying predetermined characters sets. (Recall the example of *Granny's Garden* in chapter 3.) Another example of using Mode 7 can be seen in the program "Kingdom" on the Welcome Tape (discussed in chapter 1 above). Paul Leman and Steve Swallow's article about the mode in the April 1983 issue of *BBC Micro User* notes that the program is "nearly 9K and still has impressive graphics" and continues as follows.

The effects available include:

• Seven colors and flashing characters
• Low resolution graphics (80 × 75)

- Seven background colors
- Mixing of any display and background color
- Hiding and revealing text portions on the screen
- Enlarged (double height) characters.[19]

In order for the mode to use memory efficiently, different character codes were built into the functionality of the mode as a way of creating images and text on screen. This was particularly important in displaying and creating Teletext pages when using the Teletext adapter on the BBC Micro. As was mentioned above, in the development of Teletext in Great Britain the display of data was standardized across systems. A 40 by 24 grid format was chosen as a viewing standard for pages "based on assumptions about the amount of lines needed to produce a legible character."[20] Subsequently, Mode 7 was displayed as shown here in figure 6.1. The 25th row on the BBC Micro Teletext System was used for displaying system information and prompts and was not a part of the 24 rows determined by the Teletext signals it was receiving.

The process of using Mode 7 for creating content was a topic of many magazine articles. One article in the February 1984 issue of *Micro User* explained how to create a version of *Space Invaders*; others offered "support strips" that could be printed out and placed on the top of the BBC Micro

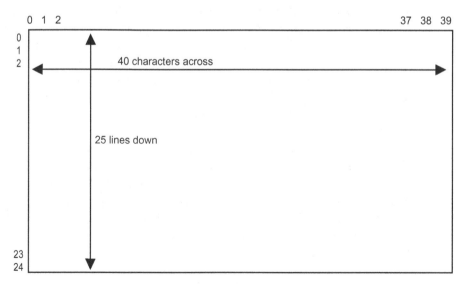

Figure 6.1 The dimensions of the Mode 7 screen.

keyboard to identify what each function key was used for.[21] An article on "a screen editor for Teletext" described the benefits of Mode 7's low memory usage while recognizing that Mode 7 wasn't easy to learn on the Micro "if only PRINT statements are used to design a complete screenful of information." The author of the latter article, Jim Notman, went on to explain that "in Teletext the ASCII codes are divided into printable characters and control codes" and that "these control codes are responsible for the many effects that are possible."[22] Reminding the reader to think about both Ceefax and Oracle pages in terms of layout and the effects that could be placed on the screen helped to show them the possibilities of programming in the mode and the outcomes of any visuals that they might want to create. Each control code corresponded to particular graphics characters or the color of the graphic to be presented. On first use, Mode 7 displayed with white text on a black background; after that, background colors, graphics colors, and blocks to be displayed could all changed depending on the code inputted by the user. For example, code 145 would produce a red graphic, code 146 would produce a green graphic, and codes between 160 and 255 would produce different combinations of "Teletext pixels" as shown here in figure 6.2.[23] Various displays and effects could be created by using spaces between the character codes; the user didn't have to place the blocks of the graphics next to one another in sequence for results to be realized.

Further uses of the Teletext screen editor discussed in Notman's article included changing characters on any line and then testing the appearances that each control code would produce, preparing title pages for programs, and "preparing pages of information and producing simple animations."[24] Simple animations produced in Mode 7 were seen in the examples in *Granny's Garden*, such as when the witch appeared to signify that the player had to start the game again. Loading screens such as those used by Acornsoft were often produced using Mode 7. Along with these functionalities, the availability of Teletext in many homes and the visual understanding of how Ceefax and Oracle pages were presented meant that classroom activities based on Viewdata and on creating pages in Mode 7 took place in schools around the country, adding another facet to the educational possibilities of the machine. The initial foresight of the BBC team to integrate Teletext capabilities into the BBC Micro meant that Mode 7 became a feature often associated with the BBC Micro, and Mode 7 was used in a variety of ways to produce different screen displays. However, it was the possibilities of Teletext and telesoftware that initially set the machine apart from other British microcomputers.

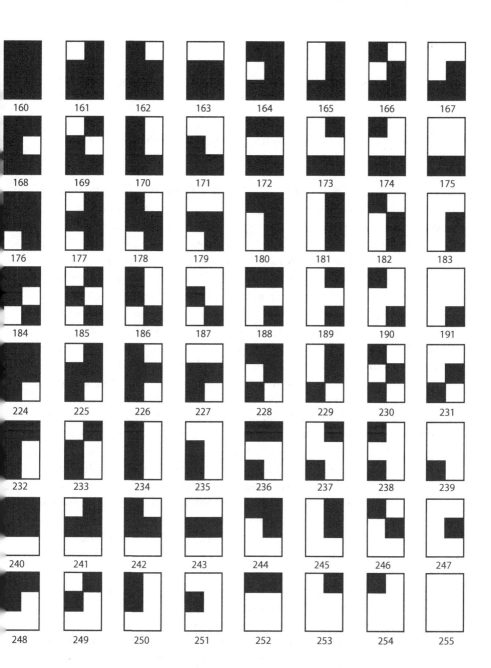

Figure 6.2   Mode 7 graphics characters and their codes.

Teletext systems have one principal drawback: they are not interactive. To help alleviate this problem, IT has developed Telesoftware, which gives a degree of interaction.

Mike Bayman, "Telesoftware Is on Its Way for the 1980s," *Electronics and Power*, January 1980

The term "telesoftware" was coined by W. J. G. Overington in May 1977 to mean "software at a distance" and was used in reference to transmitting programs to a home microcomputer by broadcast Teletext services.[25] Experimentation with telesoftware as a means for creating "intelligent" television sets was subsequently conducted in the late 1970s to see what that method of transmission could offer.[26] The trials involved microprocessor cards containing a "Signetics 2650 microprocessor and associated memory, which together form the local microprocessor."[27] These trials were seen as a means of providing an inexpensive form of microcomputing that would allow users to have access to mortgage calculators, insurance quotations, educational programs, and basic games all using the free Teletext system as a way of distributing these services. Taking advantage of the microcomputing revolution at this time and the lowering cost of microprocessing power, the possibilities of having interactive machines that didn't rely on microcomputers with command-line interfaces was at the forefront of developing early telesoftware systems. The BBC and the Independent Broadcast Authority were experimenting with telesoftware with their Ceefax and Oracle Teletext services. The interactive capabilities as to be offered by ITVs version of telesoftware were celebrated in the January 1980 issue of *Electronics and Power*: "Instead of broadcasting pages of information, a computer program can be broadcast to be run by a microprocessor contained within the t.v. set. No software cassettes or discs are necessary, nor, claims ITV, are expensive telephone calls to distant computers."[28] Here the television rather than the microcomputer was seen as the focus of the product in an attempt to hide the technology and embed it within the lives of household television owners not seeking to join the computing scene that was developing around them. Telesoftware was not unique to Teletext (it was also integrated into Prestel systems for the BBC Micro and other microcomputers at the time), but the ability to download programs through the aerial instead of a telephone line was a new venture taking advantage of the notion of transmitting software over a distance using a different type of technology. Further tests were conducted into the use of telesoftware in education by constructing a Philips Viewdata Teletext television receiver interfaced with a 32-kilobyte 8-bit microcomputer to produce the first broadcast telesoftware receiver in 1977. As was noted in a subsequent research paper, "the combination could still be used as a television and Teletext receiver but in addition operated as a stand-alone microcomputer and a telesoftware receiver, the microcomputer making use of the receiver's screen for its RGB display."[29] This project was a collaboration between the British Broadcasting Corporation and the Independent Broadcast Authority using the above-mentioned telesoftware receiver unit, developed at Mullard Laboratories, which had also played a role in earlier experimentation with "intelligent television sets." Projects involving these teams had taken place with the Teletext in Education project in 1978 and 1979. Mullard Laboratories worked with the Brighton Polytechnic Computer Centre to develop the software that allowed "pages of Teletext in the form of compressed BASIC program statements to be buffered and read by the microcomputer."[30]

From September 1981 to April 1982, in trials of how telesoftware could be used in education, thirty programs were sent over the BBC's Ceefax service or ITV's Oracle Teletext system. The research project aimed to "investigate telesoftware in three broad areas: as an interactive teaching and learning medium, as a means of providing schools with educational software, and as a means of developing educational broadcasting."[31] Television broadcasts were already used within education, usually by video-recording particular educational programs. Extending the service as was done was a natural response to technologies currently used in the classroom to facilitate learning. The possibilities of being able to use telesoftware within educational settings meant that progressing the project to be used with the Micro appeared to be a natural fit. Similarly, the links between Mullard Laboratories and the BBC Microcomputer continued through the SAA5050 character generator chip that was developed for implementing the Teletext character set. Not only was the chip used in the initial decoders used for telesoftware services developed for use without microcomputers; it was also used within other microcomputers, including the BBC Micro.[32] However, it was the Teletext adapter that was subsequently discussed in the initial trials of the Telesoftware and Primary Education project launched in July 1982 by the research team at Brighton Polytechnic. Those trials had a brief similar to that of the earlier research conducted using the Mullard Laboratories telesoftware decoder however this time the research was developed with the BBC Microcomputer and the Teletext adapter in mind. The research was focused on setting up an educational telesoftware service that could provide programs suitable for use in primary schools. For the home market the Teletext adapter could be seen as an extension of allowing users to download programs directly to their machines. For these reasons, the ability to use telesoftware was a prominent part of the Teletext adapter manual.

Once the channels were tuned, the instruction manual encouraged users to "have a go at running one of the Telesoftware programs being transmitted."[33] Using the function keys (such as f4 to select a channel and f0 to select a page), users could navigate to and view Teletext pages much as they would on a television Teletext service. However, by going to particular pages (for example, page 700 on Channel 1 of Ceefax), a user could be presented with telesoftware options to download content. Selected programs were loaded into the computer by pressing the Shift and F9 keys. The user guide mentioned that telesoftware programs could be either "disordered" or "ordered" files.[34] Disordered files were structured in numbered lines and could be loaded in any sequence, as the numbering would then be organized into the correct order once run. An ordered file was not numbered and therefore had to be loaded into the machine in the order in which it had been written. Whereas both types of files were downloaded in similar ways, the ways in which the decoder would search for problems while loading a program into memory was slightly different. Disordered programs could be searched for again and the "bad data" page could be found at any point in the process. In ordered programs, any "bad data" had to be recognized in the sequence to allow for successful loading afterward. Once programs had been downloaded, users could run them immediately and could save them to a floppy disk or a cassette tape.

Aside from the example shown at the end of the last episode of *Making the Most of the Micro*, in which a program was transmitted for viewers to record and save to cassette tape, computer programs were also transmitted by the radio for the BBC Micro and for other microcomputers, including the ZX Spectrum, the Commodore 64, and the Dragon 32. Those transmissions were generally sent at night so as to not confuse and disrupt typical broadcast programs, as the noise of the signal was not recognizable to all. A news article in the July 1983 issue of *Sinclair User* magazine noted that a Bristol radio station, Radio West, had been transmitting programs for the ZX-81 and the Spectrum during its *Datarama* broadcasts on Monday evenings after the radio show had completed its general schedule for the day. The article explained how the transmissions worked: "The programs have been transmitted on VHF/ FM and medium-wave frequencies. The VHF transmissions can be received over a fairly long distances on a domestic radio receiver with a telescopic whip antenna. Medium-wave transmissions have been used because of problems caused by ground-wave and co-channel interference. The signal has to be strong and clear if it is to be recorded for loading into a computer."[35] Those radio transmissions also allowed for content to be recorded for other microcomputing systems, including the BBC Micro. The Teletext adapter could get around the issue of transmission times by allowing users to download content at any time of day, in contrast with waiting for radio transmissions, and by using a system they had already adapted to use in the preceding ten years. However, in line with keeping to routines of transmission times, J. Billingsley and R. J. Billingsley discussed how the telesoftware programs could be "recorded at night, in the same manner as schools' sound radio programmes can be selected as and when required."[36] Although telesoftware programs were developed for home use as well as for use in schools, the initial programs developed for the system as part of the Telesoftware and Primary Education project tended to be focused on programming and computer science. Other curriculum activities also underwent trials. These included vocabulary games and programs explaining the map symbols of Ordnance Survey maps for geography classes.[37] As the possibilities of telesoftware expanded, other services were introduced, including REM, the Ceefax telesoftware newsletter introduced in the last episode of *Making the Most of the Micro*. REM gave users up-to-date information on what was happening with Ceefax's telesoftware service. Similarly, the lists of programs updated to the system were constantly changed, allowing for additional content to be seen and downloaded by regular users of the system. A "game of the week" download was envisaged as a way of delivering this exposure to new content, but the service was never as successful as had once been imagined. When demonstrating the system in 1983, Graham Clayton, the editor of the BBC's Ceefax service, suggested that most of the programs that would be available for the system in the future would be educational programs but some would be specially commissioned to go with particular BBC broadcasts, once again emphasizing a multi-platform approach to learning and distribution. Alongside this there was hope for an amateur club page allowing users to exchange programs. In this instance, the amateur club could be seen as an extension of distributing "home-brew" or "home-made" content beyond the school playground or the workplace and beyond advertisements in the back pages of magazines.

The pages of *The Micro User* began to run Ceefax Guides for software that was transmitted each week. The information box of each guide contained this statement: "Software is currently transmitted for a period of one week. The teacher's notes for the TV series Issues are transmitted from Wednesday to the following Tuesday and all other files are updated on Fridays."[38] Software downloads included basic games, compilers from earlier magazine listings, and ROM images for users to load into sideways ROM or burn onto an EPROM. The range of listings offered both education and entertainment in an attempt to expand the ways the range of software for the Micro could be distributed among its users. However, one review of the Teletext adapter mentioned potential problems that the BBC's telesoftware service faced in attracting people to put their software up on the system for download, noting that the software "can't be paid for, as viewers can't be charged and large funds are unlikely to be made available from the TV licence fee."[39] Despite the financial implications of integrating telesoftware with Teletext, the telesoftware downloads connected to the BBC Microcomputer allowed for another means of transmission both for the home and school markets that was free or at least included in the cost of the television license fee.

The BBC's telesoftware service ran until 1989, when the corporation had to decide how, and in what departments, savings could be achieved. When announcing the closing of the telesoftware service in 1989, the BBC stated: "Telesoftware was devised to provide software support to the BBC Micro in the early days, particularly in relation to Education programmes. It has always been a minor adjunct to, and not an integral part of, the BBC's commitment to the BBC Microcomputer."[40] The report went on to note that in May 1989 there were just over 31,500 Teletext adapters in domestic use, representing around 7 percent of the BBC Micro users as a target audience. The cost of the equipment did not lend itself to the home market at a time when the BBC Micro was already one of the more expensive machines on the market. The benefits of using the adapter to download programs was also lost on many users who chose to type in programs from magazines, create their own, or load them from cassette tapes or floppy disks as a more flexible and widely used medium. The sharing of programs among users of the machine also negated the need to download content for many at the time. This was recognized within the BBC's report on the closing of the telesoftware service: "The closure of the Telesoftware service in no way cuts off vital supplies of software, merely one means of their delivery."[41]

Although the number of people who adopted the BBC Micro's Teletext adapter was small in comparison with the number of people who owned

Micro machines, the closing of the telesoftware service caused an outcry among readers of *The Micro User*. The letters page of the October 1989 issue was dedicated to that topic, with the opening comments stating that "never before has our mailbag contained so many letters on one subject" and that "not one letter supporting the BBC's decision has yet arrived."[42] Readers commented that "the BBC's role has always been to educate, inform and entertain," that "all three criteria were adequately displayed to the highest order by the BBC telesoftware," and that "the BBC had a solid reputation for the long term commitment to the BBC Micro which has recently been reinforced by the launch of Acorn's new micro with the BBC name."[43] For readers, the links between the BBC and Acorn were part and parcel of owning such a machine, and disappointment with the discontinuation of the service was evident in the tone of the texts. Similarly, the lowered cost of the hardware allowed the Teletext adapter to rise in popularity near the end of the telesoftware service, after which consumers were left with adapters for which they no longer had sustained use. Despite these grievances, the use and the capabilities of the adapter can be seen as innovations that can be associated with some present-day experiences of using media technologies.

The ability to download software through the user's television set is a practice that can be seen today in a variety of forms often heralded as "new" media technologies. The rise in use of platforms that enable content to be downloaded, such as the Apple iTunes store and game-distribution platforms such as Steam, shows how we use services that are curated for us in order to download content, much like the curated pages of telesoftware content seen on Teletext services. As Tilly Blyth notes in her report on the legacy of the BBC Micro, "the early use of telesoftware by BBC Research established its position in the market" and "may have subsequently saved the BBC huge amounts in licences given that a number of devices, like TiVO boxes to TV tuners, use telesoftware today."[44] A recognition of alternative ways of distributing data and similar methods of downloading content that came before these services allows us to situate the BBC Micro within a wider context of distribution services found in histories of media technologies. Once again, the foresight of the BBC to integrate its existing services (such as Teletext) into the design of the machine shows that the platform was designed to allow users to access content in a variety of ways. This could also be seen through the BBC's involvement in promoting the networked distribution of information through its television programming content, including email and local-area networks (LANs).

After the success of *The Computer Programme* and the follow-on series, *Making the Most of the Micro*, the BBC aired a two-hour special titled "Making the Most of the Micro Live" on October 2, 1983. That show allowed viewers to call in and ask questions. A live studio audience added to the immediacy. As part of this special program, the concept of electronic mail (email) was discussed in more detail by showing British Telecom's Telecom Gold electronic mail service. The plan was for viewers with the knowledge and capability to use such a system to email in questions followed by the presenters logging in to view and answer the questions posed. However, the live nature of the show meant that this did not go as originally planned. Although the log-in details were supposed to be hidden from the camera view in order to stop the audience seeing them, the details were compromised and the infamous hacking incident of the show started to play out on screen. As David Allen remembers, the camera deliberately cut between different parts of the studio to try to prevent the password used to log in to the email account from being revealed.[45] However, once the presenter John Coll had logged in, instead of first seeing the email lists that should have appeared on the screen he was presented with the following text:

Computer Security Error. Illegal access.
I hope your Television PROGRAMME runs as smoothly as my PROGRAM
    worked out your passwords! Nothing is secure!
Hackers' Song.
"Put another password in,
we're Hacking, Hacking, Hacking.
Try his first wife's maiden name,
This is more than just a game,
It's real fun, but just the same,
It's Hacking, Hacking, Hacking."
The NutCracker (Hackers' UK)
HI THERE, OWLETS, FROM OZ AND YUG (OLIVER AND GUY)[46]

Although clearly shocked, Coll read out the message with a slight laugh, emphasizing the live element of the show and how this was intentionally used as a way of what David Allen later discussed as "showing and learning from mistakes" during the show.[47] Coll then read the rest of the emails from the public, along with a few more sent by Oz and Yug to continue their hacking fame for a little while longer. However, in a recent interview the placement of the Hackers' Song was revealed as having been the work of Jez San, of Argonaut fame, who recalled having hacked into the system with his friends, placing the message "Hi from Oz and Yug" soon afterward, and taking all the credit.[48] Although often cited in discussions of hacking within the context of microcomputing, this example also shows other possibilities of the computer network as offered by the BBC Micro beyond being used as a stand-alone machine.

Bulletin-board systems, as Jason Scott has documented, were a part of the microcomputing culture in the US, as well as in the UK and parts of Europe, allowing people to dial in by using various modem systems, to leave messages, and to connect with others.[49] As Manuel Castells notes, these systems "did not need sophisticated computer networks, just PCs, modems, and the telephone line" resulting in "several million computer users ... using computer-mediated communication in cooperative or commercial networks that were not part of the Internet" in the 1980s.[50] Although these networks were separated by their different protocols, in contrast with the immediate compatibility offered by the Internet, bulletin-board systems allowed users to communicate with one another in shared spaces often devoted to common interests. In Britain, *The Micro User* and other magazines launched their own bulletin-board systems; one example was Microweb, a portal for readers and users of the BBC Micro to leave their own messages. In many ways this helped to act as a more immediate letters page in contrast to the monthly printed magazine issues. Selected comments from May 14, 1984, the day Microweb went live, were printed in the July 1984 issue of *The Micro User*. Users discussed setting up interest groups in particular areas, praising the magazine for having its own bulletin board and having faster access to answering questions such as where to order cassettes and disks from.[51] The first caller was noted as Bob Bembridge from Tring—a fact that, the magazine noted, showed how it was possible to capture the early users of the board in a time when there was a limited user base. The board enabled users to answer each others' questions without having to write in to the letters pages of magazines showing how this collaboration could be seen as the early stages of "participatory culture" online, using the knowledge of the bulletin board's users to share the work that a printed magazine's letters page would have to do with their own dedicated team.[52]

However, this did not make the magazine redundant as an information source. Magazine articles offered a place for users to find out more about network connectivity. An article in the April 1984 issue of *The Micro User* noted that Norway and some other countries were transferring data over telephone lines using the RS423 port and a 300-baud modem.[53] The article came with an accompanying program text showing how to use the system and the benefits in doing so in terms of memory and going between a cassette-based machine and a disk-based machine. Similarly, the growth of network connectivity in relation to microcomputer use became so important that it became the theme of the last episode of *Making the Most of the Micro*. Titled "At the End of the Line," the program detailed everything from local-area networks that allowed two or more machines to be connected together in an office or school environment to electronic mail systems used on an Apple II for business purposes. The program explained the use of these technologies by giving examples of software ordering systems in pharmacies that were used on mainframe computers. Later in the program, Prestel and telesoftware were explained as two services developed in Britain that also allowed for the transmitting and possible downloading of data.[54] The downloading of content also was discussed. One of the hosts showed telesoftware hosted by Prestel and accessible by using a modem and a telephone line. The use of Prestel on the BBC Micro as a means of downloading telesoftware was also possible by using the Prestel System, a 1200/75-baud dial-up modem designed to connect the BBC Micro to the Post Office's Prestel system and was available as an add-on in the same way that the Teletext adapter could be purchased separately. Although something we take for granted today, the ability for users of the Micro to get online, share data, and communicate with others was another part of the learning required as the system developed and more users were buying machines.

Along with modem capabilities for long-distance file sharing, the BBC Micro had its own LAN networking system, which was called Econet. Econet (a network architecture that Acorn had developed for its earlier systems, including the Atom) evolved to allow BBC Micros to have Econet interfaces. The Econet interface allowed the Micros to communicate with one another and to share disks and printers. This was particularly advantageous in schools. Classrooms that had multiple Micros were able to share resources such as loading programs from a central disk drive. Praised in the April 1983 issue of *BBC Micro User*, Econet was heralded as "the low cost networking system that can allow up to 254 BBC micros to communicate with each other" and was subsequently given "an official seal of approval by Britain's 200 Information Technology Centres."[55] These centers were set up by the Department of Industry and the Manpower Services Commission to train people who had left school in computing skills, and many of them had BBC Micros for trainees to use. The low cost of the Econet system, cited at "£50 for each micro on the system—just a quarter the cost of the nearest comparable system," meant that the architecture enabled people to network as another way of expanding the possibilities of the Micro. The LAN meant that beyond printers and disk systems being shared, the teacher could view the screen of a pupil from a remote terminal, as both a monitoring device and an educational tool. Similarly, although there was an additional cost to the system, it was balanced out, as it no longer was necessary to buy multiple expensive peripherals.

Although the aforementioned peripherals required a fairly large initial financial outlay, and although the telesoftware system did not reach out to large audiences, the purposes of these systems was to enable multiple users to have access to software and hardware in new ways, with technological innovation at the heart of the educational drive. Although it is now rarely mentioned in discussions of networked technologies, since the Internet soon made the standard Teletext system obsolete, the desire to connect people to information was once again at the heart of some of the technologies initially proposed and realized by both the BBC and Acorn Computers.[56] These forward-thinking initiatives can also be seen in the development of the Domesday Project.

By 1985 the BBC Micro had comfortably positioned itself as an emerging multi-media machine for those capable of using it to its full potential. Not only did it enable various types of learning; it also supported the integration of various communication technologies.[1] Now that it was found in many primary and secondary schools throughout Britain, the British Broadcasting Corporation sought to expand the capacity of the platform's outreach once again. This time the BBC's new initiative involved an updated machine: the BBC Master, a platform that combined new peripherals and storage techniques with a unique way of enabling audiences to use and engage with content. That initiative, which was termed the Domesday Project, was a by-product of the BBC Micro era.

The Domesday Project was engineered to mark life within Britain in 1986, the year of the 900th anniversary of the completion of the Norman Domesday Survey of England in 1086. After William the Conqueror invaded England in 1066, he was crowned king. King William ordered the Domesday Survey to take place in order to document land ownership across England and as a way of locating where future land taxes could come from to help secure the defense of the country.[2] Although the document was not constructed as a visual map, the information contained within its pages could be used to map out the social and economic status of the country at a time when England was in a state of unrest. It is these related economies, such as the social state of the country that were followed through in the BBC's Domesday Project of 1986. In their initial post-mortem of the project, John Goddard and Peter Armstrong noted the differences between the two events:

For the user of the 1986 survey the most obvious contrast between it and that of the 1086 must be the technology employed in the storage and the display of information. The 1986 survey uses a video disc, micro-computer and a visual display unit rather than parchment. But there are more significant and subtle differences between the two surveys. Perhaps the most important concerns the organisation and purpose. The 1086 was an official survey conducted by an occupying power as a basis for sharing out and taxing the spoils of the conquest. In contrast, the 1986 survey was conceived very much as a "people's database" and the project carried out primarily as a public service in the Reithian tradition of British Broadcasting.[3]

The Domesday Project encompassed much of what the BBC Micro stood for in 1980s Britain. Not only did it allow potential users and the general public to contribute to what was going to be displayed on the system; it also continued to follow the precedent of the British Broadcasting Corporation's involvement with the machine. Both users and the corporation had played roles in shaping the machine and its outputs thus far, and that relationship continued in the Domesday Project. The project was set up as a way of mapping life in the UK in 1986, from the everyday to national treasures such as artifacts in museums and art galleries. In doing so, the project was presented as an interactive, hypertext experience run from two laser discs connected to the BBC Master machine using dedicated hardware created especially for the project's outcomes. In particular, the BBC was especially keen on schools being involved in the project from the outset, due to the large number of schools owning BBC Micros by the time of the project's original inception in 1984. "It was anticipated," John Goddard and Peter Armstrong write, "that the school children would be 'surveyors' of the contemporary use of the land in Britain, gathering the data in their local area and then sending it on floppy disc to the BBC."[4] But the project ended up being too expensive for every school or every library to own a copy, and in many cases so expensive that in those schools that did own a copy the children did not always have the freedom of access to the outcomes that had been envisioned. Nonetheless, the project achieved many milestones in the histories of technology, including earlier forms of the hypertext experiences, crowdsourcing, "collective intelligence," and user-generated content that we so often see mentioned in discussions of digital technology today.[5]

Vannevar Bush's vision of the Memex is often recalled in discussions of the linked capabilities of the World Wide Web and of the hypertext (a set of connected ideas or documents created online or offline).[6] Bush envisaged a machine that would allow users to link documents, search indices, and sift through information as a way of structuring archives of information, including the databases of our libraries and beyond. The idea of linking multiple types of data has existed long before users were able to interact with and imagine such machines. Similarly, the terms "hypermedia" and "hypertext" have been around since before the intro-duction of the Internet and the World Wide Web. However, it is through digital technologies and the development of particular platforms that we can see the results of constructing hypertexts as a way of creating pathways through experiences, annotating sources, and linking to other text, images, and video clips through a single page or displayed screen. Ted Nelson defines these concepts as follows: "By 'hypertext,' I mean non-sequential writing—text that branches and allows choices to the reader, best read at an interactive screen. As popularly conceived, this is a series of text chunks connected by links which offer the reader different pathways."[7] Yet the hypertext can also been seen in other sce-narios through database structures made possible by a range of storage media.

The CD-ROM's integration with computers as a storage and playback medium peaked in the 1990s. Although audio compact discs came on the market in 1982, the CD's potential as a storage device and its read-write capabilities were not embraced by computing hardware and software publishers until the late 1980s or the 1990s.[8] The multi-media presenta-tions that eventually were available on CD-ROMs ranged from artworks to hyperlinked encyclopedias such as Microsoft's Encarta, which enabled users to navigate, search, and link together ideas from databases of information.[9] In 1987 Apple released Hypercard, a hypermedia program-ming environment that was intended to be accessible to a range of users. "Using the metaphor of the Rolodex card index, and integrated with a simple scripting language, HyperTalk," Charlie Gere writes, "Hypercard enabled users to build working software, databases, hypertexts and more, as well as to integrate different forms of media and control other devices."[10]

However, the BBC's Domesday Project was first discussed in 1984, before the Hypercard and before the CD-ROM had been fully developed as workable concepts. The project would involve two distinct multi-media experiences created by researchers at the BBC, alongside commentary and artifacts from the general public as a way of documenting life within the early 1980s—an ambitious feat before the commercialization of the CD-ROM—and can be seen in many ways as a predecessor experience. But before the project could get off the ground, a new technological progression had to take place in terms of the microcomputer itself. The Domesday Project idea became so large it was no longer achievable on the much-used BBC Micro Model B, which has so far been the focus of this book. While developing the project, the BBC saw the need for another platform. Once again it would be developed by Acorn.

The Domesday Project's Hardware

In the years after the release of the BBC Micro, the platform continued to flourish among users who had access to it, and through the continuing links with the British Broadcasting Corporation. As the Micro began to grow, so did consumer demand for more powerful systems, and it was in part this demand, combined with the competition with systems, that saw the release of the next major BBC platform, BBC Master.[11] Released in the UK at the time when American microcomputer imports such as the Commodore 64 were becoming more commonplace, the BBC Master was predominantly used within the educational market, whereas the Model B was used both in schools and in homes. However, it was the development of the Master that allowed the Domesday Project to be realized. And users of the BBC Micro adapted the system in a way that later became incorporated into subsequent models. An example of this can be seen in how the BBC Micro had the ability to allow for expansion via sideways ROMs. (See chapter 2 above.) It was because a company called Solidisk began manufacturing a sideways RAM kit for the Model B that sideways RAM soon became integrated into the later BBC Master system.

In 1986, alongside the introduction of the BBC Master, a unique version of the BBC Master was manufactured for the Domesday Project. Titled the BBC Master AIV (or Advanced Interactive Videodisc), this version of the machine came equipped with a SCSI interface and a Video Filing System (VFS) ROM already installed to enable the playback of the Domesday Project laser discs on the dedicated Philips Laservision player; the Philips VP 415 Videodisc Player. In later recollections about this peripheral, Simson Garfinkel discusses the dedicated Laserdisc player's fate, calling the Domesday Project "its first and last significant application."[12] However, it was this integration of the Laserdisc as a form of data storage and selection within the project that enabled the BBC Master to be turned into an unprecedented interactive, hyperlinked experience .

The earliest optical laser discs were invented in 1958 by David Paul Gregg, who later patented the technology in 1961 and 1969. He then decided to sell the idea and the patents to the electronics manufacturer Philips. The invention of the laser disc originated in relation to the desire to distribute film content in a format different from VHS tapes. The discs arrived on the market in the 1970s. Philips manufactured Laserdisc players, and MCA, an entertainment company, made the discs.[13] As is noted in the history of the Laserdisc on the Dead Media Archive, "video and audio are stored on a Laserdisc (LD) as an analog signal. Just like a compact disc (CD) the surface of a LD is covered with pits and lands but it uses frequency modulation of an analog signal, not digital."[14] The ability to store data in this way was highlighted in an article in the December 1984 issue of *Acorn User*: "Where the breakthrough for computers will come is in the way data is stored on disc. The problem is that TV is an analogue system whereas computers are digital, so an efficient way is needed to store the computer data in a 'semi-analogue' form."[15] As a technology aimed at people who wanted to watch films at home, the Laserdisc had significant flaws. The discs were 12 inches in diameter and could hold no more than 60 minutes of content. These features did not compare well with the earlier VHS technology and the later DVD technology; however, in 1984, when the Domesday Project was being drafted, the Laserdisc was the only real candidate for the project.

It was the capacity to store large quantities of audio and video data that made the Laserdisc the final choice of a storage medium for the Domesday Project. The only other options available to the BBC at the time were floppy disks and Teletext systems, neither of which could store enough information or access the information fast enough. The Laserdisc allowed for the storage of data, which could then be played or paused— capabilities that had to be realized in order to make both aspects of the Domesday Project work. These features are highlighted in the 1984 Philips press release for the Laservision system that was engineered for the project:

This 1986 version of the Domesday Book will allow the normal still and moving picture from the video disc to be enhanced with high resolution graphics and text from the BBC Micro. These graphics will be overlaid on top of the pictures or displayed independently all on the same TV screen. The interactive style of the operation allows the user to proceed at his own pace by entering commands on the already familiar BBC Micro keyboard. We believe that not only will this prove to be the ideal carrier for Domesday but for all the follow up programme material that the BBC, and no doubt other software companies, will create for educational applications. In our view, this combined operation between the BBC, Acorn and ourselves ... sets the scene of a new era in audio visual applications.[16]

It was through discussions between the BBC and Philips that the Laserdisc player for the Domesday Project was developed. According to the summary of technical specification for the Domesday Project, the BBC/Philips AIV VP415 Laser Vision player had the following properties:

Front loading player incorporating a semi-conductor laser, elec-tronic time base corrector with sync inserter, RGB output, RGB graphics overlay, LV-ROM decode and RS 232 interface. The LV-ROM format allows up to 324 Mb of digital data to be stored on each side of the each disk (read only), as well as 54,000 analogue video frames. Data may be replaced with analogue audio where required, allowing either video/data or video/audio to exist simultaneously at any point.[17]

The ability to integrate and play back text in the form of data alongside both still images and video was fundamental to the project. The genlock (generator lock) feature used in the BBC Micro served this purpose well. By using a genlock, the display output of the BBC Master could be synchro-nized perfectly with the video signal from the Laserdisc player to give the illusion of an integrated video-and-text-based display system. The genlock made sure that the outputs from the devices started at the correct time, so that the resultant display could show the correct frame from the Laserdisc player along with the corresponding text menu systems overlaid onto the video data to allow for user interaction (a representation of which is shown in figure 7.1).

The Domesday Project was not just about capturing life in the United Kingdom within the early 1980s; it was also about innovative ways of dis-playing data. For that reason, extensive instructions for operating the system were included in manuals accompanying the Laserdiscs and the

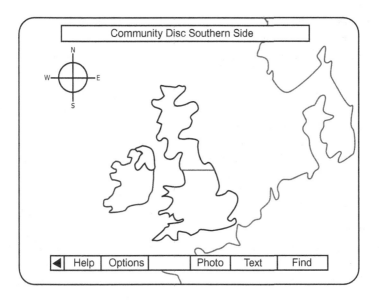

Figure 7.1 A representation of a display from the Domesday Project.

hardware. Diagrams depicting how the component parts connected to one another were included in user guides, such The Domesday Project In-Service Resources Booklet. The instructions detailed how to turn on the monitor, then the computer, and then the videodisc player to ensure that all parts of the system would load correctly. For many users, this hardware was new. Therefore, some users were expected to need some additional training in order to be able to use the extended capabilities of the familiar microcomputer.

The introduction of the additional hardware also allowed not only for discussions about what content was presented on the discs but also for discussions about the technologies that were used to present this content. Once again the aim of the Computer Literacy Project to educate audiences about the technology as well as how to use it came into play. In the educational resource booklet accompanying the Domesday setup, a "consideration of the technology and the characteristics of the hardware" was treated as just as important as an "examination of the information of the Domesday Discs."[18] Pitched in the opening pages of the resource booklet as a new form of "educational technology," the ability to use interactive video with microcomputing technologies was highlighted as offering new potentials for education, allowing students and teachers to explore combinations of sound and imagery in ways they had not experienced before. This positivist attitude toward the technology and its growth in the classroom and beyond continued in the *Teachers' Handbook for the Domesday Project*, written by Ted Wragg, then Director of the School of Education at the University of Exeter. "I have no doubt," Wragg wrote, "that by the late 1980s and the early 1990s interactive videodisc [sic] will have had the most profound effect, not only on education, but on business and information processing generally."[19] Similarly, an article in the *Radio Times* about the featuring of the project on the BBC television series *Tomorrow's World* commented: "The potential of videodiscs is enormous, and plans are already afoot to publish encyclopaedias and other reference books on disc, with sound and moving images."[20] Although the uptake of the Laserdisc was not as widespread as was once imagined, the role of the Laserdisc and the associated hardware in the Domesday Project was remarkable at the time of inception. This truly multi-media experience introduced a new way of exploring content in the classroom, and did so through two spatial experiences on the accompanying Laserdiscs, one called the Community Disc and the other the National Disc. These discs were extensive databases of information, some of it researched by the BBC and some of it contributed by the general public.

Both databases could be navigated by means of a trackerball device. Using a trackerball as an input device was nothing new; Atari and other companies had released such peripherals for their 2600 machine and for various arcade games released in the 1970s. Rather than moving a mouse around an area, the trackerball allows for the precision of selecting areas of the screen with some sort of cursor while containing the movement to the size of the trackerball area in front of the user. The trackerball device was complemented by button presses on the peripheral that allowed for actions or changes in using the system. Pressing the button on the left side of the trackerball device allowed the user to confirm that an action was to take place, such as clicking on a menu item, whereas the center button allowed users to change the picture in a sequence to view the next one on screen. Although keyboard inputs could be used to find information on both of the Domesday Project's discs, the trackerball allowed for a more natural type of movement to explore the areas depicted on screen. At the heart of each disc was a navigable experience, one in the form of a virtual museum gallery and one in the form of a map.

Both sides of this disc contain maps, text and pictures of the "community's" view of itself in the 1980s and its perception of its environment.

Fred Corbett and Gill Davidson, *The Domesday Project in Service* (BBC Enterprises, 1987)

The Community Disc part of the Domesday Project was made up of Ordnance Survey Maps, more commonly referred to as OS Maps. OS Maps are native to the British Isles, where "the great Trigonometrical Survey of the Board of Ordnance began officially in June 1791."[21] National mapping in Britain had originally been developed around the mid 1700s for military defense. A need was felt for more detailed and accurate mapping beyond the castles and fortresses previously used as landmarks, and after the Jacobite uprising of 1745 the Scottish Highlands were the first place to be mapped in this way. "Under the leadership of a lieutenant-colonel named David Watson," Simon Garfield writes, "General William Roy began a new survey of Scotland from 1747 to 1755, creating maps on a scale of 1,000 yards to an inch, something he later considered 'a magnificent military sketch [rather] than a very accurate map of a country.'"[22] It was Roy's perseverance and obsession with wanting to map the British Isles in more detail, using the ratio of a mile to an inch, that sowed the seeds for the Ordnance Survey maps. The OS Maps were created by means of triangulation, by measuring the distance between posts placed on the land to gain accurate details of land mass and positioning. Although they are not used for this purpose since the introduction of more accurate global positioning systems using satellites, these landmarks continue to be seen and used by walkers.

However, it is the detail of Ordnance Survey maps that adds distinct components to what is shown, such as bridleways, churches (with or without spires), parking, and viewpoints. Ordnance Survey Maps have their own unique qualities, which differ from the projections seen on Google Maps or Open Street Map. Each area of the UK has its own map. In contrast with the longitude and latitude we see on world maps (or even on Google Maps, which is based on the Mercator mapping system[23]), on OS Maps the whole of the UK is divided up according to what is called the National Grid Reference system.[24] Each 100-kilometer-by-100-kilometer square of Great Britain is given a set of letters that defines it, such as SP or TL. These do not correspond to county or region names but provide a reference for the Ordnance Survey System. These grids are then broken down once again into smaller 10-kilometer-by-10-kilometer grids that have numbers along both the x axis and the y axis. To find particular points on a map, first the two numbers of the map are used (for example, SP); then the x-axis number is referenced, followed by the y-axis number to give a coordinate position of a particular place. Although this system might sound confusing to someone used to using a latitude-and-longitude coordinate system, this mapping of grids proved to be useful when dividing up the places in the UK for the BBC's Domesday Project.

In order to develop the Domesday Project, the Ordnance Survey maps were broken down into a 4-by-3 grid to allow people to navigate the area. The map included four zoom levels, starting with Level 0 for the whole of the UK; Level 1 for Regions (north and south Britain, Northern Ireland, the Isle of Man, the Orkney and Shetland Islands, and the Channel Islands); Level 2, which had 40-kilometer-by-30-kilometer blocks covering approximately 70 percent of the UK; and finally level 3, which had 4-kilometer-by-3-kilometer blocks covering approximately 45 percent of the UK.[25] These blocks matched the layout of the 4:3-aspect-ratio television or monitor that the project would be viewed on, thus making the project both accessible to the viewer and practical to lay out as a database. This emerging database structure also made it easier to start compiling different parts of the Community Disc. According to a 1986 paper by John Goddard and Peter Armstrong,

Each 4 × 3 block also has associated with it 20 pages of free-form text, unedited by the BBC, in which the children or other groups have written about the area. This text was prepared with only the broadest suggestions from the BBC—principle features, local news, family life, notable events, interesting people, "a day in the life," geography, ecology and the environment, employment, games, leisure and recreation, housing, the areas, religion, etc. Finally there are three photographs for each block selected by the schools, one of which is as wide as possible a view of the "landscape."[26]

Upon signing up for the project, a school was given its own eight-digit grid reference number, which then allowed people there to find their block and plot it using an Ordnance Survey map. A Survey Guide was sent to each school containing hints and tips about how to go about compiling information for their grid area, such as going on field trips to scour the land to get a sense of their own area. Writing tips were also included with an emphasis on what was happening in the here and now rather than a historical record of their area as it once was; the purpose of the Domesday Project was to become a historical resource rather than starting as one. Details of one of the schools involved in the project were reported in the September 1985 issue of *Acorn User*, before the project was accessible as a workable piece of hardware and software. The article's author, Geoff Nairn, followed the Waldegrove School for Girls in the Twickenham area, one of 13,000 schools involved. Nairn quotes Pauline Cox, the geography teacher coordinating the school's efforts, reiterating the purpose of the project: "It's not just an historical land survey, it's more a contemporary record of Britain in the 1980s."[27]

The information that was gathered was used to form the hypertext system that users would navigate in order to show the social, economic, and "everyday" aspects of life in the 1980s. A user would click on an area and would be able to read a day in the life of a school child who had submitted their work to the project. The text and photographs were sent by post, with the printed photographs being scanned into the project to appear on the Laserdisc as digital forms. In an age before digital photography the process was time consuming and costly, yet viewing the raw data today reveals as much about a life before the "digital revolution" as it does about those writing at the time. In fact many of the writings are fairly basic as to what they offer, with school students reporting the time they got up, what they had for breakfast, and the lessons they had at school that day. The texts are very factual, listing events as daily routines that took place in the 1980s, as a way of recording the literal "everyday" without embellishment. Places on the map became a mix of both location and commentary, revealing stories and leaving histories of the individual's contribution to the project. By marking these places on a map, users were leaving behind a representation of an area and giving it a historical meaning. The way the Domesday Project achieved this was groundbreaking at the time, creating a large amount of information that users could search in order to find places, and narratives, or other related information. This was blogging before the World Wide Web. Many students couldn't have imagined viewing their work on the end platform, and many didn't, so to even have a concept of what it meant to write the piece and see it attached to the map in the end form was, for many, beyond comprehension.

The Domesday Project highlights yet another way in which the BBC Micro (and in this case the BBC Master) was a convergent medium, enabling a participatory culture among its user base.[28] The texts written by students and the involvement of numerous schools contributed to this the act of participation. The moments of creativity that we now supposedly live in through participatory culture were not discussed in this instance, as the concepts imagined for the platform could not be comprehended by those contributing to them. Nor was the project at the time ever seen on the scale it would be if it were to be online today. This was a project that can in many ways be seen as a precursor experience to the digitally located world we now live in. The Community Disc of the Domesday Project was a hypermap, linking together not only places but also media connected to those places.

In a 1997 paper titled "Principles of Hypermaps," Mennon-Jan Kraak and Rico Van Driel define a hypermap as being able to "structure the individual hypermedia components with respect to each other and the map. Hypermaps will let users navigate data sets not only by theme but also spatially."[29] This is a practice that we frequently see in our social media networks today. Instead of existing as databases of information in an offline format, we are now frequently able to locate our Facebook status updates and tweets and to use stand-alone applications such as Foursquare to show where we are to our online "friends" and associates. The Domesday Project allows for a similar perspective, although users in the early 1980s didn't have the freedom of being able to manipulate and upload the data themselves. On one level the map of the Community Disc is what Martin Dodge and Rob Kitchen, the authors of *Mapping Cyberspace*, would call a static map, yet on another level it is very much an interactive map. Here the map is "static" as it is "the equivalent of traditional cartographic maps in that they are snapshots in time" depicted by the base layer of information as provided by the Ordnance Survey maps underlying the system. Yet in a paradoxical twist, the map is also "interactive" in the sense that it moves beyond "static mappings so that the user can move through and interrogate the map from different viewpoints."[30] The discussion of the interactivity of the map goes beyond the mapped view, as although the map can shift in terms of scales and viewpoints (much like zooming in on Google Maps without going down to a layer of street-view), the Community Disc allows for an interrogation of information about an area. Here the map is no longer static in terms of location-based information, as although the base level remains in the same depiction each time, the place changes through the user's interaction with the text, videos, and images provided for the place that is found.

With the dedicated Acorn Trackerball peripheral (or a BBC Master keyboard with an embedded trackerball device), the user is able to navigate the screen space to access various parts of the map and database. Starting at the uppermost level of the map, the user is presented with clicking on northern or southern regions of the British Isles before this then zooms in to the next level of detail. Place names then become available and it is possible to zoom in further before the detail of locations on the Ordnance Survey map become recognizable to the user. Clicking at the bottom of the map then allows the user to zoom out of an area and go back up the database structure to find another section of the UK to navigate. Similar space is represented within a database function itself, as users are able to "find" information by using "map by grid reference," "map by place name," "text and photos by topic," or any "previous query" that may have existed in the system. Finding places and navigating to them on the map allows for more detail to be revealed about the area. Broad areas such as Bromley in South London give users the options of reading about "The Bromley Area and Bromley High Street Survey," or "Half-term in Bromley" (a break in the school year for a week's holiday), or an account of a user's "Swim Training". The database of information reveals itself through lists of information found about the area, making the user shift between a representation of place in a pictorial depiction, to a representation through a school child's diary or council documents related to the area in question. It is this shift in spatial layout that continues throughout the other Domesday Project disc, the National Disc, where the representation of space within the Domesday Project can also be seen in a different way—a way in which movement through the space becomes different from the mapped view.

Navigating the National Disc

Whereas the Community Disc consisted largely of personal histories, the National Disc of the Domesday Project provided a wider snapshot of British life in the 1980s. Instead of being centered on a map, the National Disc was focused around a gallery layout, and consisted of a range of national bodies putting together sets of photographs, text, and statistics about life in Great Britain at the time. The In-Service resource booklet accompanying the discs describes the "four forms in which information is available" on the discs being pictures including "photographs, moving film and surrogate walks," text including "over 2000 text items, from newspapers, magazines, journals or specially commissioned essays," data including "some 9700 sets" and maps including "approximately 500 specially drawn maps" separate to those found on the Community Disc.[31] On starting up the disc the user is presented with an opening sequence that sets the scene to the gallery sequence, depicting the virtual gallery space briefly from above to show the layout and size of the corridors, then taking the user through the "entrance" space before being confronted with a menu screen that shows a simulated gallery in all of its glory. The gallery is divided up into Popular Arts and Crafts, Society, Fine Arts, Consumerism, Royal Heritage, Environment, Sport ,and Daily Life.

Clicking on the "plan" option in the menu system displays an overview of these areas, such as the one shown in figure 7.2. The plan also displays an arrow showing users which area of the gallery they are currently in and the way they are facing in their use of the system. In many ways this is much like the map provided to players when pausing a video-game sequence of a three-dimensional world in order to help with their navigation, or markers used on mobile phone GPS systems to locate the user. The arrow display acts as a marker, placing the user within the virtual gallery space. It is a useful depiction for the user as they navigate the system, as the spatial properties of the virtual world of the 1980s disc could be confusing to those accessing it. The control system is comparable to the video-game world of *Myst*, which was not released until nearly a decade later. The user only has access to "moving" left, right, or forward through the virtual gallery space, and similarly to *Myst* these actions are not occurring through real-time three-dimensional movement, but

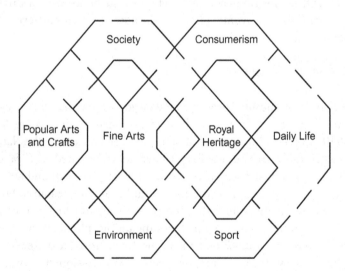

Figure 7.2 A top-down representation of the gallery space on the National Disc of the Domesday Project.

through the system drawing in different frames from the database on the disc. Manovich defines this as "branching type interactivity (sometimes also called menu-based interactivity" and goes on to comment that "navigable space can be legitimately seen as a particular kind of an interface to a database."[32] The imagery presented on the National Disc was a new type of space to many viewers. Instead of drawing on a database of Quicktime events, such as in *Myst*, the National Disc of the community project relied on the still image data being drawn from the Laserdisc, yet again focusing on the precursor production of control and experiences of multi-media CD-ROMs in the 1990s. Representations of three-dimensional spaces were not commonly found within computer media at the time, with the exceptions of games such as *Elite* (although this was rendered in a different way). Therefore, the map became a central component, as the plan allowed for a positioning of the user within the space, much as an Ordnance Survey map would in the real world.

Once the navigational elements of the system are learned, the user is free to move about the gallery space, going through doors into each of the sections listed above. The Popular Arts and Crafts section allows users to see mocked-up artworks on easels displayed images of materials that were seen as key to this area. Clicking on the images would bring up related information about them in a standard text format. For example, an image depicting "Craft in Wood and Metal" would link to a text page describing how these materials are used, and then give the user the ability to link to further related articles in the system, such as "Metalwork" or "Working with wood." These would be selected using a numbering system within the database. Linking through to these areas provide users with full screen photos linking to woodcraft and even more visual information.

Books were published (among them Alistair Ross' *The Domesday Project*) to help schools understand how to navigate through discs containing vast amounts of information and to suggest classroom activities based on the content found on the discs. In reference to the National Disc, a set of ideas surrounding the different types of homes people lived in are suggested, such as looking at surveys on the disc to see how many people owned their own home, reading about the charity Shelter, looking through a set of 2,000 pictures of a house, or using the computer to "walk" through a house and to examine its contents in great detail.[33] This walk was one of nine surrogate walks that enabled users to explore a particular environment on the disc. These are found through doorways in the gallery that the user can go through to find another world—one quite different from the gallery space they were once in. Much like a 1980s version of stepping out into Google Streetview, these walks expanded the information contained on the disc even more through these spatial activities found by accessing the information from the National Disc database. As described in the *Domesday Video Disc User Guide*, the surrogate walk is "a set of photographs portraying a physical environment from every viewpoint and stored on the disc in an organised sequence so that the user can "walk' at will through the environment and the system will always display the correct view from the current position."[34] The display of the information could be unsettling, especially in terms of the relationship between the gallery space and the surrogate walks. These walks were innovative for their time of inception and allowed for yet another perspective on life in mid-1980s Britain.

Although crude in its format, the system can be seen as a national encyclopedia about working practices and skills seen to be at the core of British life and worthy of preservation. However, the layout of the disc made the database hard to navigate spatially and its slow loading often caused frustration for the user. To make this process more straightforward, each area is selectable through a numbered menu system outside of the virtual gallery space to allow for quick linking between areas and the ability to access all parts of the system with greater ease. Clicking on the text within the gallery forwarded the user to a related theme—for example, clicking on "politics and government" on the gallery wall space would take the user to a list of texts about current political and government concerns in the 1980s, showing the near past and future as well as current information about the time in which the system was put together. Much like the Community Disc, these facts led to the documentation of life within 1980s Britain, and as such remain as a searchable archive for years to come.

By utilizing both sides of the Laserdisc, Side B of the National Disc was taken up with the final part of the project, which included a sequence of images from the years 1980–1986. There is no interaction or computer-controlled navigation in this part of the disc; instead images are displayed as a sequence without user input. Providing this aspect to the project also meant that this side of the disc could run independently of the Domesday Project's technical components and could be played on an unmodified Laserdisc Player. This made the story of the Domesday Project, the unique components created for it, and the innovative content even more important for its time and the decades since.

If the technology has not by then become obsolete, I can image future generations celebrating the 1000th anniversary of the Domesday Book in 2086 by looking back to see what your class wrote about a D-Block a hundred years previously.

E. C. (Ted) Wragg, *The Domesday Project: Teachers' Handbook* (BBC Enterprises, n.d.)

The long-term future of the Domesday Project was not foreseen. Technological obsolescence took its course, and the Laserdisc was quickly replaced by CD and DVD storage devices, by various iterations of hard drives, and then by cloud storage. This was recognized by enthusiasts and by people working at the British Broadcasting Corporation who sought to save the project before bit rot and related digital decay fully set in. The CAMiLEON project, a collaboration between the University of Leeds and the University of Michigan that began in 1999, was developed to explore the use of emulation in the context of digital preservation, and the project team investigating how to emulate a complex system used the Domesday Project as an example.[35] Similarly in 2011, the BBC launched its Domesday Reloaded Project with the tagline to "explore, compare and share the Domesday Reloaded archive."[36] Instead of trying to emulate the original archive as it was on the original Domesday discs, this project created a searchable archive of photographs and material from the 1986 project along with the D-block information. Users could view these images and offer to upload updated content in 2011 for the time the project was open to new submissions. Utilizing a similar approach to the content on the original Community disc, the 2011 user base went beyond the original schools and allowed for members of the public with Web access to upload new information. This allowed for a comparison of image data, as well as updated OS Maps for 2011 to show any changes in landscape. Both of these forms of data have since been archived online via The National Archives' UK Government Web Archive, and in the form of the two specially created touchscreen tables, one of which is held at the National Museum of Computing on the site of Bletchley Park, near Milton Keynes. The tables house a Windows 7 PC, with dedicated software to run the project. This set-up was designed by Aerian Studios, utilizing a G2 Multi-Touch touch-screen by PQ Labs. Transferring the data required the company to find solutions to seamlessly allow users to access both the original content and the 2011 Ordnance Survey maps that had been included to show an updated version of the landscape. The restrictions of the original Domesday Project meant that the Laserdisc was cleverly manipulated as a storage medium, as the still images are essentially paused on a disc created for moving-image playback. What was captured by people sending in photographs and commentary about a day at school and later scanned or transcribed into the original system was viewable only by people who were aware of the project. The original Domesday Project existed before the age of user-generated content, crowdsourcing, online forums, blogs, and social media. Therefore, to understand the platform and its outputs and restrictions is to understand the context of related conditions that form those constraints.

By moving the 1986 archives to a touchscreen device, the output of the project is changed by the properties of each platform. The Domesday Project is no longer a slow-loading trackerball-driven device, displaying a chunky arrow cursor, running on a BBC Master. In the touchscreen version, it is now a range of archives accessible by up to four people, who can manipulate the maps using touch rather than extra peripherals. This in itself affords a different experience for the user via the different material qualities and subsequent interactions inherent in each approach. However, the maps for the Domesday Reloaded Project are still driven from the Ordnance Survey maps used in the original version (along with the updated 2011 maps for comparison). These were accessed in such a way as to respond to the grid system of the Ordinance Survey cartographic display; therefore, learning to navigate the maps requires an understanding of the imposed "D-block" grid system in order to locate different places. People first using the touchscreen table sometimes encounter frustration at not being able to zoom into and access a precise point on the updated version because it is on a boundary between two grid markers. The underlying process of the system means that the map will snap to one or other of the grids, and it is not as fluid as the Google Map infrastructure that audiences are now more commonly used to. Here the platform highlights not only its affordances in the updated touchscreen device but also the underlying layer of the original platform affordances, and design decisions made in 1986 are presented to the user. With the transference to a new material aesthetic, and with an updated cultural understanding of technological processes for the user, the preserved archive takes on a new meaning. The touchscreen table and the online archives of the Domesday Project, although re-presented in new formats, mean that some of the original legacy of the BBC Micro can continue beyond its physical hardware—a legacy that remains in multiple forms today.

The BBC Micro's legacy has continued well after the machine stopped being produced, in part because of the role it played in the Computer Literacy Project and in part because of users who continue to remember the platform in various ways. Superior Software and other software publishers continued to release games for the Micro, even after sales of the platform began to decline, to support users who didn't want to upgrade and were quite happy with what the Micro offered. The modularity of the system, which allowed users to upgrade some of its components with ROM expansions and extra processors via the expansion interface called the Tube, enabled the Micro to be used for many years beyond its release. The BBC and Acorn teams wanted to see the Micro succeed in Germany and the United States as it had in the United Kingdom. The Acorn Electron was developed and released alongside the BBC Micro as a more affordable alternative aimed primarily at game players. Yet some aspects of this decision did not necessarily bode well for the future of Acorn. In this final chapter, the local legacies of the BBC Micro are discussed through the lens of the Cambridge computing scene and the unsuccessful attempts of launching similar computer literacy projects in other countries. These insights lead to much broader global legacies that can be seen today—notably the development of the Acorn RISC Machine (ARM), which was made possible by the continuation of the research ethos of the team at Acorn Computers. ARM processors are now found in numerous technologies used around the world, including the smartphone, various tablet devices, and the Raspberry Pi. Finally, we examine how attempts to boost computer literacy still remain a part of government and industry dialogue in Britain today.

Local Legacies and Abandoned Machines

A million and a quarter Micros had been sold in Britain alone. Beyond the British Isles, the BBC Micro had some success in Australia and New Zealand, and its "high sales volumes in Holland [were] reflected in the push in education and schools, as well as in the home."[1]

Alongside the Micro, the Acorn team also released the Acorn Electron. Sold as a budget version of the Micro, the Electron was developed as a way of capitalizing on the games market for microcomputers. Released on August 25, 1983, the Electron was priced at £200, nearly half the price of the Micro. But with 32 kilobytes of RAM, it lagged behind the ZX Spectrum and the Commodore 64. Advertisements for the machine included the slogan "Ask any child at school why it's worth £199" and proposed that the machine would be useful for school children to do their homework. But according to the September 1983 issue of *The Micro User*, the Electron "has no Mode 7 feature and so won't run BBC Micro software that uses it," and it "is also much slower than the BBC Micro."[2] Nonetheless, demand for the Electron often outstripped the supply. "A core component turned out to be tricky to manufacture, and only arrived in bulk in 1984, a year too late for the market."[3] Owing to a shortage of a certain component, only 30,000 of the 300,000 orders were fulfilled in time for the 1983 Christmas rush. Alongside this, the Electron came along at a time when the UK home computer market was seen to be going into decline.[4]

Acorn was eager to move into other markets, and the possibility of selling the Micro in the US was often discussed in magazines devoted to that machine. An article in the March 1983 issue of *BBC Micro User* headlined "Major Sales Drive in the USA" stated that Acorn was "planning an aggressive drive into the educational market in the US, cashing in on the tremendous amount of interest expected to be generated by the screening of the BBC's computer series on American television."[5] As that article noted, there were attempts to use other components of the Computer Literacy Programme in the US. In 1983, the television series *The Computer Programme* was shown in the US on various Public Broadcasting Service (PBS) channels. A supporting telecourse was offered by the PBS Adult Learning Service as a way of supporting the television programs, but the television program had to compete in a much wider market than the four television channels that were on offer in Britain at the time. And

1983 was also the year in which *Computer Chronicles* was first aired in the US. Although *Computer Chronicles* was not the equal of the BBC's *Computer Programme* in terms of the educational benefits of particular microcomputers, the series did document the rise of the personal computer in the same era.[6] The American public already had access to other sources of information related to computer literacy, and to the Apple II and other popular platforms.

Even though *The Computer Programme* was brought to American audiences by PBS, the holistic nature of the Computer Literacy Project, which explained how to use the Micro by using a range of other media outlets, such as television shows, was lost in transferring the machine overseas just a few years after its initial release in Britain. As Steve Furber noted in a later interview, "the perceived stability of the BBC name contributed" to sales of the machine in Britain.[7] Although the BBC was a globally known television service, the attachment of this brand to the machine for an overseas market did not allow for the same selling power as it did on home ground, and Acorn did not have the financial resources to spend huge amounts of money trying to plug into the already well established microcomputer market in North America. Figures released by David Bell in October 1985 for sales between 1984 and 1985 revealed that Acorn Corporation in the US had sold only 1,418 machines while Acorn Limited in the UK had sold 135,269.[8]

However, these were not the only factors to contend with in releasing the platform overseas. The BBC Micro had to be adapted for the American market, with a new BBC BASIC ROM that was re-written to allow for changes in language use from "colour" to "color" and for different display outputs. Mode 7, in particular, was designed for the PAL television market, to match the 625-line broadcast standard for television and Teletext signals; therefore this display mode was also affected by the change in continent. The American model of the Micro displayed only 20 lines of text in Mode 7, instead of the 25 offered by the British model, because NTSC was capable of a resolution of only 525 lines. This change in display size meant that the first few lines of the display were missing on the American model, and other parts of the display output were also often changed, causing scrolling or printing to occur in places other than those that were originally defined.

Because the North American BBC Micro was aimed primarily at the education market, it included the Intel 8271 disc interface, the Econet interface for networking the machine, and speech upgrades as standard. The voice of Kenneth Kendall (used on British models) was replaced with an American-accented voice. These machines could be recognized by the extra components build in as standard on the US Micros and by an additional caution added to the underside:

> To prevent electric shock, do not open cabinet cover. No user-serviceable parts inside. Refer servicing to qualified service personnel. Modifying, adjusting or tampering with any component inside the computer may void the warranty.

The British models had only this caution:

> before opening this case ensure that the product is disconnected from the mains power and that all **four** fixing screws are removed

The British version of the Micro showed the influence of earlier discussions of modularity and the influence of hobbyist computing. The American model did not lend itself to modifications of the sort that the British versions allowed. Although Acorn (with the help of Wong Electronics) produced 50,000 US BBC Micros for shipment in October 1984, many of them remained unsold and were subsequently shipped back to the UK and converted to the UK standard. According to Steve Furber, this was a costly exercise for Acorn:

> The USA was particularly expensive because the USA had quite strict emissions regulations that the BBC Micro had to be modified to meet. In fact the BBC—the design of the BBC Micro was really not good for the American market because it had so many ports, which was one of the things that people liked about it, but when you do the emissions test you have to stick a metre of cable in every port and so the more ports there are, the more wires there are transmitting radio interference.[9]

The different processes involved in manufacturing and selling the US version of the machine meant that it was more difficult to get the machine through the US emissions tests, resulting in what Furber describes as a "rather expensive and clumsy machine."[10] Many unsold Micros were eventually returned to Britain despite the initial claims in *BBC Micro User* that Acorn saw "no reason why sales in the United States should not even overtake those in the UK."[11]

Other models of the Micro were produced for the German and Indian markets. Again, these were not as successfully received as the models sold in the British Isles. Despite more recent websites showing images of these machines, little is known about their use, as it was not well documented.[12] Therefore, the BBC Micro platform can be seen to have a more localized history for British, Australian, and New Zealand markets, where the machine was most successfully sold and used. This history continued through Acorn's other machines of the 1980s, including the Model B+64 and the Model B+128.

All these developments came at a price. The poor sales of the Acorn Electron, along with the company's failure to gain a foothold in the American market, saw Acorn shares being devalued by 1985. This placed the company in increasing financial difficulties. Acorn needed an injection of cash to stay afloat. That came from a deal with Olivetti, a company that had just been partially bought by the American company AT&T. In an interview, Chris Curry discussed the period in 1986 when "Acorn started to get into serious trouble," stating "When we sold 25% to Olivetti, the deal was because they bought it cheaper than the share price at the time, that they would use the Olivetti distribution network worldwide to sell all the stock of BBC computers and Electrons that we had in the warehouse."[13]

In an article in the May 1985 issue of *The Micro User*, Joe Black, then head of Acorn in the US, revealed the possibility that a deal could be made to distribute a new version of the Micro in the US through Olivetti's links to AT&T, but that deal did not emerge.[14] Instead, the further downfall of the Micro both at home and abroad saw Olivetti eventually take more than 75 percent of the company, some of that share being bought by Lehman Brothers in 1996. However, the buy-out did not stop Acorn from producing other machines and working on new projects. As was noted in the preceding chapter, in 1986 Acorn Computers released the BBC Master. Not only was the Master used for the Domesday Project; it was also subsequently used in 82 percent of primary schools and 92 percent of secondary schools in Britain.[15] However, this was not Acorn's only project. Although North America did not play a role in generating much of a market for the sales of Acorn machines, members of the Acorn team did travel to the US while they were researching ideas for what became the Acorn RISC Machine, more commonly known today as the ARM.

Closing the Box

As early as 1983 the members of the Acorn team were already thinking about their next move, and particularly about the microprocessors available to them. They knew that 16-bit processors were starting to be used in other machines, and that they had to think beyond the 8-bit BBC Micro system. Steve Furber recalls that they had development kits from National Semiconductor with "what started off as the 16032 but then for marketing reasons was rechristened the 32016," and they were also aware of the Motorola 68000 and Intel chips.[16] However, those chips did not offer the performance they were after. They had already managed to get as much performance as was possible out of the Micro's 6502 chip, particularly in terms of its interrupt performance. "All of these sixteen-bit processors that were coming onto the market around '82, '83," Furber recalled, "had worse interrupt performance than the 6502. In other words, they were less able to cope with floppy disc traffic … . This seemed to us to be going in the wrong direction."[17]

The team visited National Semiconductor's Design Center in Israel to look at the development of this NS32016 chip, but the turning point for the development of the ARM architecture came in October 1983 when Steve Furber and Sophie Wilson visited the Western Design Center in Phoenix, Arizona to further investigate the 6502 microprocessor that had been used within the BBC Micro. In an interview with Tilly Blyth, Furber recalled: "We held the place in awe and respect because it was American and made microprocessors, but we discovered that they were operating out of a bungalow somewhere, they were employing school kids to do some of the silicon design on Apple IIs, and we thought 'if they can design a microprocessor, so can we!'"[18] Around the same time, Andy Hopper, who had been working at Cambridge University and at Acorn Computers, showed Hermann Hauser, Steve Furber, and Sophie Wilson some research papers about RISC machines from the University of California at Berkeley. Hopper remembers this chain of events as figuring in the development of the ARM: "It's a small but very crucial part to bring it [the RISC machines] to their attention, to Hermann's attention, who is a very, fantastic early adopter of such things, and a spotter."[19] It was this drive and innovation from members of the whole Acorn team that led Sophie Wilson and Steve Furber to design the ARM architecture.

The development of the Acorn RISC Machine began in 1983, and the first ARM chips arrived on April 26, 1985. In fact the first behavioral model of the ARM was written by Furber in BBC BASIC, and the first ARM chips were used as second processors for the Micro.[20] In an interview for the TechRadar website, Sophie Wilson, the designer behind the ARM instruction set, recalled: "When we set the project up we had a slogan internally to remind us what we thought we were doing, and that was 'MIPS for the masses,' i.e. lots of processing power for everybody. We were aiming at the mass market."[21] This differed from the research focus of UC Berkeley and Stanford, where work on the RISC architecture was being done for different reasons.

The ARM second processor to be used with the BBC Micro came at a cost. It wasn't until 1987, when Acorn released its Archimedes desktop computer, that the ARM processor debuted as the first RISC processor for low-cost personal computers. The ARM processor allowed for a graphical user interface much like those seen on Apple machines at the time. Although the Archimedes wasn't as popular as the Atari ST or the Commodore Amiga, which were both available in a competing market, the Archimedes did once again appeal to the educational market and was a more powerful and advanced machine. According to Thomas Lean, "as the games market never really developed for the Archimedes, the machines were presented as 'serious' general-purpose machines with a strong educational role. The A3000 model of 1989, endorsed by the BBC and bearing the familiar owl logo originated for the Computer Literacy Project, was one of several models to be bundled with word-processing and other applications software as the 'Learning Curve.'"[22] Once again, the Acorn Archimedes platform was most successful in Britain and in Australia. In terms of the initial developments of the ARM chipset, the resultant machines were still often local to the country of development. That was about to change.

As Sophie Wilson is eager to remind people, the ARM achieved success gradually over 30 years.[23] The recognition among other companies of Acorn's initial work on the ARM architecture in Acorn machines from 1985 on led others to get on board with the project. According to Chris Curry, Olivetti, although owning a large percentage of Acorn, did not seem interested in developing the ARM side of Acorn computers, and so Olivetti's name did not become attached to the project.[24] Therefore, in 1990 Advanced RISC Machines became a spin-off company from Acorn, and Apple Computers became a partner. The relationship between ARM and Apple grew during the development of Apple's Newton computer platform as both companies started to work on the ARM processor at the core of its design. During this time, VLSI Technology, Inc. also became an investor and the first licensee of the chip, further aiding the development of the company and its future success. It was this subsequent partnership that resulted in collaboration to create a new microprocessor standard.

The simplicity of the design of the RISC processors first created by Acorn in the 1980s enabled that company's processors to attain high performance relative to other processors on the market despite their relatively low power. This made them ideal for the Apple Newton, and it subsequently resulted in the ARM chipset's designs becoming the most prominent such designs in mobile devices. Not only do the processors use space efficiently; they also use less power. As Sophie Wilson notes, the reason for this is that the designers adopted the system-on-chip approach before anyone else did.[25] In 2007, according to a report in *The Telegraph*, "about 98 percent of the more than 1 billion phones sold each year use at least one ARM processor."[26]

Although not directly related to the BBC Micro, this sequence of events and Acorn's later collaboration with Apple on the Newton and subsequent partnership in the development of ARM shows how Acorn played a role in the development of different machines. Whereas the BBC Micro allowed users to open it up and tinker, mobile-device technologies such as Apple's iPhone and iPad products that use the ARM chipset do not facilitate the same DIY approach to the hardware. This is often characterized as, for example, the "black box effect, through which the choices and conflicts that produce a technological object are hidden in a walled off machine whose operations are simply taken for granted."[27] Far from open systems allowing for hobbyist cultures and easily accessible content creation, many mobile devices can often be seen as closed systems, not allowing as much creativity on the part of the user. The sometimes literal black box of the phone denies the user access to its inner working with a molded case and the inability to easily change even the battery pack—a far cry from the usability and "under the beige box" tinkering that was initially encouraged by the BBC Micro's design. However, it can also be seen that at the other end of the spectrum there appears to be a return to what is so often defined as "maker culture" and of digital "craft" practices around the world. Some of the technological innovations related to this rise in "maker cultures" have been subsequently realized in Britain through the continued Cambridge computing scene, which was a clear source of community and possibility during the Micro's inception in the 1980s. One technology that starts to capture some of these issues and is often associated with the microcomputing cultures of 1980s Britain and the need for increased computer literacy is the Raspberry Pi.

Continuing Computer Literacies

[T]he Raspberry Pi buzz is kind of the first time I felt an echo that the BBC Micro basically encouraged a generation to go into computing, to look at computer programming. Any number of people still say, you know, the BBC Micro set the direction of my career. If the Raspberry Pi can do the same again then it would be great.

Thomas Lean (interviewer), National Life Stories. An Oral History of British Science, Steve Furber (interviewee), August 20, 2012 (http://sounds.bl.uk/Oral-history/Science/021M-C1379X0078XX-0002V0)

Released on February 29, 2012, the Raspberry Pi couldn't be more different from the BBC Micro in size or in price. The single-board computer of the Pi measures 85.6 millimeters by 56 millimeters and weighs only 45 grams, whereas the BBC Micro Model A measured 409 millimeters by 358 millimeters and weighed 3,700 grams. Similarly, although the Raspberry Pi was released in a Model A and a Model B. referencing the strategy of Acorn Computers' initial BBC Micro models, these cost £25 or £35 respectively on launch, much less than either Micro model, although the Pi did not come with a keyboard, a case, or a power supply as standard.[28] The Raspberry Pi is the collective brainchild of the Raspberry Pi Foundation, formed in 2006 by Eben Upton, Rob Mullins, Jack Lang, and Alan Mycroft. All four of the founders noticed a "year on year decline in the numbers and skills levels of the A Level students applying to read Computer Science."[29] Subsequently, the development of the Raspberry Pi was discussed as a community activity, with a "hall of fame" of people who have contributed to its development. Because of its charity status, the foundation has a board of trustees, one of whom is David Braben, who co-developed *Elite* for the BBC Micro.[30] Braben has said that he wanted to get involved with the foundation because of "the lack of a way to teach children to learn to program."[31]

Instead of connecting to a nationwide campaign for computer literacy, the Raspberry Pi project set out to attract different types of users, ranging from young children to adult computer hobbyists and enthusiasts. In a similar vein to the Micro, the Raspberry Pi once again allows for the computer to be put into the home living room context through its ability to connect to a television through the HDMI output. The operating system and the hard drive are in the form of an SD card that can easily be plugged into the machine and changed for different versions to suit the user's needs, along with micro-USB power connectivity and the addition of an Ethernet port and dual USB connector on the Model B version. The additional composite RCA socket, along with the HDMI capabilities, makes the machine usable in both PAL and NTSC formats. In fact this functionality has seen the Raspberry Pi become successful in the United States. According to a March 2014 report in *The Guardian*, the largest market for the platform is the US, with 30 percent of total sales; the British market accounts for 20 percent of sales.[32]

Whereas other personal computing systems often adhere to the Windows or the Macintosh operating system, the Raspberry Pi takes a more open-source approach. The promoted operating system for the machine, which is based on the Debian Linux format, is called Raspian. Other versions of Linux operating systems are also available, including Pidora (based on Fedora) and Archlinux (a more "DIY" operating system that users can configure to suit their personal preferences). A RISC operating system is also downloadable as an environment specifically built for the ARM processor. All of these approaches once again promote an active engagement with the platform; a desire for users to potentially understand more than the software packages they might run on it, and start to strip the machine back to basics as a way of promoting learning further. Beyond these approaches, the other possibilities of the Pi mean there are also operating systems available to turn the Pi into a media center. One of them, the OpenElec OS, was created for running the Xbox Media Centre. The Pi also can be used to run various emulation systems, including MAME.[33]

Beyond the software capabilities of the system, the connectivity or modular nature of the Pi has seen it being used as a control box in a way reminiscent to the BBC Micro, but with peripherals, such as a camera, that allow for motion detection or video capture. Because sensors can be attached to it to monitor temperature, humidity, or other weather conditions, various other projects can also be built using the Pi. The maker culture highlighted in chapter 2 in reference to the modular functionality of the BBC Micro, as well as the ease of which users could program with the machine, is once again emulated through projects such as these to hopefully encourage another generation of young computer users. Instead of digital literacy only being concerned with how to educate people in using the basics of computers and how to connect with others online, there is a growing desire to extend this literacy beyond the black box of the machine being used. Stories of young users creating a varied set of projects attached to the ease of use of the Pi show how these "maker cultures" are emerging once again. An interview published in the June 2013 issue of *The MagPi* shows how a 13-year-old programmer's introductions to the Scratch programming environment at school and at Codeacademy sparked her interest in programming and in using the Pi for multiple processes.[34] Similarly, when asked whether there was a home enthusiast environment akin to one facilitated by the BBC Micro, David Braben replied "Yes, there seems to be. We have already outsold the BBC Micro with the Raspberry Pi. Everything from atmospheric balloons to robots to home automation projects, as well as pure programming."[35]

In many ways, the Raspberry Pi and the changes in how computing is discussed and taught in schools in the UK have bought the focus back to computer literacy. In February 2011, Ian Livingstone, a co-founder of Games Workshop and Life President of Eidos, and Alex Hope, a co-founder and Managing Director of the visual effects company Double Negative, published Next Gen, a report commissioned by the charity Nesta.[36] The report focused on the skills needed by people in order to work in the computer games and special effects industries in the UK. The outcomes for the report were made possible through a series of consultations with industry, academia, and various educational establishments. These discussions led to outcomes that highlighted the need for computer programming to be better integrated into education in the UK, particularly by bringing "computer science into the National Curriculum as an essential discipline."[37] Along with integrating Science, Technology, and Mathematics (STEM) subjects with more arts-based disciplines, the drive toward bringing back computer science as a more recognized part of the curriculum from primary through to secondary schools exposes the need for a greater awareness as to how some of these skills might be taught. The Pi is seen as a platform that could be used to fill in some of these gaps in the curriculum through the accessibility of the system and the programs that can run on it. Much like the BBC Micro, the Pi is seen as having educational potential inside and outside the classroom. Eben Upton emphasizes home use: "We have to remember this isn't really about the classroom. This is about bedrooms. This is not supposed to be the classroom computer, because schools already have computers. This is supposed to be the bedroom computer."[38]

These initiatives promoting home and school use have also seen companies expand on the Raspberry Pi even further by building upon its initial hardware and incorporating it into other products, such as Binary distribution's Fuze computer.[39] Here the Pi has been turned into a machine akin to the BBC Micro in its design, with a chunky, robust exterior and a version of FUZE BASIC as standard on the included operating system. These links are not coincidental. John Silvera, the developer of the FUZE, was inspired by the qualities of the BBC Micro, the Sinclair Spectrum, and other microcomputing platforms of the 1980s. Silvera, who had used a BBC Micro at a friend's house in the 1980s, had learned to program in BBC BASIC and in 6502 Assembly Language, and had played numerous games ("*Snapper, Arcadians, Meteors, Planetoid, Monsters*, and if I remember correctly a rather good version of *Scramble* called *Rocket Raid*"), still had a Micro in his loft many years later. Later he recalled bringing it down and setting it up for his children:

> I wanted to show my children how computers looked back-in-the-day but to my amazement [my children] were all fascinated by it. From playing simple education games to writing small programs, they were totally engrossed in it. Like most others these days we have all the modern toys in the house but it was a real surprise that something thirty years old could stop them in their tracks like this. This was the very moment the FUZE was first conceived. What if *we* could make a new computer with the accessibility of the BBC and the electronic features of devices like the Arduino and Maximite.[40]

It was because of this ambition that a breadboard and an electronics kit were bundled with some models of the Fuze. A user guide and cut out labels for using with various project cards downloadable from the Fuze website are nods to the 1980s custom of positioning strips of paper above the function keys of a BBC Micro. The design of the Fuze was taken one step further near the end of 2014 with the release of a Special Edition version of the machine that "pays tribute to the home computers of the 1980s" and looks very much like a BBC Micro.

However, the legacy of the BBC Micro in relation to present-day discussions of computer literacy goes beyond the hardware itself. In March 2015, the BBC announced a new piece of hardware, tentatively called the Micro Bit, a million units of which "will be given to all pupils starting secondary school in the autumn term."[41] The press release about the product notes that it "builds on the legacy of the seminal BBC Micro."[42] The device is discussed as being a "standalone, entry-level coding device" but also one that can connect to other devices, such as the Arduino and the Raspberry Pi. Once again the device builds upon the BBC's "hands on" philosophy, which played a role in the original Computer Literacy Project. Similarly, much like the 1980s project, the Micro Bit is part of a wider scheme, titled Make It Digital, that is to include television and radio content linked to popular television series such as *Doctor Who* and *EastEnders* and an apprenticeship scheme for 5,000 unemployed people to "boost their digital skills." Once again, the BBC is encouraging a multi-platform approach in a new age of computer literacy to promote computer programming skills and logical thinking through another range of media. However, beyond these new approaches we can also see how some of these legacies of the BBC Micro and the Computer

Literacy Project continue to live on today, not only in these other platforms but also through historical and educational institutions that continue to use the BBC Micro.

The BBC Micro today

Thanks to robust build quality and the ease with which burned-out capacitors can be replaced, the BBC Micro is still used by many people in Britain. According to Francis Spufford, "a BBC Micro controlling a geology exhibit in the Science Museum ran continuously for eight years without malfunctioning."[43] Alongside the platform's hardware strengths, the Legacy Report about the machine, published by Nesta, notes that it inspired a generation of people to learn how to program either for fun or in order to go into the computing industry or some other technology-related industry.[44] It is these aims that continue today via museum and educational projects that keep not only the platform but also the ethos of the platform alive.

Various institutions construct the theme of the 1980s classroom as a way of continuing to engage audiences with computer literacy today. The 80s Classroom set up by Replay Schools offers various packages focused on the BBC Micro, one called Programming Challenges, one called BASIC Programming, and one called Classroom Classics (in which students get to experience games such as *Granny's Garden*).[45] Similarly, the UK's National Museum of Computing provides a permanent classroom equipped with BBC Micros. School groups visiting the museum are usually given a game-programming exercise to undertake in BBC BASIC as a way to show the possibilities of computing through such a fundamental machine in British history. A classroom of the 1980s has been reconstructed at the Centre for Computing History in Cambridge, and it too welcomes visits by school groups. Its website states that "using the tried and tested BBC BASIC language, students will be taught to write and understand simple computer programs," and that "they will learn how to break down a problem into logical steps."[46] These visits are not only nostalgic remembrances for those who once used or grew up with the BBC Micro; they also enable users who were born after that platform's inception to experience computer programming in a stripped-down form without the distraction of windows and webpages. Once again, these processes show how the computer literacies enabled by the Micro continue to this day.

The Web archive of material about the Micro and emulators such as BeebEm and Beebdroid enable people to keep some of the functionality of the machine alive, albeit on different systems.[47] Games can be remembered, and people can still program in BBC BASIC, thanks to communities of users wanting to keep memories of the machine going. By 1994 development of software for the BBC Micro and the Acorn Electron had pretty much come to an end, although Superior Software kept the *Repton* back catalog going and 4Mation continued to sell copies of *Granny's Garden* and its other educational software packages for newer platforms.[48] In the case of the Domesday Project, as was noted in the preceding chapter, groups of hobbyists and preservationists also kept parts of the platform alive by making not only the hardware but also the content once captured on the Laserdisc available in more up-to-date forms. Groups of Acorn users have also continued to write games for the platform. Andrew Weston, an independent developer, created a Mode 7 text adventure titled *Dominion*, Jeffrey Lee developed *Bob and Trev*, and Dominic Beesley created *Resurrection* and *Ball Game*.[49] These efforts, along with the development work of others, saw a new software label evolve that "would promote the development and distribution of new software for retro platforms, with an initial focus on the Acorn and BBC."[50] A company called Retro Software has helped a community of users, some of whom may have never used the hardware in its original form, to embrace new ways of creating content for the BBC Micro on present-day PCs. New titles have been developed, and older ones, such as *Repton*, have been continued.[51] The website www.retrosoftware.co.uk now acts as a meeting point for users wanting to learn more about developing for the Micro, and can be seen as an online computer club in which information is shared between groups of interested users. The hobbyist of the 1980s continues, albeit in a new form with new tools.

Therefore, in spite of the more localized histories of the platform, it can be seen that the global significance of Acorn computers and some of the ethos surrounding the BBC Micro live on in other forms and through other platforms. These other, related developments see the legacy of the Micro go beyond the UK. As has been noted, at one end of the spectrum there is the development of ARM processors that are now seen in the vast majority of smartphone and tablet computing technologies discussed as "black boxes" or closed systems. At the other end of the spectrum are the Raspberry Pi and the BBC's Micro Bit computer, both of which were developed to inject creativity, modularity, and hobbyist cultures back into computing in the 2010s. Finally, there are the people who still use the BBC Micro today. It is this legacy and these hobbyist beginnings that will be remembered, as it is these groups of people that kept the platform alive during its production and mainstream use in the 1980s as a modular, expandable, programmable machine that enabled people to explore its possibilities and to create new content. As David Braben notes, one the greatest legacies of the platform is that it enabled a generation to become "immensely familiar with technology and programming."[52] It is these qualities that were seemingly passed down from the innovation and hobbyist underpinnings of the members of the Acorn team, who not only envisaged a platform that wasn't thought to be possible but also managed to educate, inform, and entertain a variety of people from 1981 until the present day.

Notes

Introduction

1. R. Fothergill and J. S. A. Anderson, "Strategy for the Microelectronics Education Programme (MEP)," *Innovations in Education & Training International* 18, no. 3 (1981): 120–129, at 120.
2. For more information about the mission and values of the BBC see BBC, "Inside the BBC—Mission and Values" (http://www.bbc.co.uk/aboutthebbc/insidethebbc/whoweare/mission_and_values/).
3. BBC Continuing Education Television Computer Literacy Project, n.d. (http://www.computinghistory.org.uk/det/7182/BBC-Computer-Literacy-Project/).
4. Paul du Gay et al., *Doing Cultural Studies: The Story of the Sony Walkman* (SAGE, 1997), 1.
5. Paul Atkinson, *Computer* (Reaktion Books, 2010), 13.
6. For more information on the history of the BBC see "History of the BBC" at http://www.bbc.co.uk/historyofthebbc/resources/in-depth/reith_1.shtml.
7. BBC, "Inside the BBC—Mission and Values."
8. See "BBC Two's Horizon Celebrates 40th Birthday with New Series This Autumn" at http://www.bbc.co.uk/pressoffice/pressreleases/stories/2004/08_august/19/horizon.shtml.
9. For more on "Now the Chips Are Down" see Magnus Anderson and Rebecca Levene, *Grand Thieves & Tomb Raiders: How British Videogames Conquered the World* (Aurum, 2012), 18; Thomas Lean, "The Making of the Micro": Producers, Mediators, Users and the Development of Popular Microcomputing in Britain (1980–1989), PhD dissertation, University of Manchester, 2008); Tilly Blyth, *The Legacy of the BBC Micro: Effecting Change in the UK's Culture of Computing* (Nesta, 2012).
10. Tilly Blyth, "Computing for the Masses? Constructing a British Culture of Computing in the Home," in *Reflections on the History of Computing*, ed. Arthur Tatnall (Springer, 2012).

11. Lean, "The Making of the Micro," 55.
12. During the 1980s in the UK, the population only had access to four terrestri-
    al television channels: BBC One and BBC Two (transmitted by the BBC), ITV
    (often called Channel 3), and Channel 4 (which began to broadcast on November
    2, 1982).
13. Christopher Evans, *The Mighty Micro* (Gollancz, 1979).
14. For more about the political climate at the time of the Micro , see Neil Selwyn,
    "Learning Love the Micro: The Discursive Construction of 'educational' to
    Computing in the UK, 1979–89," *British Journal of Sociology of Education* 23, no. 3
    (2002): 427–443.
15. Martin Campbell-Kelly et al., *Computer: A History of the Information Machine*, third
    edition (Westview, 2014), chapter 10, section 2.
16. For more about the politics in the UK during the 1980s and the relationship with
    between politics and microcomputing, see Lean, "The Making of the Micro."
17. Kenneth Baker, *The Turbulent Years* (Faber & Faber, 1993), 59.
18. Neil Selwyn, *Telling Tales on Technology: Qualitative Studies of Technology and
    Education* (Ashgate, 2002), 24.
19. Campbell-Kelly et al., *Computer: A History of the Information Machine*, chapter 10,
    section 6.
20. Kate Kirk and Charles Cotton, *The Cambridge Phenomenon* (Third Millennium,
    2012), 12.
21. Ibid.
22. See Haroon Ahmed, *Cambridge Computing: The First 75 Years* (Third Millennium,
    2013).
23. Kirk and Cotton, *The Cambridge Phenomenon*, 12.
24. Charles Crook, *Computers and the Collaborative Experience of Learning* (Routledge,
    1994), 1.
25. Maureen McNeil, "The Old and New Worlds of Information Technology in
    Britain," in *Enterprise and Heritage*, ed. John Corner and Sylvia Harvey (Rout-
    ledge, 1991), 120.
26. Ibid. 121.
27. Ibid., 124–125.
28. David Allen, The Surprising Back Story of the 1980s BBC Computer Literacy
    Project (public lecture, National Museum of Computing, November 14, 2013).
29. Ibid.
30. Blyth, *The Legacy of the BBC Micro*.
31. In 2006 Henry Jenkins defined "convergence culture" in a multitude of ways,
    ranging from "where old and new media collide, where grassroots and corporate
    media intersect, where the power of the media producer and the power of the
    media consumer interact in unpredictable ways" to "the flow of content across
    multiple media platforms, the cooperation between multiple media industries,
    and the migratory behaviour of media audiences who will go almost anywhere in
    search of the kinds of entertainment experiences they want." See Henry Jenkins,
    Convergence Culture (New York University Press, 2006), 2. The diagram of con-
    nections represented here in figure I.1 is based on a similar schematic drawn
    up by the BBC showing the links between areas responsible for the Computer
    Literacy Project (see Blyth, *The Legacy of the BBC Micro*, 15).
32. See Jenkins, *Convergence Culture*.

33. See Jay David Bolter and Richard Gruisin, *Remediation* (MIT Press, 2000). Bolter and Gruisin note that all new media (a term not restricted to digital media) draw on relationships to older media forms. This is one of the recurring themes of this book.

34. Henry Jenkins draws on Pierre Levy's concept of "collective intelligence" as a way of discussing how online audiences may "leverage the combined expertise of their members." See Jenkins, *Convergence Culture*, 27 and Pierre Levy, *Collective Intelligence: Mankind's Emerging World in Cyberspace* (Perseus Books, 1997), 20. I would argue that the collective intelligence of audiences is also made possible by a range of "offline" communities in the 1980s through outlets such as computer clubs, the school playground, and letters pages in magazines.

35. Nick Montfort and Ian Bogost, *Racing the Beam: The Atari Video Computer System* (MIT Press, 2009), 4.

36. Ibid., 3.

37. For a more detailed discussion of media archeology versus media history, see chapter 2 of Wolfgang Ernst, *Digital Memory and the Archive* (University of Minnesota Press, 2013).

38. Erkki Huhtamo and Jussi Parikka, eds., *Media Archaeology: Approaches, Applications, and Implications* (University of California Press, 2011), 3.

39. Lean, "The Making of the Micro," 117.

40. Peter Rodwell, *The Personal Computer Handbook: A Complete Practical Guide to Choosing and Using Your Micro* (Barron's, 1983).

41. Erkki Huhtamo writes that "new products are promoted as being packaged into formulas that are meant to strike the observer as novel, although they have been put together from ingredients retrieved from cultural archives." These ingredients can be described as "topoi" that can be found as recurring themes in media artifacts. Therefore, although some of the hardware or even software on the BBC Micro is not necessarily "new" in the sense that it is the first, it can still be seen as innovative and unique to the platform and thus situated in a wider context of similar techniques and processes to help shape the ensuing discussion. See *Media Archaeology*, ed. Huhtamo and Parikka, 27–47.

42. Ibid., 28.

43. Bobby Schweizer, "Platforms," in *The Routledge Companion to Video Game Studies* (Routledge, 2014), 41.

44. Katherine Hayles, "The Condition of Virtuality," in *Digital Dialectic: New Essays in New Media*, ed. Peter Lunenfeld (MIT Press, 1999), 94.

Chapter 1

1. Manpower Services Commission, Something Must Be Done (1979).

2. Blyth, "Computing for the Masses? Constructing a British Culture of Computing in the Home," 234.

3. Charles Moir, "Review—BBC Micro," *Practical Computing*, January 1982.

4. John Radcliffe and Robert Salkeld, "Towards Computer Literacy—The BBC Computer Literacy Project 1979–1983," National Archive of Educational Computing (http://www.naec.org.uk/organisations/bbc-computer-literacy-project/towards-computer-literacy-the-bbc-computer-literacy-project-1979-1983).

5. For more about the MK-14 and one user's attempts to re-create one, see "MK14 V2.0" at http://mymk14.co.uk/.
6. For more about the Acorn System 1, see Mike Cowlishaw, "Acorn 6502 Microcomputer Kit" at http://speleotrove.com/acorn/index.html.
7. Sinclair Radionics became Sinclair Instrument Ltd in August 1975, then became Sinclair Research Ltd in 1981.
8. This is a term Steve Furber now uses in retrospect; it was not used by the team to describe themselves at the time. See Thomas Lean (interviewer), National Life Stories. An Oral History of British Science, Steve Furber (interviewee), October 22, 2012 (http://sounds.bl.uk/Oral-history/Science/021M-C1379X0078XX-0003V0).
9. Douglas Fairbairn (interviewer), Oral History of Sophie Wilson, January 21, 2012, Computer History Museum, 18.
10. Lean (interviewer), National Life Stories. An Oral History of British Science, Steve Furber (interviewee), October 22, 2012.
11. Email message to author, March 9, 2015.
12. In Blyth, *The Legacy of the BBC Micro*, Steve Furber recalls the "cutting of the umbilical cord from the prototype to the development system." Furber also recalls how the portrayal of events on the day the BBC came to view the micro were exaggerated in parts in *The Micro Men*—for example, "the wire cutting episode that caused the BBC Micro prototype to come to life was actually about three hours before the BBC arrived, not three minutes after." See Lean (interviewer), National Life Stories. An Oral History of British Science, Steve Furber (interviewee), August 20, 2012 (http://sounds.bl.uk/Oral-history/Science/021M-C1379X0078XX-0002V0).
13. Radcliffe and Salkeld, "Towards Computer Literacy—The BBC Computer Literacy Project 1979–1983."
14. ACORN Computers Limited, *BBC Microcomputer Service Manual* (ACORN Computers, 1985), 2.
15. "The Micro Buyer's Survival Kit," *The Home Computer Course*, 1983, 6–7.
16. Radcliffe and Salkeld, "Towards Computer Literacy—The BBC Computer Literacy Project 1979–1983."
17. Continuing Education Department, BBC Microcomputer Hardware Specification (BBC Broadcasting Centre, n.d.).
18. "BBC Model B," *The Home Computer Course*, 1983, 89.
19. BBC Microcomputer System Technical Specification Issue 3, September 1981.
20. "BBC Model B," 89.
21. Email message to author, October 21, 2014.
22. *Making the Most of the Micro*, "The Versatile Machine" (BBC, January 10, 1983).
23. BBC, *Welcome* (British Broadcasting Corporation, 1981), 3.
24. Microvitec Cub monitors were also popular as display devices among BBC Micro users, particularly in schools. Like a PAL television set, these ran at 50 MHz and had a display size of 625 lines.
25. The line displaying "16K" would be replaced by line displaying "32K" in the Model B version of the BBC Micro.
26. BBC, *Welcome*, 5.
27. The word "affordance" is used here to mean "the perceived an actual properties of the thing, primarily those fundamental properties that determine just how the

thing could possibly be used." Donald A. Norman, *The Design of Everyday Things* (MIT Press, 1998), 9.

28. BBC, *Welcome*, 6.
29. Lev Manovich, *Software Takes Command* (Bloomsbury Academic, 2013), 2.
30. BBC, *Welcome*, 9.
31. Ibid.
32. Nick Montfort et al., *10 PRINT CHR$(205.5+RND(1)); : GOTO 10* (MIT Press, 2012), 10.
33. Manovich defines modularity as "the organization of a cultural object into clearly separable parts" See Manovich, *Software Takes Command*, 211.
34. The word "remediation" is used in reference to Jay David Bolter and Richard Grusin's book *Remediation: Understanding New Media* (MIT Press, 2000).
35. Jay David Bolter and Diane Gromala, *Windows and Mirrors: Interaction Design, Digital Art and the Myth of Transparency* (MIT Press, 2003), 86.
36. BBC, *Welcome*, 15–16.
37. Warren Sack, "Memory," in *Software Studies*, ed. Matthew Fuller (MIT Press, 2008), 190.
38. BBC, *Welcome*, 17.
39. "Roger McGough," BBC—Poetry Season (http://www.bbc.co.uk/poetryseason/poets/roger_mcgough.shtml).
40. The type of play experienced here by the user would be what Sutton-Smith defines as "play as progress" as they experimented with the machine. In his book *The Ambiguity of Play*, Sutton-Smith equates "play as progress" with both animal and children's play and although this is not always discussed through adult-centered play, this is implied. His notion of "Playful forms of play" are the most useful in thinking about some of the learning created by the Welcome cassette programs as these "are the games of those who have a creative capacity for playing." Brian Sutton-Smith, *The Ambiguity of Play* (Harvard University Press, 1997), 9 and 46.
41. BBC, *Welcome*, 18.
42. Janet H. Murray, *Hamlet on the Holodeck* (MIT Press, 1997), 126.
43. Murray states "I use the word 'encyclopedic' to refer to both a technical and cultural phenomenon: to the unequalled storage potential of the new medium and to its promise of an infinite tablet, a library as big as the world." Janet H. Murray, *Inventing the Medium: Principles of Interaction Design as a Cultural Practice* (MIT Press, 2011), 66. Although this library was relatively smaller in the early 1980s, the possibilities of the machine were still drawn upon in opening up the user to the possibilities of encyclopedic capabilities.
44. Jussi Parikka, "Copy," in *Software Studies*, ed. Matthew Fuller (MIT Press, 2008), 76.
45. David Ahl, "Hammurabi," Atari Archives (http://atariarchives.org/basicgames/showpage.php?page=78).
46. An example of a BASIC listing for Hammurabi can be found at http://www.dunnington.u-net.com/public/basicgames/HMRABI
47. David Morley, *Television Audiences and Cultural Studies* (Routledge, 1992), 201.
48. On television-viewing habits during the time under discussion, see Morley, *Television Audiences and Cultural Studies* and David Gauntlett and Annette Hill, *TV Living* (Routledge, 1999).

49. "The Computer Programme," *Just One Thing After Another* (BBC, January 18, 1982).
50. David Allen, "Confessions of a TV Producer," *Acorn User*, October 1982, 11.
51. David Allen, "The Computer Programme and beyond," *Acorn User*, August 1982, 10.
52. *Making the Most of the Micro*, "At the End of the Line" (BBC, March 14, 1983).
53. Ibid.
54. For further definitions of multiliteracies and media literacy, see Bill Cope and Mary Kalantzis, eds., *Multiliteracies: Literacy Learning and the Design of Social Future* (Routledge, 2000); Kathleen Tyner, *Literacy in a Digital World* (Erlbaum, 1998); David Buckingham, *Media Education: Literacy, Learning and Contemporary Culture* (Polity Press, 2003).
55. Buckingham, *Media Education*, 35.
56. Jussi Parikka, *Digital Contagions: A Media Archaeology of Computer Viruses* (Peter Lang, 2007), 162–163.
57. Robin Bradbeer, Peter De Bono, and Peter Laurie, *The Computer Book: An Introduction to Computers and Computing*, ed. Susan Curran and David Allen (British Broadcasting Corporation, 1982), 5–7.
58. Angelos Agalianos, Geoff Whitty, and Richard Noss, "The Social Shaping of Logo," *Social Studies of Science* 36, no. 2 (2006): 241–267, at 257.
59. See du Gay et al., *Doing Cultural Studies: The Story of the Sony Walkman*, 5.
60. *The Times* (London), January 4, 1983.
61. James Sumner, "'Today, Computers Should Interest Everybody': The Meanings of Microcomputers," in *Zeithistorische Forschungen / Studies in Contemporary History*, volume 9, 201 (http://www.zeithistorische-forschungen.de/16126041-Sumner-2-2012).
62. "BBC Micro Advert," *Electronics and Computing Monthly*, December 1982.
63. The statistics can be found on pp. 20–21 of Blyth, *The Legacy of the BBC Micro*.

Chapter 2

1. For histories of microcomputing in these countries, see Martin Campbell-Kelly et al., eds., *Computer: A History of the Information Machine*, (Westview, 2014); Melanie Swalwell, "Questions about the Usefulness of Microcomputers in 1980s Australia," *Media International Australia, Incorporating Culture & Policy* no. 143 (May 2012): 63–77; Jaroslav Švelch, "Say It with a Computer Game: Hobby Computer Culture and the Non-Entertainment Uses of Homebrew Games in the 1980s Czechoslovakia," *Game Studies* 13, no. 2 (2013) (http://gamestudies.org/1302/articles/svelch).
2. "Before Acorn became involved with consumer-orientated computers," Lean comments, "it had manufactured the Acorn System series of hobbyist, industrial and laboratory microcomputers." See Lean, "The Making of the Micro," 225.
3. See Norman, *The Design of Everyday Things*.
4. Whereas Lev Manovich recognizes the modular nature of software and how this can provide a step by step approach to learning how to use a program, among other discussions, modularity can also be discussed through the materiality of hardware, how this is constructed, and re-constructed. For discussions of "modularity" and software, see Manovich, *Software Takes Command*.

5. Lean, "The Making of the Micro," 226.

6. Montfort et al., *10 PRINT CHR$(205.5 ⌐ RND(1)); : GOTO 10*, 158.

7. John Radcliffe and Robert Salkeld, "Towards Computer Literacy—The BBC Computer Literacy Project 1979–1983," National Archive of Educational Computing (http://www.naec.org.uk/organisations/bbc-computer-literacy-project/towards-computer-literacy-the-bbc-computer-literacy-project-1979-1983).

8. John Coll, *BBC Microcomputer System User Guide*, ed. David Allen, issue 1 (British Broadcasting Corporation, 1984), 385.

9. David Allen, "The Surprising Back Story of the 1980s BBC Computer Literacy Project."

10. See Blyth, *The Legacy of the BBC Micro*.

11. Stuart Goodwin, "Sophie Wilson 2007 Interview with Stuart Goodwin," Stairwaytohell, autumn 2007 (http://www.stairwaytohell.com/articles/SG -SophieWilson.html).

12. Harry Fairhead, "Review: BBC Model B," *Electronics & Computing Monthly*, December 1982 (http://www.gondolin.org.uk/hchof/review.php?id=22&mcid =15).

13. Vivien Marles, BBC Computer Literacy Project—an Evaluation, n.d., 9.

14. Paul Shreeve, *Me & My Micro* (National Extension College Trust, 1984).

15. "Getting Down to BASIC," *Making the Most of the Micro*, BBC, January 17, 1983.

16. Wendy Chun, "On Software, or the Persistence of Visual Knowledge," *Grey Room* 18 (winter 2004): 39.

17. Christina Lindsay, "From the Shadows: Users as Designers, Producers, Marketers, Distributors and Technical Support," in *How Users Matter: The Co-Construction of Users and Technologies*, ed. Nelly Oudshoorn and Trevor Pinch (MIT Press, 2003), 32.

18. Speech! from Superior Software became a more widespread way of using speech on the Micro and was featured on Roger Walter's solo LP *Radio Chaos*.

19. Acorn Computers Limited, "Speech Upgrade Instructions," 1983 (http://acorn. chriswhy.co.uk/docs/Acorn/Tech/Acorn_SpeechUpgradeInst.pdf).

20. For a scan of the July 1986 Retail Price list for Acorn Computers Limited, see http://acorn.chriswhy.co.uk/docs/Acorn/Brochures/Acorn_APP87 _RetailPriceListJuly86.pdf.

21. For a scan of ROM fitting instructions by Computer Concepts of Hemel Hempstead, Hertfordshire, see http://acorn.chriswhy.co.uk/docs/CC/CC _ROMFittingInst.pdf.

22. Bridget Somekh and Niki Davis, "Getting Teachers Started with IT and Transferable Skills," in *Using Information Technology Effectively in Teaching and Learning*, ed. Somekh and Davis (Routledge, 1997), 139.

23. Mike Rawlings, "Sideways Storage," *Acorn User*, March 1986, 85.

24. Advanced Technology Products Limited, "Sidewise User Manual," 1983, 1.

25. "AMX Pagemaker Advertisement," *Acorn User*, June 1986, 31.

26. Tony Quinn, "Hold the Front Page," *Acorn User*, June 1986, 143.

27. John Chesterman and Andy Lipman, *The Electronic Pirates: DIY Crime of the Century* (Routledge, 1988), 68.

28. For more on maker cultures, see David Gauntlett, *Making Is Connecting* (Polity Press, 2011).

29. For more on this, see http://arduino.cc/.

30. Gauntlett, *Making Is Connecting*, 64.
31. For more on this, see http://technologywillsaveus.org/resources/thirsty-plant/.
32. Mark Hatch, *The Maker Movement Manifesto: Rules for Innovation in the New World of Crafters, Hackers, and Tinkerers*, Kindle edition (McGraw-Hill, 2014), introduction, section 3.
33. Part one of Chris Anderson's book *Makers: The New Industrial Revolution* (Random House, 2012) is titled "The Revolution" and contains references to the punk phenomenon of the 1980s and to 'zine publishing. Anderson notes that "photocopiers were becoming common, and from them arose a 'zine' culture of DIY magazines that were distributed at stores and shows and by mail." These practices were also linked to mail order and the ease of being able to distributed music for four-track tapes and vinyl pressing small-batch singles and EPs as discussed in books such as Amy Spencer's *DIY: The Rise of Lo-Fi Culture* (Marion Boyas, 2005). These practices were evident in 1980s computer culture in Britain in the selling of computer games on tapes and floppy disks, of kit computers, and of computer parts advertised in magazines.
34. See http://techshop.ws/.
35. David Skinner, Technology, Consumption and the Future: The Experience of Home Computing, PhD dissertation, Brunel University, 1992, 181.
36. Lean, "The Making of the Micro," 109.
37. Skinner, Technology, Consumption and the Future, 179.
38. Mike Harrison, "DIY Sideways ROM Board," *BBC Micro User*, February 1984.
39. Hatch, *The Maker Movement Manifesto*.
40. Coll, *BBC Microcomputer System User Guide*, 493.
41. Mike Shaw, "DIY: Making a Game Paddle," *BBC Micro User*, March 1983, 20.
42. To aid in using a BBC Micro to convert recorded voltage into values understood by users a BASIC command was provided. As was mentioned in the preceding chapter, the BBC Micro had its own variant of BASIC. One of the commands written into BBC BASIC was the ADVAL command that converted the voltage sensed in the resistor into a digital output.
43. "Everything Under Control," *Making the Most of the Micro*, BBC, February 28, 1983.
44. Jeffrey Pike, "The Truth, The Whole Truth," *Acorn User*, June 1986, 133.
45. RH Electronics Sales Limited, "Light Pen for the BBC Microcomputer User's Manual" (S-Print, n.d.) (http://acorn.chriswhy.co.uk/docs/RHE/RHE_LightPenUM.pdf).
46. Alexander R. Galloway, *The Interface Effect* (Polity Press, 2012), 30–31.
47. In a review of the BBC Buggy and the Edinburgh Turtle published in the August 1983 issue of *The Micro User*, Mike Cook notes that the Buggy was priced at £160 whereas the Turtle, which contained its own microprocessor so it didn't have to rely solely on waiting for commands input via the BBC Micro, was priced at £350. See Mike Cook, "Battle of the Buggies," *The Micro User*, August 1983.
48. Simon Beesley, "BBC Buggy," *Your Computer*, April 1983, 51.
49. Cook, "Battle of the Buggies," 27–28.
50. Seymour Papert, *Mindstorms: Children, Computers, and Powerful Ideas*, new edition (Basic Books, 1993).
51. Angelos Agalianos, Geoff Whitty, and Richard Noss, "The Social Shaping of Logo," *Social Studies of Science* 36, no. 2 (2006): 241–267, at 244.

52. "Logo on the BBC Micro," *Acorn User*, August 1982, 3.
53. BBC/Economatics, "The BBC Buggy Assembly and Operating Manual," 1983, 3.
54. "Everything Under Control," *Making the Most of the Micro* (BBC, February 28, 1983).
55. Sherry Turkle defines Claude Lévi-Strauss' notion of bricolage as "a style of working in which one manipulates a closed set of materials to develop new thoughts." See Turkle, ed., *Evocative Objects: Things We Think With* (MIT Press, 2007), 308.

Chapter 3

1. Saul Metzstein, "Micro Men" (BBC, October 8, 2009).
2. WHSmith stores also sell magazines, newspapers, books, stationery, and digital media.
3. In Britain, children typically enter secondary school between the ages of 11 and 16, as if they choose to continue secondary education they may remain in secondary school until age 18. Primary school is for children between the ages of 5 and 11. Some primary, middle, and secondary schools have different age requirements.
4. Kenneth Baker, *The Turbulent Years* (Faber & Faber, 1993), 61.
5. For more on the Micros in Schools scheme, see Blyth, *The Legacy of the BBC Micro*, 29–30.
6. Selwyn, "Learning Love the Micro: The Discursive Construction of 'educational' to Computing in the UK, 1979–89," 431.
7. "Making the Most of the Micro," Getting Down to BASIC" (BBC, January 17, 1983).
8. See Joe Telford, "Teaching Toddlers," *Acorn User*, August 1984, 104; Mike Bibby, "Spreading the Micro Gospel in Education," *Acorn User*, March 1983, 46.
9. Clive Kelly, "Where Infants Pick up a Micro Instead of a Crayon," *The Micro User*, August 1983, 22.
10. Acornsoft advertisement in *Acorn User*, March 1984, 88.
11. Blyth, *The Legacy of the BBC Micro*, 37.
12. Mark Green, *"Granny's Garden* Creator Interview," Pixelatron, August 7, 2010 (http://pixelatron.com/blog/grannys-garden-creator-interview/comment-page-1/#comment-3830).
13. Martin Campbell-Kelly, *From Airline Reservations to Sonic the Hedgehog: A History of the Software Industry*, new edition (MIT Press, 2004), 208.
14. Mizuko Ito, "Education vs. Entertainment: A Cultural History of Children's Software," in *The Ecology of Games*, ed. Katie Salen (MIT Press, 2008).
15. Richard Jones, "Search for the Mary Rose—and Discover the Direction Software Should Take," *The Micro User*, January 1984, 51.
16. It isn't clear which version of *Adventure* Matson played. In any case, his comments about the playing the game can be found in an interview with Mark Green available at http://pixelatron.com/blog/grannys-garden-creator-interview/comment-page-1/#comment-3830
17. Nick Montfort, *Twisty Little Passages* (MIT Press, 2003), 4. In *Inventing the Medium* (p. 426), Janet Murray favors the term "interactor" over "user" to describe people interacting with the texts presented to them.

18. Although Baker states that some microcomputer programs in schools did not encourage written-literacies, *Granny's Garden* encouraged these literacies in other activities that could be conducted in relation to the game content. See Clive Baker, "The Microcomputer and the Curriculum: A Critique," *Journal of Curriculum Studies* 17, no. 4 (1985): 449-451, at 449.

19. On Easter Eggs in games, see Mia Consalvo, *Cheating: Gaining Advantage in Videogames* (MIT Press, 2007), 19.

20. Cave-exploration games and text adventure games are mentioned early in Jason Scott's 2010 DVD documentary *Get Lamp*. The cave in the game *Adventure* is mentioned later in the documentary by one of the game's developers, Don Woods.

21. James Paul Gee defines a "virtual identity" as "one's identity as a virtual character," a real-world identity as who the player is in real life, "a nonvirtual person playing a computer game" and "projective identity" in terms of the player playing as a character (the *as* is emphasized by Gee as stressing the "interface between—the interactions between—the real-world person and the virtual characters." See Gee, *What Video Games Have to Teach Us about Learning and Literacy*, 48–54.

22. The character Grotbags was introduced in the ITV television series *Emu's World*, first aired in Britain in 1982.

23. For a more recent discussion of what failure means in games, and of how it can act as a catalyst to encourage us to continue playing, see Jesper Juul, *The Art of Failure: An Essay on the Pain of Playing Video Games* (MIT Press, 2013).

24. Katie Salen and Eric Zimmerman, *Rules of Play: Game Design Fundamentals* (MIT Press, 2004), 81.

25. Ibid., 80.

26. Gee, *What Video Games Have to Teach Us about Learning and Literacy*, 88.

27. 4Mation Educational Resources, *"Granny's Garden* Manual" (4Mation, 1983), 8.

28. Montfort, *Twisty Little Passages*, 38.

29. Mark Green, *"Granny's Garden* Creator Interview," Pixelatron, August 7, 2010 (http://pixelatron.com/blog/grannys-garden-creator-interview/comment-page-1/#comment-3830).

30. Ibid.

31. Ibid.

32. Lean, "The Making of the Micro," 189.

33. David Smith and Sue Segger, "Granny Comes to Holyport: The Use of an Educational Adventure Game with Children with Severe Learning Difficulties," *European Journal of Special Needs Education* 1, no. 1 (1986): 23–28.

34. Katie Salen, "Toward an Ecology of Gaming," in *The Ecology of Games* (MIT Press, 2008), 9.

35. 4Mation Educational Resources, *"Granny's Garden* Manual," 7.

36. For a more detailed discussion of Mode 7, see chapter 6.

37. An author's note near the back of the *Granny's Garden* game manual jokingly says that Granny is drinking gin while the children are playing in the garden.

38. Although this quotation pertains to a later-released version of *Granny's Garden* for PCs, the structure and the main themes of the game were the same. See David Whitebread and Angela McFarlane, "Developing Children's

Problem-Solving: The Educational Uses of Adventure Games," in *Information Technology and Authentic Learning: Realizing the Potential of Computers in the Primary Classroom* (Routledge, 1997), 31.

39. Buckingham, *Media Education*, 37.

40. Livingstone puts children and young people in the categories "traditionalists," "low media users," "screen entertainment fans," and "specialists," but we can see how these categories can be used to discuss other types of media and computer uses. See Sonia Livingstone, *Young People and New Media: Childhood and the Changing Media Environment*, Kindle edition (SAGE, 2002), chapter 3, section 4.

41. Richard Cobbett, "Crap Shoot: *Granny's Garden*," *PC Gamer*, January 22, 2011 (http://www.pcgamer.com/2011/01/22/crap-shoot-grannys-garden/).

42. See http://www.4mation.co.uk/cat/granny.htm.

43. Mike Matson, telephone interview with Thomas Lean, in Lean, "The Making of the Micro," 165–166.

Chapter 4

1. For more on the pre-crash histories of video games, see Mark J. P. Wolf, *Before the Crash: Early Video Game History* (Wayne State University Press, 2012).

2. Graeme Kirkpatrick, *Computer Games and the Social Imaginary* (Polity Press, 2013), 58.

3. See Alex Wade, "The State of the Art: Western Modes of Videogame Production," in Proceedings of the 2007 DiGRA International Conference on Situated Play; Leslie Haddon, "The Home Computer: Making of a Consumer Electronic," *Science as Culture*, no. 2 (1988): 7–51; Aphra Kerr, "The UK and Irish Game Industries," in *The Video Game Industry: Formation, Present State, and Future*, ed. Peter Zackariasson and Wilson, Kindle edition (Routledge, 2012). Kerr also recognizes Haddon and Skinner's work on how the BBC Micro played a role in software development during the 1980s, although she does not explicitly discuss computer-game software.

4. According to Graeme Kirkpatrick, "on average, around 25 per cent of magazine content in the early years of the decade was devoted to game programs readers could copy into one of the small computers of the day." See Kirkpatrick, *Computer Games and the Social Imaginary*, 76.

5. Email message to author, February 27, 2015.

6. Melanie Swalwell discusses the microcomputer scene in New Zealand in a similar context, with active learning through the typing and tracing of code an integral part of the user's participation in and engagement with the gaming scene at that time, something that she terms to be the "will to mod." Her accounts of users entry in the world of programming again links to the copying of code in some cases and the experiences of "learning by doing" that was actively encouraged within the wider contexts of microcomputer creation and consumption at this time. See Swalwell, "The Early Micro User: Games Writing, Hardware Hacking, and the Will to Mod," in *Proceedings of DiGRA Nordic 2012 Conference: Local and Global—Games in Culture and Society*, 2012.

7. Simon Dally, "The Name of the Game," *Acorn User*, August 1982, 20.

8. Kirkpatrick, *Computer Games and the Social Imaginary*, 60.

9. See Jesper Juul, "High-Tech Low-Tech Authenticity: The Creation of Independent Style at the Independent Games Festival," in *9th International Conference on the Foundations of Digital Games*, 2014 (http://www.jesperjuul.net/text/independentstyle/).

10. Kerr, "The UK and Irish Game Industries," Section 2. The figure of 150,000 copies was later explained as sales from both the BBC Micro and Acorn Electron versions of the game. See Jimmy Maher, "Elite (or the Universe on 32K Per Day)", The Digital Antiquarian, 2013, http://www.filfre.net/2013/12/elite/

11. Van Burnham, *Supercade: A Visual History of the Videogame Age 1971–1984* (MIT Press, 2001), 293.

12. See http://uk.ign.com/articles/2000/07/24/the-top-25-pc-games-of-all-time.

13. Anderson and Levene state that Acornsoft was founded in 1979. See Anderson and Levene, *Grand Thieves & Tomb Raiders: How British Videogames Conquered the World*, 32. However, an incorporation document emailed to myself from Chris Jordan, previously of Acornsoft, shows Acornsoft was formed on October 14, 1980.

14. David Johnson-Davies, *Atomic Theory and Practice* (ACORN Computers, 1980).

15. The show asked people to send in their game designs as drawing or on cassettes and didn't anticipate that anyone would program a whole game. The prize was a BBC Micro; because the Olivers already owned one, they were given a "high resolution monitor" (a Commodore product) instead. They subsequently sold *Black Box* and *Gambit* to Acornsoft for £200. For more on the Oliver Twins, see http://www.olivertwins.com/history/page/2.

16. Retro Gamer Team, "Snapper," *Retro Gamer*, March 13, 2010 (http://www.retrogamer.net/retro_games80/snapper/).

17. Jonathan Griffiths, "Snappy Writing," *Acorn User*, January 1984, 53.

18. Anderson and Levene, *Grand Thieves & Tomb Raiders*, 66.

19. Retro Gamer Team, "Geoff Crammond," *Retro Gamer*, January 7, 2014 (http://www.retrogamer.net/profiles/developer/geoff-crammond/).

20. Tony Quinn, "Revving up at Silverstong," *Acorn User*, July 1985, 157.

21. In 1982, before coming to Cambridge to study mathematics, Bell had created a successful game called *Free Fall*. On his website (http://www.iancgbell.clara.net), Ian Bell defines Free Fall as the "first beat-em-up," jokingly suggesting that he had invented two gaming genres.

22. Email message to author, June 20, 2014.

23. Ibid.

24. For a further history of arcade-game clones in 1980s Britain, see Alison Gazzard, "The Intertextual Arcade: Tracing Histories of Arcade Clones in 1980s Britain," *Reconstruction* 14, no. 1 (2014) (http://reconstruction.eserver.org/Issues/141/Gazzard.shtml).

25. Email message to author, June 20, 2014.

26. Andrew Hutchison, "Making the Water Move: Techno-Historic Limits in Game Aesthetics of *Myst* and *Doom*," *Game Studies* 8, no. 1 (2008) (http://gamestudies.org/0801/articles/hutch).

27. Edge Staff, "The Making of 3D Monster Maze," Edge, 2006 (available at http://wayback.archive.org/web/20070513045033/http://www.edge-online.co.uk/archives/2006/04/the_making_of_3_1.php).

28. Rory Cellan-Jones, *Elite*: Classic 1980s Game to Be 'Kickstarted' with Sequel," BBC News Online, 2012 (http://www.bbc.co.uk/news/technology-20187897).

29. Anderson and Levene, *Grand Thieves & Tomb Raiders*, 112.

30. Steven Levy traces the origins of the terms "hack" and "hacker" to pranks played by MIT students in the days before mainstream computing and notes that the term was used with pride. "It was be understood," Levy writes, "that, to quality as a hack, the feat must be imbued with innovation, style, and technical virtuosity." See Levy, *Hackers: Heroes of the Computer Revolution* (O'Reilly Media, 2010), 10.

31. Email message to author, June 20, 2014.

32. David Braben, "Classic Game Postmortem—ELITE" (GDC, 2011), http://www.gdcvault.com/play/1014628/Classic-Game-Postmortem.

33. Email message to author, June 20, 2014.

34. Ibid.

35. Braben, "Classic Game Postmortem—ELITE."

36. Email message to author, June 20, 2014.

37. Ibid.

38. Anderson and Levene, *Grand Thieves & Tomb Raiders*, 116–117.

39. Braben, "Classic Game Postmortem—ELITE."

40. Francis Spufford, *Backroom Boys: The Secret Return of the British Boffin* (Faber & Faber, 2003), 103.

41. Ibid., 105.

42. Fell, "*Elite*—An Outstanding New Game from Acornsoft."

43. Anderson and Levene, *Grand Thieves & Tomb Raiders*, 109.

44. Tristan Donovan, *Replay: The History of Video Games* (Yellow Ant, 2010), 120.

45. This is defined by Mark J. P. Wolf in his categories of space in video games. Wolf categorizes Battlezone within his definition of "interactive three-dimensional environment" as a way of positioning the player in the first-person viewpoint. *Elite* seeks to do this, but it also plays with the graphics moving on the z axis to highlight the three-dimensionality of the space in each of the three viewpoints to generate the illusion of moving through space. See Wolf, *The Medium of the Videogame* (University of Texas Press, 2001), 63–65.

46. Ed Byrne, "*Elite*," in *Space Time Play. Computer Games, Architecture and Urbanism: The Next Level*, ed. Friedrich von Borries, Steffen P. Walz, and Matthias Böttger (Birkhaüser, 2007), 104.

47. "Micromail," *The Micro User*, January 1985, 176.

48. Jesper Juul, *The Art of Failure: An Essay on the Pain of Playing Video Games*, 5.

49. "The Great *Elite* Battle Is Joined," *The Micro User*, April 1985, 127.

50. "National *Elite* Championships for Micro Show," *The Micro User*, May 1985, 23–24.

51. Ibid.

52. Michael Nitsche defines the "fictional space" of the gameworld as one "that lives in the imagination, in other words, the space 'imagined' by players from their comprehension of the available images." See Nitsche, *Video Game Spaces* (MIT Press, 2008), 16.

53. Raiford Guins, *Game After: A Cultural History of Video Game Afterlife* (MIT Press, 2014), 182.

54. Jenkins defines transmedia storytelling as "stories that unfold across multiple media platforms, each medium making distinctive contributions to our

understanding of the world, a more integrated approach to franchise development than models based on urtexts and ancillary products." See Jenkins, *Convergence Culture*, 239.

55. Maher, "Elite (or the Universe on 32K Per Day)"
56. See http://www.frontier.co.uk/about/.
57. See the original Kickstarter page for *Elite: Dangerous* at https://www.kickstarter.com/projects/1461411552/elite-dangerous.
58. For more about "spreadable media," see Henry Jenkins, Sam Ford, and Joshua Green, *Spreadable Media: Creating Value and Meaning in a Networked Culture* (New York University Press, 2013).
59. Kirk and Cotton, *The Cambridge Phenomenon*.

Chapter 5

1. Richard Hewison, "Level 9—Past Masters of the Adventure Game?" (http://l9memorial.if-legends.org/html/rh.html)
2. Tony Quinn, "Rock with the Caveman," *Acorn User*, September 1984, 155.
3. Crispin Boylan, "Interview: The Superior Software Years and the Future," The BBC Games Archive—Digital Memories, 1998, http://www.beebgames.com/rhinterv.php.
4. Ibid.
5. Christopher Payne, *Top Tips for Games Authors* (Superior Software, 1986), 2.
6. Boylan, "Interview: The Superior Software Years and the Future."
7. Ibid.
8. Ibid.
9. Email message to author, February 27, 2015.
10. Ibid.
11. Ibid.
12. Phil Tudor, "*Repton* Is a Sparkler," *The Micro User*, October 1985, 78; Bruce Smith, "A Gem of a Challenge," *Acorn User*, September 1985, 155.
13. David Andrews, "*Repton* Revisited to Good Effect," *The Micro User*, February 1986, 89.
14. Edge Staff, "The Making of: *Repton*."
15. Ibid.
16. James Newman, *Playing with Videogames* (Routledge, 2008), 163.
17. See Donovan, *Replay: The History of Video Games*, 142.
18. Jon Revis, "Graphics Come Pretty Basic," *The Micro User*, November 1985.
19. Wade, "The State of the Art: Western Modes of Videogame Production."
20. David Lawrence, "The Games Page," *Acorn User*, January 1987.
21. James Riddell, "Nasty Newcomers," *The Micro User*, December 1986, 21.
22. Edge Staff, "The Making of: *Repton*."
23. "Hacman: Discover the Inner Secrets of Arcade Games," *The Micro User*, April 1987, 51.
24. David Lawrence and David Acton, *Repton Infinity Instruction Manual* (Superior Software, 1988).
25. See Repton Continuum at http://aw.drobe.co.uk/REPTON/.

26. Hanna Wirman, "On Productivity and Game Fandom," *Transformative Works and Culture* 3 (2009), http://journal.transformativeworks.org/index.php/twc/article/view/145/115.

27. Swalwell, "The Early Micro User: Games Writing, Hardware Hacking, and the Will to Mod," 11.

28. Anderson and Levene, *Grand Thieves & Tomb Raiders: How British Videogames Conquered the World*, 128.

29. Tony Leah, "Heading for the Century," *Electron User*, February 1989.

30. See http://www.superiorinteractive.com.

Chapter 6

1. Castells situates the "network society" in relation to events "around the end of the second millennium" in which "a number of major social, technological, economic, and cultural transformations came together to give rise to a new form of society." See Manuel Castells, *The Rise of the Network Society: Information Age: Economy, Society, and Culture v. 1*, second edition (Wiley-Blackwell, 2009), 354. Van Dijk expands on this in his book titled *The Network Society*, defining such a society as "a modern type of society with an infrastructure of social and media networks that characterizes its mode of organization at every level." See Jan A. G. M. van Dijk, *The Network Society*, third edition (SAGE, 2012), 23.

2. Richard H. Veith, *Television's Teletext* (Elsevier, 1983), 14.

3. *Eng Inf: The Quarterly for BBC Engineering Staff*, winter 1983–84 (http://bbceng.info/Eng_Inf/EngInf_15.pdf).

4. Ibid.

5. Veith, *Television's Teletext*, 14.

6. Paul Gregg, "Teletext: New Life for an Under-Rated Source?" *Business Information Review* 1, no. 2 (1994): 63–74.

7. See Teletext System User Guide (ACORN Computers Ltd, 1983), 42. It is also noted in the user guide that "not every magazine and every page is necessarily transmitted."

8. Veith, *Television's Teletext*, 16–17.

9. Prestel originally went under the name "Viewdata," but that name could not be registered as it consisted of two words in general use. However, "Viewdata" continued to be used and was often used since as a way of separating British Teletext and videotex systems from similar systems found in Canada, France, Germany, the United States, and Japan. See ibid., 107.

10. Prestel User Guide (ACORN Computers Ltd, 1984), 2.

11. See Lev Manovich, *The Language of New Media* (MIT Press, 2001), 218. Manovich defines the database as "collections of individual items, with every item possessing the same significance as any other."

12. Veith, *Television's Teletext*, 15.

13. Steve Gold, "Teaching Old Dogs New Tricks," *The Micro User*, March 1985, 130.

14. "Orders Pour in for Teletext Adapter," *The Micro User*, July 1983.

15. David Allen, "Here Comes Auntie," *Acorn User*, September 1982.

16. Magazines such as *The Micro User* and *Acorn User* offered discounted Teletext adapters through mail order in some issues of their magazines, such as the May 1988 issue of *Acorn User* offering the adapter at a discounted price of £134 (inclusive of value-added tax and delivery).

17. Gordon Horsington, "Save Programs, Save Pounds," *The Micro User*, May 1987.

18. Jerome Aumente, *New Electronic Pathways: Videotex, Teletext, and Online Databases* (SAGE, 1987), 10.

19. Paul Leman and Steve Swallow, "Teletext Mode 7," *BBC Micro User*, April 1983, 7.

20. Veith, *Television's Teletext*, 83.

21. See Tom Blackburn, "Alien Invasion," *The Micro User*, February 1984; Jim Notman, "A Screen Editor for Teletext," *The Micro User*, August 1984; Notman, "Take the Toil out of Typing in Your Programs," *The Micro User*, May 1984.

22. Notman, "A Screen Editor for Teletext."

23. Christopher Stop, "Choose Chunky Mode 7 Letters," *The Micro User*, November 1984.

24. Notman, "A Screen Editor for Teletext."

25. W. J. G. Overington, "Telesoftware," *Computing* 5, no. 18 (1977): 25.

26. J. Hedger and R. Eason, "Telesoftware: Adding Intelligence to Teletext," *IEE Proceedings* 126, no. 12 (1979): 1414.

27. Ibid.

28. Mike Bayman, "Telesoftware Is on Its Way for the 1980s," *Electronics and Power*, January 1980.

29. M. White, "Telesoftware—a New Educational Resources?" *The Radio and Electronic Engineer* 54, no. 3 (1984): 114–116.

30. Ibid.

31. L. T. Mapp, "Telesoftware for Beginners," *Journal of Educational Television* 7, no. 1 (1981): 25–27.

32. White, "Telesoftware—a New Educational Resources?"

33. ACORN Computers Limited, "Teletext System User Guide," 9.

34. Ibid.

35. "Programs Programme," *Sinclair User*, July 1983.

36. J. Billingsley and R. J. Billingsley, "Software Distribution Via Broadcast Television Signals," *Electronic Letters* 21, no. 10 1985): 444–445.

37. White, "Telesoftware—a New Educational Resources?"

38. See, for example, "Ceefax Guide," *The Micro User*, May 1988.

39. Malcolm Hall, "Teletext for Your Micro," *Acorn User*, October 1983.

40. "BBC Announces Closure of Telesoftware Service (1989)," http://teletext.mb21.co.uk/gallery/ceefax/telesoftware/closure.html.

41. Ibid.

42. "Telesoftware: The End of an Era?" *The Micro User*, October 1989.

43. Ibid.

44. Blyth, *The Legacy of the BBC Micro*, 12.

45. Allen, "The Surprising Back Story of the 1980s BBC Computer Literacy Project."

46. See "Making the Most of the Micro Live" (BBC, October 2, 1983).

47. Allen, "The Surprising Back Story of the 1980s BBC Computer Literacy Project."

48. Paul Drury, "Desert Island Disks: Jez San," *Retro Gamer*, 2015.

49. Jason Scott, *BBS: The Documentary*, 2005, https://archive.org/details/BBS.The .Documentary.

50. Castells, *The Rise of the Network Society: Information Age: Economy, Society, and Culture v. 1*, 2209.

51. "Microweb," *The Micro User*, July 1984, 102.

52. Henry Jenkins defines "participatory" as offering a contrast to "older notions of passive media spectatorship." "Rather than talking about media producers and consumers as occupying separate roles," he adds, "we might now see them as participants who interact with each other according to a new set of rules that none of us fully understands." Jenkins, *Convergence Culture*, 3.

53. Are Leistad, "The Norwegian Connection," *The Micro User*, April 1984, 91.

54. "At the End of the Line," *Making the Most of the Micro*, BBC, March 14, 1983.

55. "Econet given the ITC Seal of Approval," *BBC Micro User*, April 1983.

56. On page 165 of Gauntlett and Hill's book *TV Living*, Teletext is characterized as "quite mundane." Respondents discussing their use of Teletext describe it as having "blocky graphics" and looking "severely dated." Others see the growth of the Internet at this time as something that would supersede much of Teletext's use.

Chapter 7

1. In many ways the BBC Micro could be seen as a Gesamtkunstwerk linked to multi-media practices. As Charlie Gere notes, "historically multimedia can be traced back to any number of beginnings, including Greek tragedy, to various other practices involving combining sounds, words and images, or to Richard Wagner's concept of the total artwork, the Gesamtkunstwerk." See Gere, *Digital Cultures* (Reaktion Books, 2002), 86.

2. England, in 1086, was defined as anywhere south of the River Ribble and the River Tees, which were the boundaries between England and Scotland at the time.

3. John Goddard and Peter Armstrong, "The 1986 Domesday Project," *Transactions of the Institute of British Geographers* 11, no. 3 (1986): 291.

4. Ibid.

5. In his book *Convergence Culture*, Henry Jenkins uses the term "collective intelligence" from the theorist Pierre Levy to "refer to the ability of virtual communities to leverage the knowledge and expertise of their members, often through large-scale collaboration and deliberation." (See Jenkins, *Convergence Culture*, 281.) Although the information for the Domesday Project was not collected through online provision, it was only possible by crowdsourcing information from local areas in order to gain insights into the daily life of some of their inhabitants as well as photographs taken in those areas. People contributing to the project had to collaborate, albeit without always knowing who they were collaborating with to make the project a success.

6. Vannevar Bush, "As We May Think," *Atlantic Monthly*, July 1945 (http://www .theatlantic.com/magazine/archive/1945/07/as-we-may-think/303881/).

7. Ted Nelson, *Literacy Machines* (self-published, 1981).

8. For more on the histories of CDs and DVDs see Anne Friedberg, "CD and DVD," in *The New Media Book*, ed. Dan Harries (BFI, 2002), 33.

9. Microsoft discontinued sales of Encarta in June 2009. More information available at, http://www.microsoft.com/uk/encarta/default.mspx

10. Gere, *Digital Cultures*, 141.

11. The BBC Micro had also been upgraded in 1985 to Model B+, which came in 64K and 128K versions.

12. Simson Garfinkel, "The Myth of Doomed Data," *MIT Technology Review*, December 3, 2003 (http://www.technologyreview.com/news/402333/the-myth -of-doomed-data/).

13. MCA had a large back catalog of films at this time, so the partnership meant that hardware and film content could be sold simultaneously, without the need to find a company to provide the film content.

14. For more on Laserdiscs, see "Laserdisc" in Dead Media Archive (http:// cultureandcommunication.org/deadmedia/index.php/Laserdisc).

15. Geoff Nairn, "Acorn and BBC Go for Interactive Video," *Acorn User*, December 1984.

16. Peter Jones and Mark Southworth, "Philips to Develop New Laservision for Domesday Project," November 5, 1984 (http://www.microcomputer.org.uk/ documents/press/philips-lvrom-release.php).

17. David Rhind, Peter Armstrong, and Stan Openshaw, "The Domesday Machine: A Nationwide Geographical Information System," *The Geographical Journal* 154, no. 1 (1988): 56–68.

18. Fred Corbett and Gill Davidson, *The Domesday Project in Service* (BBC Enterprises, 1987), 10.

19. E. C. (Ted) Wragg, *The Domesday Project: Teachers' Handbook* (BBC Enterprises, n.d.), 7.

20. Madeleine Kingsley, "Domesdata," *Radio Times*, November 1986, 3.

21. Simon Garfield, *On the Map: Why the World Looks the Way It Does* (Profile Books, 2012), 183.

22. Ibid., 184.

23. For a further discussion about the histories of Mercator's map projections see ibid., 130–134.

24. Source: 'Using the National Grid' at http://www.ordnancesurvey.co.uk/ oswebsite/education-and-research/teaching-resources/using-the-national -grid/index.html.

25. Rhind, Armstrong, and Openshaw, "The Domesday Machine: A Nationwide Geographical Information System."

26. Goddard and Armstrong, "The 1986 Domesday Project," 293.

27. Geoff Nairn, "Countdown to Domesday," *Acorn User*, September 1985, 17.

28. See the preceding chapter for a discussion of participatory culture.

29. Mennon-Jan Kraak and Rico Van Driel, "Principles of Hypermaps," *Computers & Geosciences* 23, no. 4 (1997): 457.

30. Martin Dodge and Rob Kitchen, *Mapping Cyberspace* (Routledge, 2001), 72.

31. Corbett and Davidson, *The Domesday Project in Service*, 27–28.

32. Manovich, *The Language of New Media*, 127 and 248.

33. Alistair Ross, *The Domesday Project* (Black, 1987), 22–23.

34. Peter Armstrong and Mike Tibbets, *Domesday Video Disc User Guide* (BBC Publications, 1987), 110.

35. Paul Wheatley, "Digital Preservation and BBC Domesday" (presented at the Electronic Media Group, Annual Meeting of the American Institute for Conservation of Historic and Artistic Works., Portland. Oregon, 2004).
36. For more about the preservation of the project, see http://www.bbc.co.uk/history/domesday/story.

Chapter 8

1. Blyth, *The Legacy of the BBC Micro*, 22. See also Arthur Tatnall, "The Australian Educational Computer That Never Was," *IEEE Annuals of the History of Computing* 35, no. 1 (2013): 35–47.
2. "Beeb's Baby Brother Is on the Way!," *The Micro User*, September 1983, 9.
3. Anderson and Levene, *Grand Thieves & Tomb Raiders: How British Videogames Conquered the World*, 137.
4. Kirk and Cotton, *The Cambridge Phenomenon*, 54; Haroon Ahmed, *Cambridge Computing: The First 75 Years* (Third Millennium, 2013), 127.
5. "Major Sales Drive in the USA," *BBC Micro User*, March 1983.
6. The history of the Computer Chronicles can be found at http://www.stquantum.com
7. Lean (interviewer), National Life Stories. An Oral History of British Science, Steve Furber (interviewee).
8. Blyth, *The Legacy of the BBC Micro*, 23.
9. Lean (interviewer), National Life Stories. An Oral History of British Science, Steve Furber (interviewee).
10. Ibid.
11. "Major Sales Drive in the USA," *BBC Micro User*, March 1983.
12. For examples, see http://acorn.chriswhy.co.uk.
13. Ellee Seymour, "How Olivetti Stitched up Acorn," ElleeSeymour ProActive PR, February 24, 2012 (http://elleeseymour.com/2012/02/24/how-olivetti-stitched-up-acorn/).
14. "Acorn Is Poised for Another Go at the US Market," *The Micro User*, May 1985, 23.
15. Blyth, *The Legacy of the BBC Micro*, 21.
16. Lean (interviewer), National Life Stories. An Oral History of British Science, Steve Furber (interviewee).
17. Ibid.
18. Blyth, *The Legacy of the BBC Micro*, 50.
19. Thomas Lean (interviewer), National Life Stories. An Oral History of British Science, Professor Andy Hopper (interviewee), March 22, 2010 (http://sounds.bl.uk/Oral-history/Science/021M-C1379X0010XX-0002V0).
20. Douglas Fairbairn (interviewer), Oral History of Sophie Wilson, January 21, 2012, Computer History Museum.
21. In the article MIPS is noted as standing for, "Microprocessor without Interlocked Pipeline Stage, a RISC—or Reduced Instruction Set computer microarchitecture." See Dan Grabham, "From a Small Acorn to 37 Billion Chips: ARM's Ascent to Tech Superpower," Techradar.pro, July 19, 2013 (http://www.techradar.com/news/computing/from-a-small-acorn-to-37-billion-chips-arm-s-ascent-to-tech-superpower-1167034).

22. Lean, "The Making of the Micro," 249.

23. Dan Grabham, "From a Small Acorn to 37 Billion Chips: ARM's Ascent to Tech Superpower," Techradar.pro, July 19, 2013 (http://www.techradar.com/news/computing/from-a-small-acorn-to-37-billion-chips-arm-s-ascent-to-tech-superpower-1167034).

24. Ellee Seymour, "How Olivetti Stitched up Acorn," ElleeSeymour ProActive PR, February 24, 2012 (http://elleeseymour.com/2012/02/24/how-olivetti-stitched-up-acorn/).

25. Email message to author, October 31, 2014.

26. "History of ARM: From Acorn to Apple," *The Telegraph*, January 6, 2011 (http://www.telegraph.co.uk/finance/newsbysector/epic/arm/8243162/History-of-ARM-from-Acorn-to-Apple.html).

27. Ted Friedman, *Electric Dreams: Computers in American Culture* (New York University Press, 2005), 2.

28. These costs have since changed for example in August 2014, the Element14 community website stated that they were £24.87 for a Model B and £18.65 for a Model A (http://www.element14.com/community/community/raspberry-pi). There have since also been other models of the Raspberry Pi that have been released including the Raspberry Pi 1 Model B+ and the Raspberry Pi 2 Model B (https://www.raspberrypi.org/products/raspberry-pi-2-model-b/)

29. See http://www.raspberrypi.org/about/. "A Levels" are a qualification in England, Wales, and Northern Ireland that students can take when they are usually aged between 16 and 18. These are one of the qualifications sought before gaining entry to university or the workplace.

30. Ibid.

31. Email message to author, June 20, 2014.

32. Shane Hickey, "The Raspberry Pi Computer—How a Bright British Idea Took Flight," *The Guardian*, March 9, 2014 (http://www.theguardian.com/technology/2014/mar/09/raspberry-pi-computer-eben-upton-cambridge).

33. MAME stands for Multiple Arcade Machine Emulator. It is currently used to "emulate several thousand different classic arcade video games from the late 1970s through the modern era." See http://mamedev.org

34. Adrian Harper, "Amy Mather: The Future of Young Hackers?" *The MagPi*, June 2013 (http://www.themagpi.com/issue/issue-13/article/amy-mather-the-future-of-young-hackers).

35. Email message to author, June 20, 2014.

36. See Ian Livingstone and Alex Hope, Next Gen, at http://www.nesta.org.uk/publications/next-gen.

37. Ibid., 7.

38. Steven Osborn, *Makers at Work* (Apress, 2013), 158.

39. See http://www.fuze.co.uk

40. Email message to author, May 30, 2014.

41. Jane Wakefield, "BBC Gives Children Mini-Computers in Make It Digital Scheme," BBC News, March 12, 2015 (http://www.bbc.co.uk/news/technology-31834927).

42. "The Micro Bit," BBC Media Centre, March 12, 2015 (http://www.bbc.co.uk/corporate2/mediacentre/mediapacks/makeitdigital/micro-bit).

43. Spufford, *Backroom Boys: The Secret Return of the British Boffin*, 77.

44.	Blyth, *The Legacy of the BBC Micro*.
45.	See http://www.replayschools.co.uk/80s-classroom/
46.	See http://www.computinghistory.org.uk/pages/12058/Schools/
47.	See http://www.mkw.me.uk/beebem/
48.	Peter Edwards, "The Beginnings of Retro Software," *Micro Mart*, April 23, 2009, 106.
49.	Ibid., 107.
50.	Ibid.
51.	*Repton: The Lost Realms*, a sequel to *Repton 3* developed by Paras Sidapara and Tom Walker, can be found at http://www.retrosoftware.co.uk/wiki/index.php/ Repton:_The_Lost_Realms.
52.	Email message to author, June 20, 2014.

Index

Printed in the United States
by Baker & Taylor Publisher Services